FOUNDATIONS OF MODERN POLITICAL SCIENCE SERIES

Robert A. Dahl, Editor

FOUNDATIONS OF MODERN POLITICAL SCIENCE SERIES

PRENTICE-HALL, INC., Englewood Cliffs, New Jersey

CONGRESS AND THE PRESIDENCY

Second Edition

NELSON W. POLSBY

University of California, Berkeley

FOUNDATIONS OF MODERN POLITICAL SCIENCE SERIES

Robert A. Dahl, Editor

CONGRESS AND THE PRESIDENCY, Second Edition

by Nelson W. Polsby

Design by John J. Dunleavy

(p)   0-13-167619-9   (c)   0-13-167627-X

PRENTICE-HALL INTERNATIONAL, INC., London
PRENTICE-HALL OF AUSTRALIA, PTY. LTD., Sydney
PRENTICE-HALL OF CANADA LTD., Toronto
PRENTICE-HALL OF INDIA PRIVATE LTD., New Delhi
PRENTICE-HALL OF JAPAN, INC., Tokyo

Current printing (last number):

10   9   8   7   6   5   4   3   2   1

Again, for Linda, Lisa, and Emily

PREFACE

To the Second Edition

Walter Bagehot published a superb commentary on the English constitution in book form in 1867; in the same year the Reform Act put it out of date. Woodrow Wilson had better luck with *Congressional Government*, as his short preface to the book's fifteenth printing in 1900 indicates. Nevertheless, he said, "inasmuch as [these pages] describe a living system, like all other living things subject to constant subtle modifications, alike of form and of function, their description of The Government of The United States is not as accurate now as I believe it to have been at the time I wrote it." (Woodrow Wilson, *Congressional Government*, 1st ed., 1884, New York: Meridian Books, 1956, p. 19.)

What can happen to Bagehot and Wilson can happen to Polsby. Although for all we know the United States government may be living on borrowed time, it is still a living system, and so it should surprise no reader that in the six years that have elapsed since I wrote *Congress and the Presidency* there have been some changes in these institutions. I have not canvassed them all here, but some things that I could only dimly make out then have become clearer to me with time, events, and the progress of scholarship—a little of my own and a lot by others. And I suppose it is fair to say that a few other matters that I thought were reasonably clear are less so to me now.

Readers may wonder if, in revising the book, I have given consideration to currently fashionable "radical" and "new left" critiques of the American political system. It will not tax anyone's credulity, I am sure, for a Berkeley professor to report that he is aware that such critiques exist. I am not persuaded, however, that this book is the proper place to take full account of them. Radicals, in common with many other American intellectuals, betray little interest in how political institutions actually work. They are more concerned with what they conceive to be the outcomes in society than with the complexly interrelated institutions and processes that produce outcomes. The focus here, for better or worse, is on institutions and processes. For the most part, these are real. They exist in time and space, create, spend, and redirect resources, and affect peoples' lives. They should not be ignored. This is true whether or not the reader shares my view that for an increasing number of Americans, though regrettably not for all of them, these institutions have attenuated the chances that their lives would be solitary, poor, nasty, brutish, and short.

Most of what I said in the first edition, consequently, I am content to stand by for this one. I have brought a few allusions in the text up to date and added sections of commentary and amplification where I thought it appropriate or helpful to do so—notably on the Kennedy and Johnson Presidencies, on reapportionment and electoral reform, and on the role of the Senate in the political system.

In spite of the light work I have tried to make for myself, I am, as always, awash in scholarly obligations. I want to thank, in particular, the following friends and colleagues who read and commented on part or all of this second edition, sometimes in great detail: Robert A. Dahl, Elizabeth Brenner Drew, H. Douglas Price, Seyom Brown, Richard F. Fenno, Fred I. Greenstein, Kai T. Erikson, Leslie Gelb, David Cohen, Aaron Wildavsky, Raymond Wolfinger, Andrew McFarland, Paul Sniderman, Robert Jervis, Bill Cavala, William K. Muir, Jr., Robert Axelrod, Byron Shafer, and Jack Citrin. John Palladino, Sam Kernell, Robert vom Eigen, and Joan vom Eigen helped me update the manuscript, and Kathleen Peters typed everything with her usual skill, speed, and imperturbability. The responsibilities, mistakes, and fanciful little touches throughout are, however, all mine.

My work on *Congress and the Presidency* since the first edition has been facilitated by the Carnegie Corporation through its grant to the American Political Science Association's Study of Congress, the Institute of Governmental Studies and the Institute of International Studies of the University of California, the Social Science Research Council, the Rockefeller Foundation, and the Center for Advanced Study in the Behavioral Sciences.

And I am still greatly indebted to the three ladies to whom this book is dedicated for the fun and amusement they provide when, as sometimes happens, I can get neither from Congress and the Presidency.

Nelson W. Polsby

Berkeley, California
1971

PREFACE

To the First Edition

It is a remarkable fact that American political institutions have survived—indeed flourished—through the strenuous challenges attending the birth of our nation, an explosive expansion westward, civil war, industrialization, urbanization, mass immigration, several depressions, two world wars, and sundry and miscellaneous hostile challenges from abroad. The constitutional order under which these institutions operate has now remained intact for 175 years, longer than virtually any other government in the world. American political institutions are, by any modern standard, impressively venerable. They are also enormously interesting. I hope in this book to suggest why the operations of Congress and the President, in particular, give so much pleasure to the professional student of politics, purely as spectator sport. In addition, to be sure, these two institutions continue to have critical importance in shaping our futures, as they have our collective present and past.

In writing this book, I have relied in part on reading in the scholarly literature and the newspapers, in part on documentary and other primary material, and also on interviews and personal observations. These latter have been made possible over the last few years by generosity from several sources: Ford Foundation grants to the Public Affairs Center of Wesleyan University, which made funds available to me for research assistance; The Social Science Research Council, which has aided me at almost every turn in my pursuit of first-hand knowledge about Congress and the Presidency; and my colleagues in the Government Department at Wesleyan, especially Clement E. Vose, who as chairman made it possible and pleasurable to harmonize teaching and research.

Just as a thief or an embezzler may be kind to his mother, loyal to his friends, and civil to his neighbors, so a short and selective book about Congress and the Presidency may display inadvertent virtues. In this case, any such are probably the result of the strenuous efforts of my friends and colleagues, H. Douglas Price, Theodore Lowi, Fred Greenstein, Joseph Cooper,

Micah Naftalin, Robert L. Peabody, John Bibby, Roger Davidson, Edwin Olson, Elizabeth Brenner Drew, Basil Moore, Aaron Wildavsky, Raymond E. Wolfinger, Lewis A. Froman, Jr., and Richard F. Fenno, Jr.; or of my assistants, Peter Morrison, Paul D. O'Brien, Michael Leiserson, John Neff, and Andrew Kleinfeld; or of my typists, Sheila Jones, Martha McCaughtry, and Karen DiStefano; or of my editors, Alfred Goodyear, James J. Murray III, and, especially, Wilbur Mangas, and Robert A. Dahl; or of my wife, Linda. Most of these people read at least parts of the manuscript. All had comments and suggestions that either improved the book or my disposition and sometimes (rarely!) both. But the reader will have no difficulty in assigning responsibility for errors in a book that intends to be only a first approximation, leaves much unsaid, and hence depends so heavily upon an author's own judgment. Indeed, in a book of this kind, the author has no incentive to protest his own inadequacies in a preface because they are so eloquently displayed throughout the volume in question.

Nevertheless, a brief warning. Sometimes I have sacrificed discussion of an institution to a consideration of analytical writing about it. At other points I was moved to do the reverse. Many of the judgments expressed in these pages are by no means widely accepted, and some of them may turn out to be quite wrong. The restrictions of the present format have provided me with an excuse to follow my interests rather than the demands of symmetry or comprehensiveness that a larger text would have imposed. I can only hope that the result will stimulate the reader to work back into the books and articles with which my interpretations agree and disagree, and forward into an enriched understanding of the lively institutions of American democracy.

Nelson W. Polsby

Middletown, Connecticut
1964

CONTENTS

xi

CHAPTER FIVE

NATIONAL POLICY-MAKING I: THE LEGISLATIVE LABYRINTH

　　The Origin of Bills. Reference to Committees. In Committee. Hearings. The Mark-up. The Calendars. The Rules Committee. Floor Action in the House. Floor Action in the Senate. The Conference. The President Acts. Summary and Review: Power in the Process.

CHAPTER SIX

NATIONAL POLICY-MAKING II: THE BUDGETARY PROCESS

　　Presidential Planning: March–June. Presidential "Ceilings" and Agency Estimates: June–November. Presidential Oversight: September–December. Congressional Action: January–July (or Later). Summary: The Politics of Budget-Making.

CHAPTER SEVEN

CONFLICT AND COOPERATION

　　Dimensions of Conflict. Sources of Conflict. Instruments of Conflict. The Legitimacy of Conflict. Sources of Cooperation.

TO EXPLORE FURTHER

INDEX

CONGRESS
AND
THE PRESIDENCY

CHAPTER ONE

ON THE AMERICAN POLITICAL SYSTEM

In 1884, a young student of politics named Woodrow Wilson published a book called *Congressional Government*. In it, he said he was going to "point out the most characteristic practical features of the federal system . . . with a view to making as plain as possible the actual conditions of federal administration . . . striving to catch its present phases and to photograph the delicate organism in all its . . . parts exactly as it is today."[1] Nowadays, Wilson's book is regarded as a classic commentary for its time on the American system of government.

Despite the obvious immodesty of the aim, the object of the present book is to follow, as best it can, in Wilson's footsteps. For us, the task will be somewhat simplified by concentrating on those two great institutions of our national government whose officers are directly elected by the people and together share responsibility and accountability to the people for all the manifold policies that govern our nation. Congressional and presidential policymaking are important because they embody our theories of democratic government and decisively shape outcomes that affect all of us. And both Congress and the Presidency are altered with the times. Thus, in every generation, the study of Congress and the Presidency is a continuing obligation.

Since *Congressional Government* was written, a great many changes have overtaken our country and expressed themselves through changes in our politics. From a vantage point today, the resiliency and endurance of the American Constitution are much more worthy of note than they seem to have been for Wilson, who wrote when our government was less than a century old and still in the shadow of the post-Civil War Reconstruction. The Presidency was then in eclipse; now, owing to the insatiable coverage of the mass

---

[1] Woodrow Wilson, *Congressional Government* (New York: Meridian Books, Inc., 1956; 1st ed., 1884), pp. 23, 24, 30.

media, the immense growth of the Federal bureaucracies, and, particularly, the urgent pressure of foreign affairs, the Presidency clearly dominates the Federal system.

Some things, however, have remained the same. The ways of Congress are still labyrinthine and inscrutable. It is still more a working legislature than a debating society. However, the distribution of powers between its branches has shifted in interesting ways. The Senate, primarily because of its practices of debate and its greater involvement in policy-making as an advisor and sometime public adversary of the President, has gained a superior toehold in the consciousness of politically aware citizens. The House, on the other hand, is, as it was in Wilson's day, preeminently the home of a recognizably old-fashioned legislative politics. More often and in more ways, the House is where the domestic plans and programs of liberal Presidents receive their stiffest and most detailed scrutiny and where they most often fail. Through its detailed appropriations procedures, the House maintains a close contact with the machinery of the executive branch; thus it retains substantial power even in a day and age when the bulk of the news coverage goes to presidential activity of almost any kind and to senatorial speechmaking.

HOW MANY BRANCHES OF GOVERNMENT?

The United States Constitution provides for three branches of national government: a legislature, to make the laws; an executive, to "take care that the laws be faithfully executed"; and a Supreme Court, whose jurisdiction is spelled out in some detail. Over the years, as the nation and its government have grown in size and complexity, organizations besides the original three—for example, political parties and interest groups—have assumed a share in government. Government corporations and "independent" regulatory agencies have been established in the interstices of the original three branches. Media of mass communication have sometimes been designated as a "fourth branch of government."

And each of the original three branches has increased in size and become more specialized. In 1816, the first year for which statistics are available, the entire executive branch numbered 4,479. Today it employs more than 2.9 million civilians and almost 3.5 million men and women in uniform.[2] They are organized into a tremendous number of agencies and bureaus, some responsible directly to the President, others responsible to administrative officers selected by the President with the advice and consent of the Senate, of which a few are supposed to be independent of both Congress and President. Congress, meanwhile, has grown from a Senate of 28 and a House of Representatives of 65 to 100 and 435, respectively. In 1792, each congressman represented an average of 34,436 constituents. Today, the average is more than

[2] For the 1816 figures, see *Historical Statistics of the United States; Colonial Times to 1957* (Washington, D.C.: Government Printing Office, 1960). The 1968 figures on executive branch employees are 2,940,944 civilians and 3,489,876 military personnel. *Statistical Abstract of the United States 1969* (Washington, D.C.: Government Printing Office, 1969) pp. 398, 257.

450,000. And, finally, what was originally a five-man Supreme Court has grown to nine men and has been supplemented by an entire Federal judiciary, consisting of 90 courts of original jurisdiction and 11 appellate courts.[3]

The various branches of government have also changed and modified their functions. The most notable modification came early (1803) when, in *Marbury v. Madison*, the Supreme Court claimed the right to examine the constitutionality of acts performed by the other two branches.[4] In addition, the judiciary has from time to time engaged in administrative activities, as, for example, in their supervision of local plans for school desegregation. And the courts have also in effect legislated "interstitially," in areas where Congress was vague, ambiguous, or silent. The executive branch, likewise, engages in judicial proceedings through the actions of administrative tribunals, such as the Subversive Activities Control Board, which has the power, after a quasi-judicial proceeding, to require organizations to register under an act of Congress. Agencies of the executive branch legislate by issuing regulations covering classes of events, such as a regulation changing the order in which different groups of citizens become eligible for the draft. Finally, committees of Congress take care that the laws are faithfully executed by undertaking intensive investigations of executive agencies from time to time. These investigations entail reviewing and overseeing the details of decisions reached by the executive departments. Public investigations of private citizens and nongovernmental organizations also provide Congress with a device that in many of its particulars imitates the judicial process.

The point of these observations is to suggest that, in this day and age, the Constitution is a fallible and incomplete guide to national policy-making. Instead of three branches of government, each with its clearly defined sphere of competence and activity, there may be five branches of government in any particular issue area, or seven, or twenty, or only one. The number of "branches" involved varies from time to time and from issue to issue. And the roles these branches play may vary greatly too. An executive agency may "legislate" a regulation. An aggrieved interest group may "appeal" to a congressional committee, which in turn may instruct another agency to grant relief. The first agency may then ask the President to intervene and "adjudicate" the dispute—and so on, with "legislative," "executive," and "judicial" roles mixed and distributed throughout the national government.

Finally, alliances may spring up across traditional boundary lines at the same time that fierce competition is contained within the constitutional branches. Sometimes the competition between (let us say) the United States Army Corps of Engineers and the Reclamation Bureau of the Department of Interior for jurisdiction over a particular public-works project becomes in-

---

[3] *U.S. Government Organization Manual 1969–70* (Washington, D.C.: Government Printing Office), pp. 44–54. In addition, there are specialized courts, including the Tax Court of the United States, territorial courts, the United States Court of Claims, the United States Customs Court, and the United States Court of Customs and Patent Appeals.

[4] Although this decision was controversial at the time, some scholars now feel that the Court was acting under a mandate clearly implied by the Constitution. See Charles L. Black, Jr., *Perspectives in Constitutional Law* (Englewood Cliffs, N.J.: Prentice-Hall, 1963), pp. 2–3.

tense; each side brings in allies and defenders from different committees of Congress and from other branches of the Federal bureaucracy—sometimes up to and including the President.[5] In order to understand how a conflict such as this one plays itself out, a person must suspend his belief in what Woodrow Wilson called a literary theory, which views the branches of government as locked in airtight compartments, fixed in number and each operating in its own frictionless universe. Rather, the political activities of Congress and the Presidency that we shall be describing are examples of coalition politics, where there are sometimes only a few "branches" of government to consider, sometimes many.

THE CONTEXT OF POLICY-MAKING

It is quite impossible to classify and count in any meaningful way for our purposes all the complex problems facing the government, but to get a rough idea of what is involved, reflect on the governmental decisions lying behind the following headlines from the front page of a national newspaper on *one* day in 1964.[6]

RIGHTS BACKERS SEEKING CLOSURE WITHIN 2 WEEKS; JOHNSON URGES SUPPORT

RUSK WARNS NATO AGAINST ASSUMING A DETENTE EXISTS

TIES OF SENATORS TO BAKER QUERIED

REP. CANNON DIES; LED FUNDS PANEL

MC NAMARA OPENS TALKS IN VIETNAM

U.S. TRAINING TAIWAN TROOPS; ROLE IN VIETNAM HELD POSSIBLE

FIGURES ON SOVIET ARMS FOR INDIA INDICATE THAT U.S. SENDS LESS

GOLDWATER SEES NEW RACE STRIFE UNLESS GOP WINS

Clearly, the range of decisions, the number of difficult technical problems, the number of different actors involved in the day-to-day operations of our national government is remarkable. Obviously, no single President, no matter how shrewd and skillful, no matter how well supplied with staff aid, can hope to give his personal attention to even a substantial fraction of these issues and decisions. Nor can a Congress. In spite of the fact that there are as many as 435 representatives and 100 senators, they make laws only if *co-ordinated*. A majority in each House (and, usually, the President's assent) must be secured for each law passed by Congress. There is simply not enough time for either Congress collectively or the President individually to deal effectively with all the problems that come up.

Therefore, both Congress and the President *sample*. Specific techniques they use to handle the decision-making situations they ultimately face will be

[5] See, in this case, Arthur Maass, *Muddy Waters* (Cambridge, Mass.: Harvard, 1951).
[6] *The New York Times*, May 13, 1964.

discussed in detail later. Right now, let us look at a few of the principles on which sampling is based.

There is a tendency, first, for Congress and the President to address those problems, regardless of their intrinsic importance, that are forced on them by the calendar. For example, laws are often written so that they expire after a certain date—indeed, in the case of laws giving money to the armed services, the Constitution requires that they do so.[7] If national policy-makers want to continue such a law in force, they must act promptly to renew it before it expires or they risk the dismantling of valued administrative machinery, the loss of personnel, the misplacement of records, and the interruption of service. And so, of course, they do generally attend to the renewal of expiring laws, even when other matters are pressing. Another example: the Constitution gives the President the duty "from time to time [to] give to the Congress Information of the State of the Union."[8] In practice, this has meant a major speech at the opening of each congressional session. Since the Constitution prescribes when Congress shall convene (noon, January 3 of every year, unless another day is appointed by law),[9] the President knows he has a deadline to meet. Other longer-range matters must be pushed aside when that deadline approaches. Thus, the first bias in sampling is to do things that the calendar says must be done promptly.

The number of deadlines fixed by the Constitution is not great, but the calendar is inexorable in other ways. Suppose, for example, the President wants Congress to pass a law empowering him to furnish new types of foreign aid. In what way does the calendar constrain him?

There is already a law in effect that deals with the general subject of foreign aid. The President (and his advisors) must decide whether they want to wait until this bill comes up for renewal and tack the new proposals onto it or whether they want to make the program they have in mind a special issue. If they decide to make this a special issue, they must find someone appropriate in each house of Congress to introduce the bill they want (usually a senior member of the committee to which the bill will be assigned). But first they must draw the bill up and make sure it says what they want it to say. This takes time, especially if more than one Federal agency is concerned with the bill, because each agency will want to look the bill over and signify its approval or disapproval or suggest modifications. Furthermore, the President normally wants a draft of the bill reviewed by outside experts to make sure his proposal is a sound one and to alert the people who are going to have to execute the law to the trend of his thinking.

The executive agencies involved ordinarily want to supply their congressional supporters with strong and relevant arguments for the bill. They also want to make up statements of their own to submit when congressional committees hold hearings on it. This means they want to coordinate the submission of the bill with *their* priority lists for legislation.

---

[7] Article I, Section 8, says, in part, "The Congress shall have power . . . to raise and support armies, but no appropriation of money to that use shall be for a longer term than two years."

[8] Article II, Section 3.

[9] Twentieth Amendment, Section 2.

The relevant committees of the House and Senate may have other pressing legislation before them. So *their* priorities must be considered. Yet the President's term of office is only four—or, at most, eight—years. It takes time to move the wheels of government, perhaps not enough time to do all he wants to do. So the second bias in national policy-making is toward doing things that can be done quickly.

A third bias, equally understandable, orients decision-makers toward problems that appear to be especially acute rather than chronic. When a crisis occurs, men must act. A threatened nationwide railroad strike may demand immediate legislation. Other matters must be put aside. Missile bases may be erected in Cuba. The President cannot wait. In a sense, then, events govern the priorities established by our national decision-makers. They must keep themselves sufficiently open to the pressure of events to move promptly when necessary. But this precludes attending to as many "basic" or chronic demands as they otherwise might tackle.

The pressures of time and events, the multiple competing demands on our national government, mean that, unavoidably, policy-makers are less systematic, less orderly in their decision-making than they would be if they could fully control their environments. Even so, they do make choices. They do pursue policies in part of their own devising. They can regulate many of the demands placed on them. But they must pursue their goals in a complicated world that sets boundaries and constraints on them and that continually forces them into compromises not only in their policy preferences, but also in the ways in which they allocate their time and attention.

IS THE SYSTEM DEMOCRATIC?

A fair-minded preliminary characterization would probably concede that, in general, Americans enjoy a "democratic" political system. In the early 1970s, among presumably well-educated people, this is sometimes regarded as a quaint, irrelevant, or even complacent view—quaint because it is more likely to be held by persons over thirty, irrelevant because it fails to address pressing social issues, and complacent because the use of the honorific term *democracy* implies a satisfaction with things as they are and an incapacity to recognize or decry injustice. Perhaps what is needed is some other term, without honorific connotations, that concedes the existence of injustice but that nevertheless denotes a system relatively (but not perfectly) open to participation by those possessing requisite skills and interests, relatively (but not perfectly) responsive to the demands of a variety of participants, and run (but not flawlessly) according to a relatively stable and equitable set of rules. Criteria such as these have in the past served to distinguish more and less democratic political systems and have been helpful to observers who wanted to monitor changes in political conditions within one country. Thus, an observer might find it useful to contrast the legal, political, and social position of black persons in various parts of the United States before Emancipation, during Reconstruction, after the imposition of Jim Crow laws, and today. Or he might compare the condition of our most deprived social groups today with that of Jews in modern-day Poland, Catholics in Northern Ireland, Armenians in Turkey, Chinese in Indonesia, Ibo in Nigeria, or Watusi in Rwanda.[10] Or he might gauge the relative size of privileged and unprivileged groups in different societies. He might ask how widely opportunities to develop the skills requisite to political action are distributed in the population. By such inductive means the relative position of the United States can be established.

To be sure, such an exercise would establish only one context within which the American political system might be viewed, because it leaves open questions of improvement and the extent to which the system approximates or approaches ideal standards. The value of an inductive approach is that it encourages the acquisition of knowledge. Knowledge is helpful in turn in developing the competence necessary to work a complex political system. Thus an inductive approach may facilitate the achievement of ideals more effectively than the mere reiteration of the ideals themselves.

An empirical approach may also contribute to the closer examination of ideal standards. Consider the ideal of majority rule. It would be incorrect to say that our system is one in which majorities always rule, and this fact sometimes confuses observers who believe that the rule of the majority is always a necessary or even a sufficient condition for a political system to be democratic. It is possible, however, to think of several situations in which simple majority rule could operate but in which the system would not be satisfactorily "democratic" from the standpoint of most Americans. For example, duly constituted agents of a majority could deprive members of the minority of the right to participate in future elections. Or heavy majorities could be registered in elections in which no alternatives were permitted. Or there could be occasions when a minority felt intensely about an issue but the majority, which did not care strongly one way or another, still prevailed. In each of these cases, even though majority rule operated, the government would be less open, less responsive, less stable, less equitable, and therefore less democratic than Americans would probably like or accept. Indeed, our national government operates in many instances to thwart the rule of the majority. Here are several brief examples.

1. The electoral college, through which we select our Presidents, provides that individual votes be counted state by state. By custom, the presidential candidate receiving the most votes within a state is declared the winner of all the state's electoral votes. This means that a presidential candidate who loses the state of New York by one vote but wins Delaware by ten thousand votes receives only three electoral votes, while his opponent receives forty-three electoral votes. The underlying principle of majority rule is, of course, equality in the weight of each vote. Yet the votes of millions of New

---

[10] These examples are meant to stack the deck only against those who assert that the American political system is the worst one they ever heard of. A more complex and interesting formulation of the problem would be to study the United States in the context of societies with similarly mixed populations and compare our solutions to the problems of government with theirs.

Yorkers who voted for the loser are in effect not expressed in the final tabulation. Indeed, in this instance, the candidate who receives the majority of popular votes in the two states would receive only a bit more than 6 percent (3/46) of the electoral vote.

The electoral college thwarts the majority-rule principle in still another way—by giving small states more electoral votes than they would be entitled to if each popular vote were weighted exactly the same. In 1968, for example, 6,682,361 New Yorkers voted for President. They chose forty-three electors, one for each of their forty-one members of the House of Representatives, and one for each senator. At the same time, 74,782 Alaskans chose three electors (for one House member and two senators). If each New Yorker's vote were weighted equally with each Alaskan's, it would have been necessary in 1968 for New York to have had 268 electors, not 43.

2. Malapportionment is widespread. In the Senate, each state has two votes, regardless of its population. The senators from the nine least populous states, with 2.4 percent of the nation's population, can cancel out the votes of the senators from the nine most populous states, representing a majority (52.0 percent) of the nation's people.[11]

In the House of Representatives, however, the most common cause of malapportionment has been attenuated. Within each state, congressional district lines are drawn by the state legislature. As long as state legislatures were themselves grossly malapportioned, as many were, congressional districts stood in jeopardy of being malapportioned also. Before the Supreme Court began to attack legislative malapportionment, in a series of decisions that began in 1962,[12] great disparities in the populations of congressional districts were not uncommon. Sometimes adjacent districts would have populations varying from a little over 200,000 to over 1 million.

Today, this sort of extreme disparity is not possible under the law. Within each state the populations of congressional districts must approach equality. Some malapportionment is bound to occur, however, because all states have at least one congressman, even though their populations are much smaller than the nationwide average for Congressional districts (one congressman for every 468,000 people).[13]

Needless to say, the Supreme Court was not able completely to abolish political maneuvering with respect to districting. State legislatures are still

---

[11] This arrangement is written into the Constitution (Article I, Section 3). It is most difficult to change, because Article V of the Constitution provides that "no state, without its consent, shall be deprived of its equal suffrage in the Senate."

[12] The main decisions were *Baker v. Carr*, 369 U.S. 186 (1962), which took jurisdiction in state apportionment cases; *Wesberry v. Sanders*, 376 U.S. 1 (1964), which required substantial equality of United States House districts; and *Reynolds v. Sims*, 377 U.S. 533 (1964), which forced the apportionment of both houses of bicameral state legislatures on the same population basis. For a thorough discussion of these and other cases, see Robert G. Dixon, *Democratic Representation* (New York: Oxford, 1968). In *Wells v. Rockefeller*, 389 U.S. 421 (1969), the Court defined more exactly—and more narrowly—what "substantial equality" meant.

[13] Dixon, *op. cit.*, p. 455, shows that, based on 1960 population figures, states having two congressmen are most likely to lose out under the present formula for allocating congressmen among the states.

political bodies, even though politically they are balanced somewhat differently than they used to be. The one-man, one-vote rule is now more or less followed in House districting, but the system is far from tamperproof. Thus, the legislatures, while accepting the constraint of population equalization the Court placed on them, have nevertheless still managed on occasion to draw congressional districts with shapes as bizarre as the Massachusetts senatorial district that in 1812 was dubbed "the gerrymander."[14] Moreover, a political Pandora's box opens every ten years when the results of the decennial census are tallied. Adjustments then must be made in the allocation of seats among the states, making a wave of reapportionments necessary within each affected state. However, the alternative would be greater numerical malapportionment, so in this respect—and to some degree—the political system has moved toward majority rule since 1964.

3. Many of the practices of the Senate and House thwart majority rule within each body. Often their internal decisions are made by application of the rule of seniority rather than by vote or in committees rather than on the floor. In the House a great deal of business has been kept off the floor by the actions of the fifteen-man Rules Committee. In the Senate unlimited debate permits a determined minority to prevent legislative action indefinitely. Filibusters cannot be terminated by a simple majority vote, only by two-thirds of the senators present and voting.

4. Even after both houses of Congress act favorably on a bill and it is signed by the President, its constitutionality may be challenged in the courts. If the Supreme Court holds a law to be unconstitutional, it is voided in spite of the majorities of popularly elected legislators that passed it and the President who signed it.

But might not these majority-thwarting institutions also be responsible for the openness, responsiveness, and stability of our system and hence actually be democratizing influences? It is not at all clear that this is so. What makes our system democratic is more complicated than that; it concerns the fact that each center of special power is for various reasons responsive to somewhat different segments of the population. Furthermore, many power centers share in the making of public policy. This means that public policy is likely to respond to a variety of interest groups. As long as different factions with differing policy preferences control different centers of power and large numbers of those who are willing and able to learn how to participate have ready access to one or more centers, the system is likely to be reasonably

---

[14] Connoisseurs of the art form particularly admire the Thirty-fifth Congressional District of New York, which was drawn by a Republican legislature in an unsuccessful attempt to unseat Democratic Congressman Samuel Stratton. Until it was changed in early 1970, this district wandered all over upstate New York in search of a Republican majority. Another example is the state of Missouri, which in late 1969 was apportioned by the Democratic-controlled state legislature into ten congressional districts more exactly equal in size than those in any other state in the union. The city of St. Louis was carved into small, irregular pieces and parceled out among five congressional districts, including one (the First) that a Republican leader said was shaped like a "flying turkey." This same leader referred to another district (the Eighth) quite accurately as "the moose." See *Congressional Quarterly Weekly Report* 27 (Sept. 5, 1969) p. 1644.

democratic. But what makes groups and factions willing to ally with others and admit outsiders? Here we come to four additional, critically important prerequisites of democracy:

1. Frequent election of public officials means that it is constitutionally possible to replace public officeholders.

2. The existence of a competitive party system means that sufficient alternatives are presented at elections to make the replacement of officeholders not unlikely or at least not politically impossible.

3. The consent of many different politicians must be secured to enact public policy. These politicians may vary in numerous ways: according to their constituencies if elected (safe, not so safe, rural, urban, large, small, one-party, two-party), according to their terms of office if appointed (for life, for a long, set term, at the pleasure of the President), according to their conceptions of their role and their responsibilities, according to their technical knowledge, according to their policy preferences, and so on. These different politicians must deal with one another in order to accomplish their own policy goals.

4. Politicians are generally sufficiently uncertain of the outcomes of elections to be willing, between elections as well as at election time, to accommodate, if they can, the intensely expressed preferences of most groups in the population. And their uncertainty extends to the activities of other politicians. Hence, men (say, Southern congressional committee chairmen) relatively inaccessible to a particular group (say, Northern Negroes) must beware the activities of men more accessible to this group (such as the President). *Uncertainty* is the glue that holds together many of the disparate parts of a complex, stable democracy.

The operation of the uncertainty principle depends on a further condition, namely, that among groups, there be extreme differences in intensity of preferences on issues, with each issue at the focus of concern for one or only a few narrowly specialized groups. In short, if politics is conducted at relatively low temperatures, that is, if friction between contending groups is not intense, it is possible for politicians to seek to accommodate the preferences of most of those who make demands on them. At high temperatures, politicians have to choose sides among interest groups. They exchange uncertainty (about what people in an undifferentiated political environment *might* do) for certainty (about what friends and enemies *will* do); they seek less to avoid hypothetical costs than to avert certain costs. In these circumstances, the diversity of power centers in American politics and the differences in their accessibility to different interest groups become more important than the uncertainty of politicians in keeping the political system open and responsive.

AMERICAN POLITICS IS COALITION POLITICS

I have spoken of the diversity of power centers in the American political system and of the low temperature and pressure at which most policies are prepared. This continues to be true even when some major policies are hotly debated in the public arena. For example, while thousands of newly concerned citizens focused their attention on military involvement in Southeast Asia, immense leeway for elite participants continued to exist in such matters as the regulation of broadcasting, the setting of farm price supports, the acquisition of land for national parks, and scores of other government policies. With respect to these, an observer could note the extent to which political resources are not efficiently or energetically employed to change outcomes and the extent to which policies are unplanned, uncoordinated, piecemeal, and trial-and-error in their conception and execution.

These characteristics of policy-making are not necessarily deplorable. Rather, one would expect policy-making processes of this kind under the following conditions: (1) The constitutional order is highly stable and generally accepted. (2) The society is large, heterogeneous, literate, and mainly prosperous. (3) Political resources and their legitimate use are widely dispersed throughout the population. This would mean in effect that, if most citizens who wanted to could participate in politics and if the demands made on political institutions were moderate and somewhat attainable by those who were willing to seek widespread agreement among politically active segments of the population, then coalitions would—as they often do in American politics—contribute to the legitimacy of governmental decisions by gaining the assent of relevant publics for governmental activity.

Generally fortuitous circumstances of American life and history, such as abundant natural resources and territory, peace during our period of modernization, the absence of a feudal heritage, the ability of our expanding economy to absorb and welcome successive waves of immigrants, and the sheer complexity of the government and the diversity of problems that face it, all contributed to the early development of our system of coalition politics. Once in operation, the system has maintained itself not only by continuing to foster its preconditions but also by indoctrinating, training, and selectively recruiting skilled people for political positions.

As long as political resources are widely (even though unequally) dispersed in a political system, the success of any participant depends on his ability to make alliances, his skill at setting policy goals that will distribute rewards to enough interests to make it possible for him to achieve what he wants to achieve. This is generally accomplished by consent, not coercion. But in order to understand contemporary policy-making by Congress and the Presidency, it is necessary to know more than that they bargain and search for coalitions. Circumstances, variations in the kinds of resources available to politicians and the goals they are seeking, make some coalitions easier to assemble than others. Thus we must sketch in greater detail the resources and goals of Presidents, senators, and congressmen in order to see how they adjust to and transform their political environment.

CHAPTER TWO

THE PRESIDENCY

THE PRESIDENTIAL COALITION

Perhaps the easiest way to begin a discussion of the American Presidency is to describe the presidential coalition, the combination of interests and political forces that has tended, at least since the New Deal, to form around candidates for President from both political parties. The presidential coalition has its roots in the political strategies of presidential nomination and election, which in turn are shaped by a few central facts of life.

There is, for example, the fact that presidential elections are contested essentially between two parties, either of which can win.[1] Winning the Presidency is the supreme goal of both political parties, and they have learned to adapt their strategies to this task. Parties nominate men who they believe can win, and they write platforms that attempt to appeal to a broad spectrum of voters and interest groups. But some voters and interest groups are more strategically placed than others. Voters in large, industrialized, two-party states are particularly well situated. The reason for this is the method of counting votes in the electoral college that is almost universally followed—the so-called unit rule. Enforced by custom or state regulation, the unit rule provides that the presidential candidate who wins a popular majority, no matter how narrow, in a state shall receive the state's entire electoral vote.

The number of electoral votes each state casts is determined by its number of senators (two for each state) and representatives in Congress (which varies according to population). Thus the populous states have large electoral votes and are particularly important. The candidate who wins most or all of them, even by a hair, will probably win the Presidency. Both parties realize

[1] See Nelson W. Polsby and Aaron B. Wildavsky, *Presidential Elections* (New York: Scribner, 1968), for an extended discussion of political strategies in presidential elections.

this and shape their strategies accordingly. They tend to nominate men who come from the larger states and who, in the progression of their own careers, have made alliances with urban interest groups, such as labor unions, Negroes, and other ethnic blocs, and these groups' representatives. In their policy preferences, these groups, by and large, are conventionally described as "liberal"—welfare minded, favoring civil rights legislation, and demanding of governmental services.

Although Democrats rather than Republicans are more likely to have firm alliances with groups representing these interests, over the last three decades *both* parties, on the whole, have pursued the strategy of wooing voters in the large, industrialized areas as the first order of business in presidential campaigns. This has given rise in the Republican party to the charge by conservatives that "me-too" candidacies have weakened Republican electoral effectiveness. But there is scant reason to believe that more conservative Republican candidates would have won. On the contrary, most politicians, including those most instrumental in selecting Republican candidates, believe that candidates as conservative as, say, the late Senator Robert A. Taft, who was greatly revered throughout his party, could not possibly win a presidential election. Public as well as privately sponsored opinion polls have generally borne out this conclusion, and so does the 1964 campaign, in which the Republican nominee rejected the "me-too" strategy with disastrous consequences. Thus it is not surprising that Republicans (as well as Democrats) have tended to select as their candidates for President men from the large states, men whose allies are more likely to be industrialists and Wall Street bankers, corporation lawyers and suburban voters rather than the farmers, small-town professional men, and merchants who contribute so much to the grass-roots leadership of the Republican party. Whatever their personal preferences, successful Republican presidential nominees in recent years have harbored few illusions about the necessity for recognizing the manifold demands that are made on big government.[2]

Thus, in the first instance, the nature of the Presidency is shaped by the process that nominates a President and elects him to office. This process tends to bring to the Presidency candidates whose alliances and promises, if not their personal inclinations as well, spell active government, a government that makes plans and meets demands. There is a passive theory of the Presidency, one that insists on congressional initiative—as if a bicameral body of 535 were designed to be fast on its 1,070 feet. But even modern exponents of

[2] Here is an example of Richard Nixon's thinking on the subject: "They tell me, 'You didn't hit them hard enough. Why don't you give them hell like Truman?' I explain that I not only have to appeal to partisan Republicans but also have to get Democrats to cross over. But the women don't understand that. Occasionally I say a good word for Johnson or Humphrey. *It's a device, of course, to show I'm fair-minded*, but the women don't see that. That's why the women liked Barry so. He didn't give a damn about Democrats. But to win, you have to" (italics in original). (Jules Witcover, *The Resurrection of Richard Nixon*, New York: Putnam, 1970, page 135.) The most recent Republican attempt to argue the case for a more conservative governing coalition is Kevin Phillips, *The Emerging Republican Majority* (New Rochelle, New York: Arlington House, 1969). For a number of reasons, I find this argument unpersuasive. See Nelson W. Polsby, "An Emerging Republican Majority?" *The Public Interest*, vol. 17 (Fall, 1969) pp. 119–126.

a passive Presidency, such as the late General Eisenhower, could not success-fully be passive Presidents. If responsiveness to the needs of the presidential coalition were not enough to provoke presidential activity, other factors have made the contemporary Presidency active even when the President was not.

ENERGY FOR THE SYSTEM

Why, in our complex and interdependent political system, does so much de-pend on the President? "A President has a great chance; his position is almost that of a king and a prime minister rolled into one," said Theodore Roose-velt.[3] That is true. But why is it true? A number of factors, some historical and some institutional, have converged on the President in modern times and have changed radically the character of the office as it was conceived of by the authors of the Constitution.

Of the historical factors, none has been more obtrusive, more demand-ing, or more critical than the progressive entanglement of the United States in foreign affairs. The Constitution gives the President an unmistakable, far-reaching, and almost exclusive mandate in this area; the few enumerated duties of the Chief Executive include the power to receive ambassadors from foreign countries, the power to make treaties (with the advice and consent of the Senate), and the rank of Commander in Chief of the armed forces. As the rapidly advancing technology of mankind has shrunk the world, the rele-vance of these powers to the prosperity and tranquillity of the United States has increased greatly.

A second historical factor in the rise of the President has been the sheer growth of the executive branch, which he heads. As our land area and popu-lation have increased and diversified over the last two centuries, the national government has been faced with a variety of new demands—for help, for relief, for services of all kinds. A preferred method for dealing with these de-mands has been the founding of new agencies within the executive branch. Once they are set in motion, these agencies do not merely respond passively to the accelerating needs of an expanding population; they behave creatively, seeking ways to increase their powers and their size. Here, too, the Presi-dent's constitutional powers place him at the top of an expanding situation. The Constitution gives him the right, as Chief Executive, to nominate (the Senate consenting) and appoint the policy-making officers of the executive branch and to require their opinions in writing on matters of state. The vague constitutional mandate to see that the laws are faithfully executed means, in effect, that virtually all agencies created by Congress pursuant to public laws automatically come under the President's purview.

A third historical reason for the rise of the Presidency can be traced to the relationship, in a modern democratic society, between political leaders and followers, as it is filtered through news media. In the judgment of the purveyors of news, the great mass of citizens is not so gripped by political issues that their interest in them can be sustained without the leaven of so-

[3] Letter to Lady Delamere, March 7, 1911.

called human interest. In the early days of the Republic, when there was a party-controlled press, rank, vituperative, partisanship, and personal name-calling provided a rich emotional diet for the consumer of political news. The President was never far from the center of these controversies, since the Presidency, because of its powers to enhance the fortunes of a political party by staffing the government, has always been the most important office of all. Today, in a relatively bland era of "responsible," "objective" news coverage and vastly increased suffrage, the President still remains in the center of the limelight.[4] The media now ask him to play a more sacerdotal role, as a kind of guardian of national morale, a focus for affectionate emotions, an animate symbol of American sovereignty. Hopefully, he will have a sense of humor and a lively family—the media will in any event do their best to endow him with them.

This burden of group emotions and status aspirations that we ask our Presidents to bear has obvious political uses. Most recent Presidents have yielded regularly to the temptation to make political hay—either in behalf of their party or in behalf of their policies—by donning the mantle of nonpartisan sanctimony that the contemporary press fashions for them. In any case, whatever an American President does or says is news—automatic, instantaneous news—everywhere in the world. By manipulating the flexible boundaries between public business and private confidences, between firm policy commitments and trial balloons, a clever President can turn his status leadership to enormous political advantage.   *Nixon*

Historical changes associated with the growth, industrialization, and modernization of our country have, then, had a great deal to do with the emergence of the President as the principal figure in American national government. Characteristics of the institution apart from these historical changes also enhance the importance of the Presidency.

Consider the scope of the responsibilities allotted to him. These are virtually as broad as the coverage of the entire body of Federal law. They extend, for example, to the regulation of the economy. Various agencies of the executive branch or appointees of the President have powers to grant subsidies, approve or disapprove corporate mergers, raise and lower tariffs, let contracts (with variations as to their timing, amounts, and geographic locations), condemn land, and regulate credit. This list is not exhaustive.

The President's position at the peak of the executive branch (which,

[4] See Elmer E. Cornwell, Jr., "Presidential News: The Expanding Public Image," *Journalism Quarterly*, vol. 36 (Summer, 1959), pp. 275–283, for an ingenious demonstration of the increase, in this century, of news media attention to the President as compared with Congress. Other indications of the emotional centrality of the President in American life are contained in Leila Sussman, *Dear F.D.R.: A Study of Political Letterwriting* (Totowa, N.J.: Bedminster, 1963), and in studies of public opinion when Presidents die in office. A good summary of this literature is contained in Harold Orlansky, "Reactions to the Death of President Roosevelt," *The Journal of Social Psychology*, vol. 26 (November, 1947), pp. 235–266. See also Bradley S. Greenberg and Edwin B. Parker (eds.), *The Kennedy Assassination and the American Public* (Stanford, Calif.: Stanford, 1965); Martha Wolfenstein and Gilbert Kliman (eds.), *Children and the Death of a President* (Garden City, N.Y.: Doubleday, 1964); and Fred I. Greenstein, "The Psychological Functions of the Presidency for Citizens," in Elmer E. Cornwell (ed.), *The American Presidency: Vital Center* (Chicago: Scott, Foresman, 1966), pp. 30–36.

unlike the other two branches of the government, is formally organized under a single head) means that he may compel the cooperation of executive agencies in behalf of the policies he wishes to pursue.

A final institutional factor that enhances the position of the President is the discretionary character of the office. He is free to pursue those policies that are of greatest concern to him; he is not required to give equal attention to all problems and all agencies. Hence, it can be expected that most agencies most of the time will conduct their business according to the same pattern no matter who is President. But when a President desires to do so, he can change a particular agency's policies—if he is willing to bear the costs in terms of time, energy, and perhaps also the enmity of bureaucrats and the interest groups who are served by the agency involved.

Within the executive branch, the President must delegate powers, but he need not share them. The policy preferences he brings to his job, his conception of his role, the demands of the interest groups who are his allies, and the suggestions of his friends, his Cabinet, and his staff—all provide sources for presidential policies. His position at the head of an enormous hierarchy, whose concerns reach virtually everywhere, and the wide discretion of his office provide the President with the institutional tools that make it possible for him to move vigorously if he chooses. As we shall see in later chapters, these tools also permit him to move with initiative into areas where he must share powers, such as in the legislative process.

WAYS OF BEING PRESIDENT

There are as many different ways of being President as there are men willing to fill the office. Circumstances permit only one man at a time actually to be President, however, and face the problems of a particular era, and thus it is very difficult to make meaningful comparisons among Presidents and the ways in which they have conducted themselves in office. The temptation to try apparently is still overwhelming. Again and again, commentators attempt to illuminate the problems and possibilities of the presidential office by evaluating the performance of present or recent incumbents. Furthermore, writers on the Presidency have reached something of a consensus in their evaluations —even though these have been heavily influenced by value premises that are only partially articulated in the course of discussions in which they distill out of historical experience personal qualities and administrative practices that seem to be helpful in the conduct of the Presidency. These pages will provide room for only a few modern examples of this process of evaluation.

Herbert Hoover (Republican, 1929–1932). Most contemporary discussion of the Hoover Presidency focuses upon the economic disaster of 1929 to 1933, an event that Mr. Hoover understandably called "The nightmare of my years in the White House."[5] Although the great crash took place only seven months after he took office and robbed him a year later of effective majori-

---

[5] *The Memoirs of Herbert Hoover*, vol. 2, *The Cabinet and the Presidency 1920–1933* (New York: Macmillan, 1952), p. vi.

ties in both houses of Congress, the Presidency of Herbert Hoover is considered retrospectively almost exclusively in the light of two questions: Why did he let it happen? Why did he not do something to alleviate its effects?

Stated baldly, the questions seem unfair. Surely no Republican President, elected at the end of a fifty-year wave of industrial expansion and business dominance in national politics, was in a strong position either to prevent the Depression or to relieve its effects, no matter what his personal style. Nevertheless, attention has been called to what surely must have been of very marginal importance—Mr. Hoover's administrative fastidiousness, his habit of checking personally into minute details:[6]

> Exposure to detail can be carried too far. . . . Herbert Hoover is perhaps the classic instance of the man who went too far. For example, Hoover personally read and approved every letter sent by the Budget Bureau to executive agencies "clearing" their individual replies to congressional inquiries on legislation. In suggesting that a President be his own staff director I would not urge that he routinely do the work of the whole staff. One admires Hoover's industry but not his judgment of what to take upon himself and what to leave to others.[7]

Another remark by Neustadt about the Hoover Presidency is even more telling—he refers to Mr. Hoover as "caught in the trap of fighting history."[8] As we shall see, the criterion of judgment this implies plays an important role in the assessment of Presidents. Mr. Hoover's constitutional principles forbade to him many sorts of action that another President might have taken in a crisis.[9] His unwillingness in an acute domestic emergency to use the powers other men have found in the office grievously handicapped his Presidency and deprived it of the esteem of students of the Presidency to this day.

⟹*Franklin D. Roosevelt* (Democrat, 1933–1945). All Presidents receive vigorous criticism; for only a fortunate few does praise pour forth in comparable volume and intensity. Franklin Roosevelt is certainly of the elect group.[10]

---

[6] See *ibid.*, pp. 216ff, and esp. 217; and Victor L. Albjerg, "Hoover: The Presidency in Transition," *Current History* (October, 1960), pp. 213–219. In 1949, Mr. Hoover was rated next to the bottom of the "average" category as a President by fifty-five social scientists. See Arthur M. Schlesinger, Sr., *Paths to the Present* (New York: Macmillan, 1949), pp. 93–111. A more recent ranking by a similar group of historians rated Mr. Hoover nineteenth out of thirty-one, fifth from the bottom of the "average" category, ten notches below Truman, who was rated "near great." Arthur M. Schlesinger, "Our Presidents: A Rating by 75 Historians," *New York Times Magazine* (July 29, 1962), pp. 12ff. A recent, perceptive discussion of Hoover's presidential style is James D. Barber, "Classifying and Predicting Presidential Style: Two 'Weak' Presidents," *Journal of Social Issues*, vol. 24 (July, 1968), pp. 51–80.

[7] Richard Neustadt, *Presidential Power* (New York: Wiley, 1960), p. 214.

[8] *Ibid.*, p. 162.

[9] In this connection, see E. P. Hayes, *Activities of the President's Emergency Committee for Employment* (Concord, New Hampshire: private printing, 1936), pp. 2–3, 6–10, 15, 38, 96, and passim. For a more sympathetic discussion of President Hoover's economic policies, see Herbert Stein, *The Revolution in Fiscal Policy* (Chicago: University of Chicago Press, 1969).

[10] The 1949 and 1962 Schlesinger surveys, *op cit.*, placed Roosevelt third in rank behind Lincoln and Washington, as a "great" President, a judgment in which Clinton Rossiter concurs, *The American Presidency*, rev. ed. (New York: Harcourt, Brace & World Harvest Books, 1960), p. 152.

The elements of his effectiveness as a President are, for many commentators, extensions of his personality. He loved being President, rather than merely worked at it. In the view of most contemporary writers, effectiveness as a President entails the enhancement of the powers of the office at the expense of those beneath in the executive branch. Thus they give high marks to Roosevelt's preoccupation with concentrating power in his own hands. One of the most important factors in this quest was Roosevelt's capacity for opening up unconventional sources of information. He read widely in the newspapers, saw hundreds of visitors, kept an ear open for politically revealing gossip, and systematically cultivated informal reporting mechanisms.

One source of informal information was the set of complaints generated from subordinates to whom the President had assigned overlapping jurisdictions, as it was his policy to do. By settling the conflicts arising among his appointees, President Roosevelt could retain control over policy-making.[11] Arthur Schlesinger, Jr., says:

> His favorite technique was to keep grants of authority incomplete, jurisdiction uncertain, charters overlapping. The result of this competitive theory of administration was often confusion and exasperation on the operating level; but no other method could so reliably insure that in a large bureaucracy filled with ambitious men eager for power the decisions, and the power to make them, would remain with the President.[12]

Francis Biddle, Roosevelt's Attorney General, shows how this tactic of the President's could cause great difficulty even among members of his Cabinet. Speaking of the Secretary and Undersecretary of State, Biddle writes:

> Hull came to distrust Welles and finally to hate him. The President knew this long before the Secretary came to him with the final ultimatum—one of them must go. Yet before that the President did little to better their relationship, often bypassing Hull by taking up a matter with Welles. . . . The President cared little for administrative niceties.[13]

Unavoidably commentators also mention other personal qualities of Mr. Roosevelt—his buoyant personality, his flair for the dramatic, his superbly modulated radio voice.[14] Because he used these qualities and his love of

[11] Arthur Schlesinger, Jr., says that this characteristic of Roosevelt's Presidency was widely criticized at the time; this is one general point in the discussion of the Presidency at which many analysts have reversed themselves, owing most, perhaps, to the influence of Schlesinger and Richard Neustadt. See Schlesinger, *The Coming of the New Deal* (Boston: Houghton Mifflin, 1958), pp. 521ff.

[12] *Ibid.*, p. 528. See also an admiring memoir by Frances Perkins, *The Roosevelt I Knew* (New York: Viking, 1946).

[13] Francis Biddle, *In Brief Authority* (Garden City, N.Y.: Doubleday, 1962) p. 182.

[14] Fillmore H. Sanford, reporting on a public opinion poll conducted in 1949 in Philadelphia, gives evidence of Roosevelt's overwhelming popular appeal four years after his death. Respondents gave Mr. Roosevelt his highest marks for gregariousness. A second theme of approval is related to Mr. Roosevelt's image as helper of materially deprived groups, such as "the poor" and "labor." "Public Orientations to Roosevelt," *Public Opinion Quarterly*, vol. 15 (Summer, 1951), pp. 189–216.

power in the service of a vigorous Presidency in both the domestic crisis of the Depression and World War II, Mr. Roosevelt's Presidency has had a special claim on the attention of historians.

Harry S Truman (Democrat, 1945–1952). Harry Truman initially was the victim of the Rooseveltian penchant for making the office of the Presidency coextensive with his own personality, for Roosevelt failed to prepare his successor properly. Louis W. Koenig says:

> Roosevelt was not in Washington a month altogether during the 82 days that Truman was vice-president. The Roosevelt papers disclose that the two met by appointment only twice. Truman himself estimates that he saw Roosevelt only eight times the year before his death, and these meetings contributed little to Truman's preparation for the Presidency.[15]

Mr. Truman never forgot the difference between the man and the office. A major contribution of Mr. Truman's to the history of the Presidency was the progressive institutionalization of the office under his aegis, a systematic rejection, whether conscious or not, of Mr. Roosevelt's preference for an informally run Presidency centering entirely on himself. Under Mr. Truman, the Council of Economic Advisors and the National Security Council came into being and the Bureau of the Budget took on new importance as the center through which presidential control of executive agencies and the President's legislative program could be maintained.[16] "During my administration, [Mr. Truman wrote] there was a continuing audit on the part of the Budget Director in all departments. I had people checking all programs to see how they were shaping up within the framework that had been established."[17]

Although Mr. Truman institutionalized the Presidency, he retained many features of centralization that Mr. Roosevelt had encouraged by his own methods. Richard Neustadt says: "Truman saw the Presidency as the place where the buck stopped; he saw the President as the man in charge of government, as maker of a record for his party, and as a voice for the whole body of Americans. The job he had to do, as Truman saw it, was to make decisions and to take initiatives. . . ."[18]

Mr. Truman said: "I wanted it to be made clear that as long as I was in the White House I ran the executive branch of the government, and no one was ever allowed to act in the capacity of President of the United States except the man who held that office."[19]

Mr. Truman's way of being President apparently arose from many sources—from a strongly ingrained personal preference for decisiveness and from a sense of history fed by his own wide reading in American history and

---

[15] "Truman's Global Leadership," *Current History*, vol. 39 (October, 1960), p. 226.

[16] See, in particular, Harry S Truman, *Memoirs, Year of Decisions* (Garden City, N.Y.: Doubleday, 1955), pp. 58–59, 95–99, 226–227; *Years of Trial and Hope* (1956), pp. 31–38 and passim. Both, © Time, Inc.

[17] *Ibid.*, pp. 35–36.

[18] Neustadt, *op. cit.*, p. 175.

[19] Truman, *Years of Trial and Hope, op. cit.*, p. 194.

biography. He had a conscious political theory of the Presidency, a theory of the duties that in a democracy rest upon elected officials to take the responsibility for major public decisions and to render themselves accountable to the people who elected them and also a theory of presidential representation that harked back to Andrew Jackson. "One thing I always liked about Jackson [Mr. Truman wrote] was that he brought the basic issues into clear focus. People knew what he stood for and what he was against, and . . . that he represented the interests of the common people of the United States."[20]

Whereas Mr. Roosevelt's method of keeping control of his administration was to listen to complaints, to collect tidbits of information, to keep his ear to the ground, Mr. Truman's approach was more methodical. He did his homework, carefully went over materials that were prepared for him, and consulted with the people to whom he had delegated specific tasks. As he said: "I believed that the best way to obtain different views, without encouraging rivalries among different members [of the Cabinet] was to have complete airings in the open at full Cabinet meetings. . . . I would, of course, see Cabinet members individually, but theirs were special problems that affected only their own departments. . . ."[21]

Considering the recency of his administration, the highly partisan fervor that often surrounded his domestic program and his political activities, and the very low ratings that at times he achieved in public opinion polls, the judgment of contemporary historians on Mr. Truman is remarkably uniform and favorable. No doubt this is largely owing to their evaluation of Mr. Truman's foreign policies. Many of these policies, such as Greek-Turkish aid, the Marshall Plan, and the Point Four Programs, sent an unprecedented flood of American resources abroad. American entrance into the U.N. and the North Atlantic Treaty Organization also gave us close peacetime diplomatic ties with other countries—something we had never had before. Both sets of policies were pursued on the premises that the world had been shrunk by modern techniques of transportation, communication, and warfare and that America's interests were bound up in the prosperity and safety of her allies. This was a difficult and unfamiliar doctrine to expound to Americans, yet Mr. Truman presided over the change that brought the United States face to face with worldwide responsibilities on a continuing, peacetime basis and through the arduous trial of limited war in Korea. Thus Mr. Truman's stature as a President is tied not to the techniques he used to gather power in his own hands but rather to the purposes to which he put the powers that he had.[22]

Dwight D. Eisenhower (Republican, 1953–1960). Dwight D. Eisenhower came late in life to partisan politics. Elected by enormous majorities, he nevertheless faced a Congress controlled by the opposite party for six of his

[20] *Ibid.*, p. 193.

[21] Truman, *Year of Decisions, op. cit.*, pp. 329–330.

[22] See Koenig, *op. cit.*; Schlesinger, "Our Presidents," *op cit.*, Elmer Davis, "Harry S Truman and the Verdict of History," *The Reporter* (February 3, 1953), pp. 17–22; and Herbert Elliston, "The Stature of Harry Truman," *The Atlantic Monthly* (February, 1956), pp. 69–71. An excellent discussion of foreign affairs in the Truman administration and an affectionate portrait of President Truman is contained in Dean Acheson, *Present at the Creation* (New York: Norton, 1969).

eight years in office. Greatly beloved as a leader, he is still generally adjudged by scholars to have been a disappointing President.[23] A brief discussion of some of the sources of this disappointment may tell us something about what we expect of our Presidents and something of the trials and frustrations, as well as the opportunities, of the presidential office.

One widely quoted diagnosis of what went wrong with the Eisenhower Presidency—actually a prediction about what would go wrong with it—is attributed by Richard Neustadt to Harry S Truman.

"He'll sit here," Truman would remark (tapping his desk for emphasis), "and he'll say, 'Do this! Do that!' *And nothing will happen.*"[24]

There was much reflection and experience behind this remark. Mr. Truman knew as few men could know the difficulties of operating a complicated political organism—one designed to be, at best, only partially responsive to presidential priorities, or programs, or persuasion. Nevertheless, the conspicuous failures of the Eisenhower administration—the ones that caused the most difficulty and attracted the most publicity—were in general not the product of an apparatus—executive *or* legislative—unresponsive to presidential wishes. Rather, the Eisenhower administration suffered from difficulty in formulating policies to which the government could respond at all or without untoward effects. Passivity or ambiguity at critical moments in policy formation seems to have presented a greater problem to the Eisenhower Presidency than lapses of efficiency in policy execution.

It is instructive, for example, to recall President Eisenhower's unwillingness to do anything to strengthen the hand of the executive branch against the attacks of Senator Joseph McCarthy of Wisconsin, despite the President's strong personal antipathy for the Senator. McCarthy's charges against the State Department and the International Information Administration had already gained wide currency and notoriety by the time Eisenhower assumed office. The problem was alarming, of great magnitude, and unmistakably damaging to the morale and effectiveness of a large and vital part of our government. Observers, hoping that a Republican presidential victory in 1952 would cut McCarthy off from his base of support in the party, could take little comfort from the few clues the new administration gave about how McCarthy would be handled. During the campaign, candidate Eisenhower had excised from a speech in Milwaukee a paragraph praising General George Marshall, the target of one of the Wisconsin Senator's most elaborate attacks. In the early months of the new administration, Scott McLeod, well known on Capitol Hill as a McCarthy ally, was appointed Assistant Secretary of State for

---

[23] The 1962 Schlesinger *New York Times Magazine* poll of seventy-five historians, *op cit.*, rated Eisenhower next to the bottom of the "average" category—three steps below Hoover and bracketed by Chester A. Arthur and Andrew Johnson. Out of a large number of sympathetic, well-informed, but nevertheless unfavorable assessments see, for example, Dean Albertson, in Albertson, (ed.) *Eisenhower as President* (New York: Hill and Wang, 1963), introduction; Neustadt, *op. cit.*; Rossiter, *op cit.*; Emmett J. Hughes, *The Ordeal of Power* (New York: Atheneum Publishers, 1962; Dell, 1964); Richard Rovere, *Affairs of State: The Eisenhower Years* (New York: Farrar, Straus & Cudahy, 1956). For favorable verdicts, see Merlo J. Pusey, *Eisenhower the President* (New York: Macmillan, 1956); and Arthur Larson, *Eisenhower: The President Nobody Knew* (New York: Scribner, 1968).

[24] Neustadt, *op. cit.*, p. 9 (italics in the original).

Personnel and Security, an extremely sensitive post from the standpoint of frightened employees in the Department.

The new Republican management team in the Information Administration had an especially difficult job, because in the early days of the Eisenhower administration, McCarthy was concentrating a heavy barrage of criticism at that agency. The assistant to the agency director describes an attempt to get help at a meeting with a top Eisenhower aide:

> [We told him] morale was terrible and had primarily affected the better personnel, who were dismayed by the seeming impotence of the "new team's" leadership, or absence of it. Would the President give us his backing if we had . . . a showdown?
>
> [The man from the White House] blandly answered that he wouldn't dream of approaching the President on the subject. It was Eisenhower's "passion," he said, "not to offend anyone in Congress."[25]

Later, McCarthy went after other agencies in the executive branch. The cumulative effects of his irresponsible behavior finally resulted in a vote of condemnation by the Senate. The election of 1954 deprived him of his committee chairmanship, and he died soon afterward. Throughout the entire two-year period, however, Eisenhower never attacked McCarthy.

> Some of my good friends and most trusted advisors [Eisenhower wrote] would, periodically, become infuriated at his irresponsible actions and urge me to censure him publicly. . . . It seemed that almost every day I had to point out that if I were to attack Senator McCarthy, even though every personal instinct so prompted me, I would greatly enhance his publicity value without achieving any constructive purpose. . . . Lashing back at one man, which is easy enough for a President, was not as important to me as the long term value of restraint. . . . As the months went by, my advisors gradually became practically unanimous in agreeing with my methods for defeating McCarthyism.[26]

In the case of McCarthy, it is clear that the fact that "nothing happened" in the White House was the result of deliberate choice. Historians may argue over President Eisenhower's conviction that this strategy contributed to McCarthy's eventual decline; our purpose here is only to illustrate the restraint which was such an important feature of Eisenhower's presidential style, even when he reports that his personal instincts strongly urged a less passive response.

President Eisenhower promoted a passive presidency in other ways. Much authority previously held by Presidents was delegated downward. According to Sherman Adams, Eisenhower's chief of staff for six White House years, this included such matters as control over patronage. With respect to

---

[25] Martin Merson, *Private Diary of a Public Servant* (New York: Macmillan, 1955), p. 73. See also Norman Dorsen and John G. Simon, "A Fight on the Wrong Front," *Columbia University Forum* (Fall, 1964), pp. 21–28.

[26] Dwight D. Eisenhower, *Mandate for Change* (Garden City, N.Y.: Doubleday, 1963), pp. 319–321. Larson, *op. cit.*, pp. 12–14, was an Eisenhower advisor and one of those who agrees.

foreign policy, Adams says: "Eisenhower delegated to [Secretary of State John Foster] Dulles the responsibility of developing the specific policy, including the decision where the administration would stand and what course of action would be followed in each international crisis."[27]

Adams makes other illuminating comments about Eisenhower's administrative style:

> Because Eisenhower disliked talking business on the phone, [Presidential Assistant Wilton] Persons and I and a few other staff members would speak for him on the telephone on many matters that required his personal attention.[28]
>
> . . . Eisenhower was not much of a reader. He was impatient with the endless paperwork of the Presidency and always tried to get his staff to digest long documents into one page summaries, which was sometimes next to impossible to do. . . .[29]

As any President must, President Eisenhower fashioned the Presidency to suit many of the needs of his own personal administrative style. Withdrawal from partisan politics, a dislike of rough and tumble, a preference for decision-making at the staff level, leaving him relatively free from detail—all characterized his method of being President. If this freed him for other things, it also had its costs. Sometimes, the President was not thoroughly briefed on matters that he would have been better off knowing about.

An authoritative commentary on the famous Dixon-Yates case discusses one such occasion:

> When repeated public questions arose—and the cry about it climbed to a fever pitch, the Administration's disinclination to pursue the matter was so great that the President was put in the position of making untenable statements whose accuracy could have been checked by a phone call. . . . The President's apparent lack of information concerning Dixon-Yates has led to charges that he was misled by his advisors. . . . [Nevertheless] it is clear that the Chief Executive either directly or through acceptance of the going procedure, shapes the major channels of information and advice upon which he must base his decisions. While it is important to know how well the President has been served by the men he has chosen to advise him, it is at least as revealing to discover how well the President has permitted himself to be served. This is especially true of a President like Eisenhower who has taken considerable pains to introduce organizational reforms into the White House. There is no evidence to suggest that President Eisenhower was dissatisfied with his own work.[30]

---

[27] Sherman Adams, *Firsthand Report* (New York: Popular, 1962), p. 92. In *Alliance Politics* (New York: Columbia, 1970), Richard Neustadt suggests that there was less loss of presidential control over foreign policy than Adams seems to imply. See pp. 103–106.

[28] Adams, *op cit.*, p. 83.

[29] *Ibid.*, p. 78.

[30] Aaron B. Wildavsky, *Dixon-Yates, a Study in Power Politics* (New Haven, Conn.: Yale, 1962), pp. 307–308.

As the author of this passage points out, the weakness in the machinery, if it is a weakness, cannot properly be attributed to a lack of responsiveness to President Eisenhower's own preferences. This was also the case with perhaps the most striking purely administrative snafu of the Eisenhower years, which took place at the presentation of the budget for the fiscal year 1958.

On the very day that President Eisenhower sent the Federal budget to Congress, he authorized and approved a statement by his Secretary of the Treasury criticizing the budget as too large. Warning of a "depression that will curl your hair," Secretary George Humphrey urged that the Eisenhower budget be cut by the Democratic Congress. Incredulous reporters, seeking repudiation of Humphrey's statement from the President, learned that "that written memorandum—I not only went over every word of it, I edited it, and it expresses my convictions very thoroughly."

Several commentators have said that this contradiction was greatly damaging to the Eisenhower Presidency.[31] It hurt the relations of trust, confidence, and mutual support that Presidents try to build with the executive departments and agencies by reaching agreement on a budget. It exacerbated partisan divisions between the Republican President and the Democratic-controlled Congress and that year jeopardized the mutual security program on which our allies were heavily dependent. Finally, it damaged President Eisenhower's prestige within the professional community of Washington, that large amorphous group in and out of government that consists of congressmen and their staffs, newsmen, lawyers, lobbyists, agency executives, and embassy people—men who as a part of their daily routine keep an eye on political affairs in the nation's capital. To them, that President Eisenhower would allow—indeed, encourage—the repudiation of his own budget on the day it was presented was simply bad political craftsmanship.

But the question is, was this a result of presidential difficulty in persuading some part of the administration to "go along"? Was Eisenhower having trouble persuading people "to do the things they ought to . . . do"?[32] Evidently not. Eisenhower's administrative machinery admirably captured his ambivalence toward his own budget.[33] He said "do this," and the budget was sent to Capitol Hill; "do that," and Humphrey's attack was mounted.

What administrative innovations did Eisenhower introduce to further institutionalize the White House? Under Eisenhower, each presidential assistant had fixed responsibilities. Only Sherman Adams, his chief of staff, reported directly to the President; everyone else was subordinate to Adams in a highly explicit White House chain of command. Cabinet meetings grew in size to include perhaps twenty or thirty regular participants. (UN Ambassador, Budget Director, several White House staff members, Mutual Security Administrator, and so on), and a Cabinet secretariat was established to follow

[31] See Neustadt, op. cit., pp. 64–80, 108–123; Hughes, op cit., pp. 205–209; Adams, op. cit., pp. 354–375; and Charles J. V. Murphy, "The Budget and Eisenhower," Fortune (July, 1957), pp. 96ff.
[32] This is a condensation of President Truman's analysis of the actual power of the Presidency, the power to "persuade," quoted by Neustadt, op. cit., p. 10.
[33] See especially ibid., p. 118.

up on decisions reached in Cabinet meetings and to keep the agenda.[34] A congressional liaison operation was set up in the White House under General Wilton Persons, who had previously performed similar functions for the Department of the Army. As in previous administrations, a separate press office was also maintained. But aside from the accretion of activities in the White House and the rather more rigid separation of functions than was usual, the main feature of the Eisenhower system of staff organization was the channeling of all lines of communication to the President through Sherman Adams, and later, after Adams resigned, through his successor, General Persons. Eisenhower protected himself from overexposure; some commentators say that the net result of this and of the zealousness of his assistants to protect him during and after his three episodes of serious illness in office was that he was seriously underexposed to alternatives, to information, and to the opportunities to make decisions. But there is little doubt that Eisenhower preferred it that way. His philosophy of government welcomed self-limitation. Other Presidents might suffer, as Harry Truman undoubtedly did, from an inability to get the machinery of government to accomplish the goals they set. President Eisenhower's main burden apparently was a reluctance to formulate goals or a distaste for those goals the demands of the system thrust on him.

John F. Kennedy (Democrat, 1961–1963). John Kennedy, the youngest man to serve as President since Theodore Roosevelt, operated in office quite differently from his predecessor, who was the oldest President. Kennedy was a rapid, serious, and voracious reader, had analytical skills of a high order, and hence processed through his own mind a vast quantity of information. This alone provides a great contrast to Eisenhower. Unlike Eisenhower, Kennedy saw virtually nothing of his full Cabinet, preferring to meet with smaller groups and task forces.[35] And the White House staff was far less rigidly compartmentalized than during the previous administration. In some positions, however, there was a fairly clear division of labor, with special assistants for appointments, the press, foreign and security matters, and congressional relations. All of Kennedy's assistants had direct access to the President, and he to them.[36]

Because John Kennedy was a man of great charm, because of the overpowering tragedy of his assassination, and because of the brevity of his time in office, it has been difficult for observers to reach balanced judgments about the contribution he made to the Presidency. He came to office as the choice of less than 50 percent of the voters, the winner of the closest presidential election in the twentieth century. His presence at the top of the Democratic ticket was a test of the readiness of American voters to accept the leadership of a Roman Catholic. Analysis of the election suggests that for a

[34] See Robert Donovan, *Eisenhower: The Inside Story* (New York: Harper, 1956), for an authorized account of Cabinet meetings during Eisenhower's first term.
[35] See, for example, Joseph Loftus, "Cabinet Holding Informal Talks," *The New York Times* (July 25, 1961); and Richard F. Fenno, Jr., "The Cabinet: Index to the Kennedy Way," *New York Times Magazine* (April 22, 1962), pp. 13, 62–64.
[36] Perhaps the most interesting contemporary account of Kennedy's White House is Joseph Kraft, "Kennedy's Working Staff," *Harpers* (December, 1962), pp. 29–36.

sizable number of voters the issue of Kennedy's religion overrode other considerations, and this worked against Kennedy in the popular vote, although not in the electoral college.[37] An important consequence of Kennedy's weakness as a candidate in 1960 was a sharp reduction, in comparison to the off-year election of 1958, in the number of Democrats elected to the House of Representatives.[38]

Thus Kennedy began his Presidency under severe constraint. There could, under the circumstances, be no dramatic "hundred days" such as his well-wishers would have liked.[39] It is not surprising that Kennedy, as a Democrat succeeding a rather conservative Republican, undertook important reorientations of national priorities in a number of areas; however, deprived of his full term of office, he was unable in many cases to see them through.

It is not easy to sort out the main themes of the Kennedy Presidency. With respect to Congress, there was great caution. Even before he was inaugurated, Kennedy favored enlargement of the Rules Committee, but this was not something he could achieve himself or without a coordinated effort based within the House. He also gave carefully measured aid and comfort to his allies in Congress who pressed for liberalization of the Ways and Means and Appropriations Committees after the election of 1962. The legislative record of Kennedy's three years was not distinguished when compared with that of the triumphant Eighty-ninth Congress (1965–67), which, under Johnson, enacted Federal aid to education, the poverty program, and Medicare, or the latter half of the Eighty-eighth Congress, which enacted a tax cut and a sweeping civil rights bill. There is every reason to believe, however, that the efforts of the Kennedy years in setting priorities, in mobilizing the Federal bureaucracies and the press, and in packing key committees of the House made a significant contribution. It can hardly be doubted that Kennedy would have been a much stronger candidate in 1964 than he was in 1960 or that Goldwater would have been a weaker opponent for him than Nixon was in 1960. Thus it is not implausible to speculate that had Kennedy lived to run again, an overwhelmingly liberal Eighty-ninth Congress would have been available to him (as it would have been to virtually any Democratic President in that year) and that the final enactment of so many New

---

[37] See Polsby and Wildavsky, op. cit., pp. 21–22; and Ithiel De Sola Pool, Robert P. Abelson, and Samuel L. Popkin, Candidates, Issues and Strategies (Cambridge, Mass.: Massachusetts Institute of Technology Press, 1964), pp. 117–118. The best original data on the attitudes of voters in the 1960 election is from the Michigan Survey Research Center. See Angus Campbell, Philip Converse, Warren E. Miller, and Donald E. Stokes, Elections and the Political Order (New York: Wiley, 1966) pp. 67–69, 78–124. On p. 92, the authors calculate that Kennedy's Catholicism was probably responsible for a net loss of 2.2 percent of the two-party vote nationwide.

[38] The Democrats lost twenty-one seats in the 1960 election. Normally, at congressional elections held in the middle of a President's four-year term, the President's party loses substantial ground in the House. The twentieth-century average is forty-five seats. In the 1962 elections, however, the Democrats lost only three seats. Many observers interpreted this, incorrectly, as a sign of President Kennedy's popularity rather than as an indication of his unpopularity in 1960.

[39] Tom Wicker, for example, complains of the lack of a Kennedy "hundred days." See JFK and LBJ: The Influence of Personality upon Politics (New York: Morrow, 1968), esp. p. 147.

Deal–Fair Deal measures, which a generation of Democrats had advocated, would have been credited to him.

Because the legislative record is relatively easy to score, Presidents and President watchers use it to evaluate and compare Presidencies. One of the least attractive aspects of the Kennedy-Johnson succession was the passionate squabbling that developed between supporters of both men over who could claim credit with posterity for New Deal–Fair Deal–New Frontier–Great Society legislation.[40] Since getting credit for something helps a politician's career, it is understandable that an active politician and his partisans should claim all they plausibly can. When his career is over, however, and analysts with less at stake begin to weigh in with their judgment, the record can be studied in a new light.

To an analyst committed to neither man, the most significant feature of the Kennedy-Johnson legislative record would surely be its continuity. Both men largely accepted an agenda that had been part and parcel of their national party's basic outlook for a generation. Both came relatively late to an all-out commitment to that agenda, but by the time they reached the Presidency, their commitment to it was firm. Both added and subtracted marginally from the basic Democratic agenda, and both were in major respects constrained by events beyond their control from pursuing it as vigorously as they might have wanted. And, certainly, both brought to its execution highly individual styles of work.

Nowhere were their styles more at odds than in the attitudes that underlay their stance toward the social and political forces that impinged on White House decision-making. Kennedy reached out to visitors with questions about the outside world. He encouraged competition among contending groups in his administration, giving high marks to those who fought for their ideas.[41] He welcomed trial balloons, in which subordinates would suggest a

---

[40] For informed discussion on the legislative effectiveness of both men, see Joseph Cooper and Gary Bombardier, "Presidential Leadership and Party Success," *Journal of Politics,* vol. 30 (November, 1968), pp. 1012–1027; and Dan Cordtz, "Lyndon's Legislation," *The Wall Street Journal* (August 11, 1965).

[41] See, for example, Roger Hilsman, *To Move a Nation* (Garden City, N.Y.: Doubleday, 1967) p. 56. "The minute I got back to my desk, the phone rang from the White House. 'By now,' a voice said, 'you will have been told that you are to be the new Assistant Secretary of State for Far Eastern Affairs.' I said that I had. 'You will also have been told to refrain from intruding into military and strategic matters.' I admitted this, too. 'Well,' said the voice, 'the President wants you to understand that it was precisely because you have stood up to the Defense Department that you were chosen, and that he expects you to continue.' "

Examples from another domain can be found in Arthur Schlesinger, Jr., *A Thousand Days* (Boston: Houghton Mifflin, 1965), p. 138, on the appointment, which Kennedy initially opposed, of Kermit Gordon to the Council of Economic Advisors. "Finally [Council Chairman-designate Walter] Heller called on Kennedy . . . hoping to get the matter settled. While he waited, he discussed the problem with Ken O'Donnell. O'Donnell asked whether Gordon was really the best man for the job. Heller said emphatically that he was. O'Donnell then said that he should stick to his guns and tell the President-elect that he had to have Gordon. Heller did so when he saw Kennedy a few minutes later. Kennedy said 'Oh, all right,' picked up the phone and called Gordon in Williamstown." At another point (p. 656), Schlesinger says: "It was one of the Council's jobs to venture out ahead of policy. The President would say to Heller, 'I can't say that yet, but you can.' "

possible line of policy to newspaper reporters, so he could use the reactions from outsiders—interest groups, congressmen—in shaping decisions. Like the skipper of a small boat, Kennedy attended to the winds and the tides, running with the wind when he could, tacking when he thought he had to, bailing energetically when, as in the Bay of Pigs episode and on a few other occasions, his administration was momentarily swamped. More than once Kennedy gave voice to a sense of elements "out there" that he could struggle with but not control.[42]

Perhaps the most measured assessment of the achievements of the Kennedy administration by an insider has been that of Richard Neustadt.[43] Of the themes he identifies in the Kennedy Presidency, he gives overwhelming weight to the management of relations with Russia and the management of our defense posture, which was based on avoiding miscalculations and misapprehensions and providing a means of responding to military challenges that was not tied to the use of nuclear weapons. This entailed a sizable expansion of America's military capability, a corresponding expansion of the military budget, and a drastic, important shift in the balance of power within the government—away from military and toward civilian leadership in the setting of priorities with respect to the evaluation of strategic doctrines, in the allocation of missions among the services, and in the choice of weapons systems.

More than any events in foreign affairs, the two early and short-lived crises over Cuba set the tone for Kennedy administration decision-making. The Bay of Pigs episode of April, 1961, three months after Kennedy's inauguration, was an unmitigated disaster, in which President Kennedy and his foreign policy advisors were persuaded by top officials in the CIA to proceed with plans that had been in the making for some time. The utter miscarriage of the plan shook Kennedy's confidence in the military and intelligence bureaucracies he had inherited and gave credence to the maxims of advisors like Richard Neustadt, whose book *Presidential Power* argued that each major decision of the government had to be looked at in the White House from the President's own political perspective, as the only sensible precaution

---

[42] William Manchester reports that a tiny plaque on Kennedy's desk read: "Oh God, Thy sea is so great and my boat is so small," *Death of a President* (New York: Harper & Row, 1967) p. 8. The rather bombastic rhetoric of Kennedy's much-admired oratory on large occasions thus did a gross injustice to the essentials of his style as a presidential leader, if we can judge from offstage eyewitness reports such as Hilsman, *op. cit.* See, for example, p. 53, a quotation, in indirect discourse, of Kennedy discussing problems he was having with the State Department: "Everyone had his own style and people above as well as below, always had to do some adapting." On another occasion, Kennedy said, "There is always inequity in life. Some men are killed in a war, and some men are wounded, and some men never leave the country. . . . It's very hard in military or in personal life to assure complete equality. Life is unfair." Theodore C. Sorensen, *Kennedy* (New York: Harper & Row, 1965) p. 42. Sorensen comments (pp. 370, 371), "He assumed that we would all have to live indefinitely with national and international tensions and imperfect humans and solutions. . . . He entertained no delusions about himself or others, neither affecting nor accepting any pretensions of grandeur."

[43] Though never employed full time in Kennedy's White House, as he had been in Truman's, Neustadt was a frequent visitor and consultant from his post as a professor of government at Columbia University. See Neustadt's "Kennedy in the Presidency: A Premature Appraisal," *Political Science Quarterly*, vol. 79 (September, 1964), pp. 321–334.

against Presidential entrapment by the big bureaucracies of the national government.[44]

When, some eighteen months later, intelligence photographs showed that Russian offensive missiles were being planted on Cuban soil, Kennedy convened, in utmost secrecy, a task force of top foreign policy advisors, dominated by political executives he had appointed, to debate the alternatives. They settled on a strategy of blockade that gave the Russians an opportunity to withdraw. The Russians pulled out, producing euphoria in the Kennedy administration. Recalling the decision-making atmosphere years later, when Vietnam was proving so troublesome, a high official was quoted as saying "There was a confidence—it was never bragged about, it was just there, a residue perhaps of the confrontation over the missiles in Cuba—that when the chips were really down, the other people would fold."[45]

In domestic politics, three main themes of the Kennedy administration stand out—civil rights, modern economics, and reorganization of the Defense Department—and all were in one way or another carried forward by Kennedy's successor.

Before President Kennedy installed Robert McNamara as Secretary of Defense, the Defense Department was commonly assumed to be ungovernable by civilians.[46] Major decisions were bargained out among military potentates without much participation by the Secretary. This was not an altogether stagnant system, however—incentives to innovate in strategic doctrine were created by the desire of each of the major services to expand at the expense of the others. Nor were civilians totally absent from the decision-making process—at various times, both Presidents Truman and Eisenhower imposed stringent budgetary limits within which interservice rivalry had to take place.

In fact, during the Eisenhower years it was budgetary limits leading to reliance on the doctrine of "massive retaliation" that provided a context for the Kennedy-McNamara reforms. The armed services found it far easier to accept drastic reallocations of missions, consolidation of procurement, and civilian control of the choices among weapons systems while the military budget itself was increasing. In the three years of the Kennedy Presidency, the Defense Department budget increased an average of 7.3 billion dollars per year over the allocation it received in the last Eisenhower year. "Massive retaliation" gave way to "graduated" or "flexible" response as the central strategic doctrine of the United States. The greater expense was justified on

[44] Neustadt, *Presidential Power, op. cit.*, passim. For accounts of the Bay of Pigs, see Schlesinger, *One Thousand Days, op. cit.*, pp. 233–247; Sorensen, *op. cit.*, pp. 291–309; and Hilsman, *op. cit.*, pp. 26–39.

[45] David Halberstam, "The Very Expensive Education of McGeorge Bundy," *Harpers* (July, 1969), p. 36. On the missile crisis, see Schlesinger, *One Thousand Days, op. cit.*, pp. 794–841; Sorenson, *op cit.*, pp. 607–718; Hilsman, *op cit.*, pp. 159–229; and, especially, Elie Abel, *The Missile Crisis* (Philadelphia: Lippincott, 1966).

[46] See Paul Y. Hammond, *The Cold War-Years: American Foreign Policy Since 1945* (New York: Harcourt, Brace & World, 1969), for a good overview. Samuel P. Huntington, *The Common Defense* (New York: Columbia, 1963); Jack Raymond, *Power at the Pentagon* (New York: Harper & Row, 1964); and Paul Y. Hammond, *Organizing for Defense* (Princeton, N.J.: Princeton, 1961) are also useful accounts of the pre-McNamara Pentagon.

the grounds, first, that building American capability to fight limited wars would decrease the probability that America's enemies would start them and, second, that a more flexible posture of defense opened a greater range of diplomatic options for the Kennedy administration in its maneuvers over the fate of Berlin, the Middle East, Cuba, and Southeast Asia.

As a rising tide of domestic disturbances in the late 1960s turned the focus of public attention from foreign to internal affairs and as the war in Vietnam claimed an increasing share of national resources, the basic contours of the Kennedy-McNamara strategy became harder to discern in the perspective of history. There is no doubt that this strategy gave America the capacity to make a sizable commitment in Vietnam, that ultimately this commitment became extremely costly, and that resources that otherwise might have been applied to the amelioration of domestic problems were used there. Moreover, in at least some quarters doubt has been expressed that increased American capability to fight limited wars may have discouraged more vigorous Soviet intervention in the Middle East, kept them from annexing Berlin, forced them to pull missiles out of Cuba, and temporarily thwarted the more ambitious Communist designs on most of Southeast Asia. And since the defense of the Kennedy strategic doctrine (which President Johnson also largely pursued) rests on claims that it prevented dire events that consequently did not happen, the doubts of skeptics can never be definitively resolved.

It is true, however, that in a tense world increasingly populated by nations having the capacity to build and deliver nuclear weapons, none of these weapons has been employed militarily since the American bombing of Nagasaki in 1945. And while our relations with the Soviet Union have not been ideal, since the Cuban missile crisis of 1962 direct confrontations between the two major powers have been avoided.

If the strategic consequences of Kennedy's reorganization of the Defense Department are hard to sort out, the administrative consequences are equally unclear. Secretary McNamara forced program justifications to new levels of detail, precision, and subtlety, and he established civilian control of the Pentagon. He consolidated decentralized intelligence and procurement activities in the Defense Department. But he was not able to cure the perennial problem of drastic cost underestimates in contracting for major weapons hardware that his new control system was designed to monitor. McNamara's reforms did not vanquish or appreciably rationalize the Byzantine politics of the Eisenhower era's "military-industrial complex," which consisted of shifting and competing coalitions of manufacturers and suppliers of goods and services to the armed services, the various branches of the services, and interested congressmen. But their net effect was to deal in the civilian leaders of the government on a more powerful basis.[47]

[47] A favorable assessment is William Kaufman, *The McNamara Strategy* (New York: Harper & Row, 1964). Less favorable is Richard Harwood and Laurence Stern, "McNamara: Debate Puts His Record on Trial," *Washington Post* (June 15, 1969). See also an informative follow-up on the Harwood-Stern article, by Joseph Califano, "Correcting the Record on McNamara," a letter to the editor of the *Washington Post* (July 1, 1969); and Paul Y. Hammond, "A Functional Analysis of Defense Department Decision-making in the McNamara Administration," *American Political Science Review*, vol. 62 (March, 1968), pp. 57–69.

The great economic achievement of the Kennedy administration was the tax cut of 1964 (actually enacted after Kennedy's death). It was explicitly designed to incur a deficit over the short run in the Federal budget but, by stimulating private consumption, to increase incomes and hence tax receipts over a slightly longer period.[48] Although the theory of economics on which this was based had been widely accepted for thirty years and although the government since Herbert Hoover's day had undertaken smaller scale applications of this theory, the tax cut of 1964 was the frankest, best publicized, and most explicitly didactic application of Keynesian economics ever undertaken by the Federal government. But perhaps the greatest virtue of the tax cut was that it succeeded in stimulating the economy and in winning political friends for modern economics in the service of national policy.

The Kennedy administration's record in civil rights is as difficult to disentangle from current events outside the President's control as is its record in foreign affairs. President Eisenhower had hesitated to give moral support to those pressing for civil rights. President Kennedy was very much dependent in Congress on Southern committee chairmen and Southern votes to enact his program. Moreover, he had appointed his brother Attorney General, chief officer of the government in charge of enforcing rulings of the Supreme Court on desegregation in education and public facilities. In so doing, Kennedy accepted an extra measure of political responsibility—and vulnerability—for acts of the Justice Department.

There is general agreement that in the field of civil rights the Kennedy Presidency distinguished itself administratively (as did the Johnson administration), peaceably integrating the University of Alabama (despite the well-publicized defiance of Governor George Wallace), protecting Martin Luther King from an irate mob in Birmingham, and desegregating interstate bus terminal lunchrooms by executive order. The Civil Rights Act of 1964, a high priority of both the Kennedy and Johnson administrations, was a historic law that was triumphantly and shrewdly assisted over its most difficult hurdle, the Senate, by Democratic Whip Hubert Humphrey. It provided for initiatives to be taken by the Federal government to enforce the prohibition of racial discrimination in public accommodations and to protect many of the constitutional rights of citizens. These initiatives could take the form of suits by the Justice Department or the cutting off of Federal funds from state and local projects that practiced discrimination.

The Kennedy administration had an unmistakable style, which was exemplified by phrases, such as "beautiful people" and "jet set," that came to be applied to its members. The Kennedy brothers, themselves quite youthful and reared in an atmosphere emphasizing competition, toughness, self-control, and victory, gathered around them persons having similar mannerisms. It was easy and not always fair for the more homespun, middle-aged, and stodgy denizens of the bureaucracies and Capitol Hill to read into the

---

[48] See Walter Heller, *New Dimensions of Political Economy* (Cambridge, Mass.: Harvard, 1966), for an account of this episode by its main architect. An enthusiastic description is contained in Norman MacRae, "The Neurotic Trillionaire," *The Economist* (May 10, 1969), pp. 26–35. Another, more measured, account, placing the tax cut in historical perspective, is contained in Herbert Stein, *op. cit.*

impatience, high spirits, and fashionably smart banter of the ambitious, young Kennedy administration blades-about-town a certain callousness and self-absorption, bred of unfamiliarity with disappointment and nurtured by heady involvement with big doings.

For a time a gap yawned between the White House and the legislative liaison personnel of the executive branch on one hand and Capitol Hill people on the other, growing into what a White House aide once described as a "mutuality of contempt."[49] A friend of the Kennedy administration on Capitol Hill said: "The President's advisors are a part of the trouble. It's not that there is so much friction, it's just that we do not know them and cannot talk their language."[50] Another congressman, a liberal Democrat, agreed:

> These young men come marching up to the Capitol. They wheedle and promise and threaten. When major legislation is being handled on the floor, you will find these men in committee offices just off the floor. They call in members just before the vote and try all kinds of pressures.
>
> One House member was told that, if he did not vote as they wanted him to vote, every military base in his district would be closed. . . . There have also been threats to take defense contracts out of congressional districts. . . .
>
> They are trying to transfer ward politics to the National Capitol.[51]

An observer said:

> The most widely shared and loudly voiced grievance that Congress has against administration practices concerns the unremitting attention it receives from those it describes simply and without affection as "the young men." They badger, to hear the members tell it. They hector. They even chase. . . .
>
> Legislators who still cherish the notion that they themselves will decide how to vote appear to have been at various times amused, confused and infuriated by the discombobulation of incoming messages. . . . "Why are you calling me, son?" an august legislator asked an all but anonymous administration phoner. . . .
>
> To the White House counter-claim that pushing and prodding sometimes help and never hurt, one Congressman replies by citing the case of a young liaison man, the very sight of whom at the cloakroom door, he claims, is enough to cost the administration twenty-five votes. Under questioning he lowered the figure to three, but this time he seemed serious.[52]

[49] Richard Donahue, who worked for President Kennedy on Capitol Hill, made this comment in a speech on April 4, 1963. It was reported the next day in the *Washington Post* by Julius Duscha, "Executive Legislative Rifts Described." See also, Robert Spivack, "Seeking a Scapegoat," *New York Herald Tribune* (November 14, 1963).

[50] "What They Say about J.F.K.: Congressmen Tell What's on Their Minds," *U.S. News and World Report* (July 30, 1962), p. 32.

[51] Meg Greenfield, "Why Are You Calling Me, Son," *The Reporter* (August 16, 1962), pp. 29–31.

[52] *Ibid.*

Three years of legislative difficulty and the inevitable frustrations of try-ing to move entrenched bureaucracies had begun to mellow the more flexible and intelligent members of the Kennedy White House by the time of the as-sassination. But for such a group, whose collective impress on the Washington scene owed almost as much to a romantic Camelot mentality, a tacit assump-tion of their own chosenness and invulnerability, as to their idealism and brains, the blow of the assassination fell with devastating force. A few in the Kennedy entourage turned their bitterness on his successor and on those among their number who elected to serve the new President.[53]

Lyndon B. Johnson (Democrat, 1963–1968). Lyndon Johnson, Kennedy's successor, began to place a distinctive stamp on the office even before all the Kennedy men had left the White House staff. A less cerebral man than Kennedy, Johnson's main strengths were his prodigious energy, an extremely well-developed strategic sense, long political experience, wide political ac-quaintance, and an overwhelming attentiveness to the operational activities necessary to put across a legislative program.[54] In the early years of his Presi-dency, Johnson also enjoyed great popularity, which he nurtured by placing heavy stress on the theme of continuity with the priorities of the immediate past.

"Inside" books on the Johnson Presidency have not yet begun to flood the market, but it can safely be predicted that they will. The former President has taken with him to Texas many millions of pieces of paper, 250,000 photo-graphs (principally of himself), histories of each department and agency of the Federal government under his administration (prepared by the agencies at his request), and, one gathers, much other material.[55] Presumably, in due course, a substantial fraction of this material will find its way into public print under President Johnson's imprimatur. This alone will constitute a flood, but other authors will doubtless have their say as well.

If John Kennedy's personality and the circumstances of his departure from office have made it difficult to write about his Presidency in a measured way, this is no less true of Lyndon Johnson. Thus a contemporary account of the Johnson Presidency turns again and again to the Johnson personality, as it was and as it seemed to be, in examining his conduct of the office.

In his years in the Senate, Johnson could be observed at his most effec-tive. Johnson as President was much less so, and in part this is traceable to

[53] For an indication of this sort of sentiment, see Manchester, *op. cit.*; and for a de-scription of its effects in the Johnson White House, see Eric Goldman, *The Tragedy of Lyndon Johnson* (New York: Knopf, 1969), pp. 17–20. On page 34, Professor Goldman de-scribes the response of President Johnson's principal assistant to a story in *The Washington Post* about Goldman's appointment as a special consultant: "Jenkins' mild voice rose as he told me, 'You are not the Johnson Arthur Schlesinger. Nobody is going to be the Johnson anything of Kennedy. *This is a different administration*'" (italics in the original).

[54] A preliminary assessment of President Johnson's administrative style is contained in Tom Wicker, "Johnson's Men: 'Valuable Hunks of Humanity,'" *New York Times Magazine* (May 3, 1964), pp. 11ff.

[55] Nan Robertson, "Snapshot Album of Johnson Massive," *The New York Times* (Novem-ber 26, 1968). Henry Raymont, "Austin Is Bustling as Johnson Labors to Set the Record Straight," *The New York Times* (November 9, 1969).

personal limitations. Where policy is bargained over rather than invented or created, by circumstances as well as by men, a leader without a detailed grasp of substance can operate successfully, as Lyndon Johnson did in the Senate. But knowing who wants what and how strongly—the most important sorts of knowledge for a legislative broker—is only part of the story for a President. Presidents also have to have a feel for substantive policy—for understanding how measures will work in a real world that is immensely complex and intractable. Johnson's grasp of these matters in foreign affairs, where he was inexperienced and insensitive to fine distinctions, was unsure. Stewart Alsop has a revealing observation: "When Johnson inherited the Presidency, he at first appalled his foreign policy experts by using Iran and Iraq, and Indonesia and Indochina, interchangeably. Until he became President, those places had not been useful to him in his profession, and there had been no room for them in his mental attic."[56]

The daily pressures and pleasures of the presidential office are such that it is not possible for any President to learn very much totally from scratch. President Johnson's formidable intelligence was for over fifty years harnessed to an equally formidable parochialism—he preferred to apply his energy and ingenuity to the anticipation and solution of concrete problems rather than to speculation or the gratification of idle curiosity. When the Presidency descended upon Johnson, he fully understood the powers of the office and its potential as a constructive force in American life, but it now appears that in important ways he lacked knowledge of the rest of the world.

Some observers are inclined to attribute this handicap to the circumstances of Johnson's life—to an education at San Marcos State Teachers College rather than at some more cosmopolitan university, to the insatiable demands of Texas politics and Senate cloakrooms during the bulk of his career.[57] Philip Geyelin said:

> He had heard the fashionable concepts, be they containment or disengagement or neutralism or parallelism. But he didn't speak that language because he did not think in it; he thought in analogies to the New Deal or Munich, to "another Korea" or "another Cuba"; the Mekong Delta was to be "another TVA." He was in large measure, then, a self-taught statesman; he couldn't read the music, but he had come a long way on his ability to play by ear. . . .
>
> The trouble with foreigners, the President once said, "is that they're not like the folks you were reared with." Lyndon Johnson was reared with hill-country Texans, and his school was Congress and the New Deal. His interest and expertise were not in policies and still less in ideas.[58]

[56] Steward Alsop, *The Center* (New York: Harper & Row, 1968), p. 36.

[57] See, for example, Goldman, *op. cit.*, *passim.*, and especially p. 525.

[58] Philip Geyelin, *Lyndon Johnson and the World* (New York: Frederick A. Praeger, 1966) pp. 13, 15. Compare Frances Perkins' similar comment about Roosevelt, *op. cit.*, p. 97. "Roosevelt could 'get' a problem infinitely better when he had a vicarious experience through a vivid description of a typical case. Proceeding 'from the book,' no matter how logical, never seemed solid to him. His vivid imagination and sympathy helped him to 'see' from a word picture. Later, when the problems of unemployment became even more pressing, he heard many theoretical economic discussions, but he never felt certain about the theory until he saw a sweater mill located in a small village outside Poughkeepsie

A number of things Johnson did in office suggest that he was fully aware of this handicap. Most significant was his effort to keep so many Kennedy appointees. Three members of the first Kennedy cabinet (Secretaries Rusk, Udall, and Freeman) served out Johnson's full term. Virtually all the members of the Johnson administration who fell afoul of the dovish wing of the Democratic party in 1967 and 1968 over the Vietnam war (Rusk, Rostow, Bundy, McNamara) were originally Kennedy appointees.

Some observers maintain that Johnson's desire to maintain continuity with Kennedy administration policies led him to an initial acceptance of Vietnam escalation;[59] but it is the persistence of this policy in the face of continued disappointment that needs explaining. One plausible explanation is that President Johnson persisted because in this area he lacked the sure-footedness that is the prerequisite of ingenuity and hospitality to innovation. No doubt pride and the conviction that the policies his administration was pursuing were defensible and ultimately right also led to his persistence in them, but Johnson was not by habit an ideologically inflexible politician or one whose pride was normally invested in particular means so much as in being able to achieve a creditable result.

Although President Johnson has been quoted as saying that he believed that his strong and successful pro-civil rights policies coupled with urban riots were the principal cause of his unpopularity toward the end of his term of office,[60] his hope to settle the Vietnam war was the reason he gave for withdrawing as a candidate for reelection. Since 1948, the Solid South has not been reliably Democratic in presidential politics; moreover, since then the rest of the national Democratic coalition has more often than not abandoned the South. It was Vietnam that split the national Democratic party, not the race issue. And it was Vietnam that cast a pall over the Johnson Presidency.[61]

Information has come to light indicating that toward the end Johnson administration policy toward Vietnam began to change sharply. The manner in which this occurred reveals something of the style of the Johnson Presidency.[62] As President, Johnson put great reliance on men whom he could

---

which had employed no more than one hundred and fifty people. Roosevelt talked with the employer, who was in despair. He talked to the workers, who were frightened and confused. In this way he got the economic and human problem all at once. He had a basis of judging whether a program would be practical by thinking of how it would apply to the sweater mill."

[59] Among others, Wicker, *JFK and LBJ*, op. cit., makes this argument.

[60] David Wise, "The Twilight of a President," *New York Times Magazine* (November 3, 1968), p. 131.

[61] Richard H. Rovere comments: "It is the war in Vietnam and only the war in Vietnam that has brought him low. . . ." "Letter from Washington," *The New Yorker* (September 23, 1967), pp. 159.

[62] See Hedrick Smith et al., "The Vietnam Policy Reversal of 1968," *The New York Times* (March 6, 7, 1969); Richard Harwood and Laurence Stern, "The War and a Political Downfall: How Johnson Decided," *Washington Post* (February 9, 1969); Townsend Hoopes, *The Limits of Intervention* (New York: McKay, 1969); Clark Clifford, "Vietnam Reappraisal: The Personal History of One Man's View and How it Evolved," *Foreign Affairs*, vol. 47 (July, 1969), pp. 601–622.

President Johnson's version of the events recounted here is somewhat different from the view that emerges from the above four sources. He emphasized that he relied on advice from Secretary of State Rusk rather than from the Defense Department. See Max Frankel, "Johnson Says Tet Victory led to his '68 Peace Move," *The New York Times* (February 8, 1970).

trust personally—with whom, as he said, he had "been to the well." Many of these men had been important figures in their own right in Washington and in Democratic politics since the New Deal. One was Clark Clifford, a Washington lawyer who had been a confidential White House assistant in the Truman administration and whom Johnson picked to succeed Robert McNamara as Secretary of Defense. Virtually the first major problem Clifford faced when he took over the Pentagon in January, 1968, was a request from the commander in Vietnam for a massive new commitment of American troops. Civilian officials in the Defense Department seized on the evaluation of this request as a vehicle through which they could brief the new Secretary in detail about the problems and prospects of the war. Clifford emerged convinced that, within the ground rules imposed by our worldwide commitments, the war could not be won and that ways had to be found to limit and ultimately reduce the American investment there.

This was contrary to presidential policy; however, by the end of March, after a short period of pulling and hauling within the administration, it had become presidential policy. Clifford mounted an extraordinary effort to change the President's mind. He encouraged Johnson to convene a "council of elders" and in effect ask them to evaluate the evidence that had changed his own mind on Vietnam. Some of these men, such as Maxwell Taylor, Walt Rostow, Dean Rusk, and McGeorge Bundy, had been architects of Vietnam escalation. Others—Dean Acheson, Abe Fortas, and Clifford himself—had been sympathetic to the general line of policy. Only a few, such as George Ball, had criticized the policy from within the government. But almost all of them emerged from their deliberations convinced that Clifford was right and that administration policy had to change.

The January, 1968, Tet offensive by the Viet Cong forces, which greatly embarrassed those in the administration who were optimistic about the course of the war, and the polls, demonstrations, and presidential primaries of early 1968, which showed how unpopular the war had become with Americans (especially Democrats) also must have weighed heavily on the minds of policy-makers. But Johnson had long remained intransigent in the face of similar adversity. This persuasion from within his administration—and from men he trusted—cannot be discounted as a force in shifting the policy of the administration. Very soon after the conclusion of the "council of elders" was communicated to the President, American policy did begin to change, although this was not immediately acknowledged. General Westmoreland was denied his request for a huge new commitment of troops; procedural negotiations began with the enemy in Paris; and the President announced his determination to seek a negotiated settlement in Vietnam unencumbered by the pursuit of another term in office.

In areas where he was more at home—especially in manipulating the press, the bureaucracies, and Congress—Johnson took command of everything to a degree that greatly exceeded Kennedy. Members of his staff, compared with Kennedy's, were much less in the limelight, though many of them were of very high caliber. In some respects Johnson tried to give the appearance of running a one-man administration: whenever an agency of the government had good news, there was a standing order to send it to the White House for announcement. The resignations of Cabinet members were timed to allow the President miniscule advantages even though this entailed major inconveniences to the men involved.[63]

If Kennedy rode the waves, Johnson, Canutelike, commanded them. He resented all outside attempts, large and small, to commit him in advance to a line of policy, to a presidential appointment, to anything that would reduce his "options." Task forces were mobilized to frame new policy proposals but were required to observe the strictest secrecy.[64] Trial balloons were forbidden. Independent action by allies and subordinates was regarded as a poor substitute for coordinated service in behalf of presidential goals. In the Senate, Johnson had enjoyed six years as majority leader without the obligation to pursue a Republican President's priorities. Johnson found that by regulating the pace of Senate business he could maximize his own effectiveness.[65] In applying the lessons of those years to the Presidency, he conceded little to forces that other Presidents had appeased. No serious attempt was made to release the overwhelmingly pro-Johnson Eighty-ninth Congress from its labors in Washington early enough for incumbents of marginal House seats to campaign for reelection. Certainly, by so doing, a few of the fifty-five Democrats who lost House or Senate seats in the 1966 election could have been helped. Relations with local and state party leaders, whose preoccupations centered more on the winning of future elections than on the writing of a glorious legislative record, dwindled. Tremendous effort went into wooing the press, into finding programs with short-run payoffs, into scoring publicity coups.[66]

Much of this could be justified—and was—on the grounds that the President, as the only member of the administration who had to run for election, was the only member of the administration who needed the favorable publicity and, as the head of the government, his convenience was paramount. But, in time, this explanation seemed inadequate. Reporters noted the President's continuing appetite for adulation, his habit of intruding on and, in little ways, demeaning the people who worked most closely with him. Eric Goldman commented:

> President Johnson's attitude toward his staff was essentially feudal.
> . . . When he did not like the length of a Special Assistant's hair, he
> told him to go to a barbershop; he ordered a secretary to enroll in a
> charm school. He expected aides to be available at any time for any
> function. They were as likely to be asked to phone the tailor ("These

[63] See, for example, Joseph R. Slevin, "Hodges Shook up by Sudden Notice of LBJ's Acceptance of Resignation," *Washington Post* (January 7, 1965); and Rowland Evans and Robert Novak, *Lyndon B. Johnson: The Exercise of Power* (New York: New American Library, 1966) pp. 343–344, on the departure of Edward R. Murrow.

[64] William E. Leuchtenberg, "The Genesis of the Great Society," *The Reporter* (April 21, 1966), pp. 35–39.

[65] Evans and Novak, *op cit.*, pp. 116–117.

[66] See, for example, Tom Wicker, "Lyndon Johnson is 10 Feet Tall," *New York Times Magazine* (May 23, 1965), pp. 23ff.

damn pants hitch up too much") as to confer with an ambassador. . . .
LBJ was full of acts of *noblesse oblige.* . . .[67]

All Presidents in some way or another have been eccentric. It seems
unavoidable that anyone who lives so much of his life in the spotlight and
under pressure will display casual mannerisms that seem puzzling or unconventional to his fellowmen. But for Johnson, who never separated his private
person from his public responsibilities, who worked at presidential politics
every waking moment, the eccentricities could hardly help but reflect on
the conduct of public business.

Sometimes his theatrical instincts paid off:

> In order to discuss the application of Medicare, the American Medi-
> cal Association requested an appointment with the President, and on
> July 29th he met with eleven of its leaders at the White House. "I'd
> never seen anything like it," one of the administration officials who at-
> tended the meeting said afterward. "The President made a powerful,
> moving appeal to the doctors to accept the new law, and reminded
> them that it had been devised after long and thorough consideration by
> the people's representatives under our constitutional procedures. He
> went on in that way for some time, and then he began talking about
> what wonderful men doctors were, and how when his daddy was sick
> the doctor would come over and sit up all night with him, and charge
> a pittance. He was getting terribly corny, but he had them on the edge
> of their seats. Then, suddenly, he got up and stretched. Of course, when
> the President of the United States stands up, everybody stands up. They
> jumped to their feet, and then he sat down, so they sat down, too. He
> started off again, with another moving statement about this great na-
> tion and its obligation to those who had helped make it great and who
> were now old and sick and helpless through no fault of their own.
> Gradually, he moved back to the cornfield, and then he stood up again,
> and again they jumped to their feet. He did that a couple more times—
> until they were fully aware of who was President—and then he turned
> to a memorandum on his desk. He read them the statement in the bill
> prohibiting any government interference in any kind of medical practice
> at any time, and also the statement guaranteeing freedom of choice for
> both doctors and patients, and assured them there would be no gov-
> ernment meddling in these matters. Next, he explained that Blue Cross
> and private insurance carriers, who are the administrative middlemen
> under the law, would determine the bill's definition of 'reasonable
> charges' on the basis of what was customary for a given area. Naturally,
> the doctors went for this, because they have great influence with most
> of those outfits. Toward the end, he asked for their help in drawing up
> regulations to implement the law. Then he got up one last time, and
> said he had to leave. Before he went, he turned to Cohen, who is the
> A.M.A.'s idea of an archfiend, and, shaking a huge forefinger in his face,
> he said, 'Wilbur, I want you to stay here with these gentlemen, and
> work things out according to my instructions—no matter how long it

[67] Goldman, *op. cit.,* pp. 102–103.

takes you.' Afterward, I overheard one A.M.A. man say to another, 'Boy, did you hear how he talked to Cohen?' Of course, Wilbur had written the memorandum.''[68]

But as concern over the Vietnam war deepened and dissent became more bitter toward the end of Johnson's term, the press became less tolerant of his foibles. Although comment about them had reached print long before the downturn in his popularity, it became more and more permissible to repeat stories illustrating Mr. Johnson's hunger to domineer in small matters, his lack of cultivation, his manipulativeness and secretiveness.[69] President Johnson's defenders pointed out that many of these complaints were trivial and did not really touch the public business.[70] In other cases, Johnson was merely following the example of Franklin Roosevelt, whose secretiveness and manipulativeness in the service of preserving presidential options were so much admired by writers on the Presidency. But somehow, Johnson seemed to carry the process too far—angrily cancelling major appointments or dropping major policy proposals because news about them had leaked out too soon.[71] "By striking hard at alleged transgressors," Evans and Novak commented, "the President quickly got the message to everyone in his administration that indiscreet officials would not be tolerated. As awareness of this fact seeped deep into the collective subconscious of the federal government, the inevitable reaction was a tendency to clam up. That enhanced the President's personal control over the federal establishment and enlarged the presidential exercise of power."[72]

So it did; but this end is not desirable to the exclusion of all others. The President cannot run the government without help, and first rate help is more easily attracted by the expectation of considerate treatment. Evans and Novak continued: "Corporation officials and lawyers had heard about long hours,

[68] Richard Harris, *A Sacred Trust* (New York: New American Library, 1966), pp. 215–216.

[69] A literature sprang up about Mr. Johnson, as it does with most Presidents, that can only be described as scurrilous. It is uncommon, however, for material of this kind to have a vogue in presumably intellectual circles, as did the anti-Johnson *Macbird*, a sophomoric parody. Much more disturbing was the flow of responsible reporting and commentary giving prominence to unattractive features of Mr. Johnson's personality that seemed to be finding their way into the making and justification of public policy and into the everyday lives of his associates. See, for example, John Osborne, "Concern About L.B.J.," *New Republic* (July 24, 1965), pp. 12–14; "Report on Washington," *The Atlantic* (July, 1966), p. 13; Henry Gemmill, "Capitol Malaise," *The Wall Street Journal* (November 8, 1967); Warren Rogers, "The Truth About LBJ's Credibility Gap," *Look* (May 2, 1967); James Deakin, "The Dark Side of L.B.J.," *Esquire* (August, 1967) p. 45 ff.; Goldman, *op. cit.;* Wicker, *JFK and LBJ, op. cit.;* and Evans and Novak, *op. cit.,* all passim.

[70] A valiant attempt to deal with some of these complaints can be found in Howard K. Smith, "Prologue," in James McGregor Burns (ed.), *To Heal and to Build: The Programs of President Lyndon B. Johnson* (New York: McGraw-Hill, 1968) pp. 1–15.

[71] Details on several such incidents may be found in Evans and Novak, *op cit.,* pp. 201–504. Apparently, undue publicity was given a specific definition in the Johnson Administration: "Johnson became annoyed when he felt that Bundy was getting too much personal publicity. . . . Bundy several years later would tell a group of *Time* editors, 'The worst thing you could do with Lyndon Johnson was to go public with something, which with Lyndon Johnson meant anyone but himself.'" David Halberstam, "The Very Expensive Education of McGeorge Bundy," *Harpers* (July, 1969), p. 36.

[72] Evans and Novak, *op. cit.,* p. 504.

hard demands, and occasional abuse from above, and some of them were reluctant to join the Great Society."[73]

Nevertheless, Johnson made a number of conspicuously first-rate appointments. The Kennedy administration had been widely congratulated for bringing a fresh and extraordinarily able new group of leaders into public life. Johnson retained many of them and added a few of his own: John Gardner, for example, gave new impetus to the Department of Health, Education, and Welfare; Ramsey Clark distinguished himself as Attorney General by his concern for civil liberties; Erwin Griswold, on his retirement as dean of the Harvard Law School, became Solicitor General; the gifted Clark Clifford replaced McNamara at Defense; and Arthur Goldberg left the Supreme Court to take up the late Adlai Stevenson's UN ambassadorship.

But toward the end, the Vietnam war swallowed everything. The popularity demonstrated by Johnson's overwhelming victory in 1964 evaporated in the polls and primaries of 1968; the avalanche of new and liberal legislation that emerged from the Eighty-ninth Congress of 1965–1967 gave way to hostile Senatorial hearings and soured Johnson's private relations on Capitol Hill. When the Vietnam war devoured the Health, Education, and Welfare budget, John Gardner resigned. McNamara, increasingly skeptical of Vietnam policy, was eased out. Tension between Johnson and Goldberg, Udall, Clark, and even his old friend Clifford, became open secrets in Washington. Other high officials seem privately to have felt they stayed on too long. In a remarkable article, the usually extremely well-informed James Reston mused: "No doubt some stayed on out of compassion for the President or fear of his wrath and his fascination with the intimidating power of the FBI and the Internal Revenue Service. Others remained out of loyalty or guilt or ambition for position in the future. . . . Mr. Johnson did not make it easy for his colleagues to differ with him on fundamental issues."[74]

Like all human organizations, our political system relies heavily on the wisdom of the men who run it. Because the President alone heads the executive branch, in the end his wisdom counts for more than that of any of the men around him. Thus his weaknesses as well as his strengths, his incapacities as well as his talents are for his time in office to a greater or lesser degree embodied in and amplified by the machinery of government. Personal eccentricities in a private person normally have small consequences for his neighbors. A President's eccentricities, though publicly on display, may be gratified in small and tolerable ways—by thousands of photographs, by multiple television sets in every room, by desk buttons marked "root beer" and "Fresca."[75] Or they may manifest themselves in larger and less digestible ways. Secretiveness may preserve options but inhibit the rallying of support behind the option finally chosen.[76] The urge to dominate may focus political attention on

---

[73] *Ibid.*, p. 505.

[74] James Reston, "The Doubts and Regrets of the Johnson Dissenters," *The New York Times* (March 9, 1969).

[75] John Pierson, "The Job Is Demanding, but the Little Extras Ease a President's Lot," *The Wall Street Journal* (April 4, 1969).

[76] In "Congress and Closed Politics in National Security Affairs," *Orbis*, vol. 10 (Fall, 1966), pp. 737–753, H. Bradford Westerfield makes a parallel argument, though he does not

the leader, but unwillingness to share credit, if carried to a great extreme, may deprive the leader of the help he needs. Unwillingness to share power means the President decides what he wants to decide, but it stifles creativity and initiative in those parts of the system close enough for the President to reach but where limitations on his time and energy prevent him from acting. There seem to be no compensating advantages for a President's unwillingness to grant the normal amount of dignity to his closest associates. This trait marks a President as a person of flawed character and leads observers to misinterpret even his most disinterested and public-spirited actions.

It is difficult to tell how history will judge Lyndon Johnson's Presidency. To his contemporaries, his own personal characteristics intrude on a reading of the record—as they did so notably on the writing of it.[77] If his contemporaries are thankful that Johnson had it in him to rise nobly to many occasions —in civil rights, the trauma of the succession, and the grand design of his domestic program—they also regret that often between occasions he fell to petty and vindictive behavior, insensitivity, and maudlin self-justification that in the end may have cost him and his fellow citizens more than he ever intended.

Richard M. Nixon (1969–   ). It is simply too early to do justice or even a convincing injustice to Richard Nixon's Presidency.[78] However, the running commentaries that have accompanied the early years of the Nixon Presidency have stressed a number of themes that may prove useful when the time comes to take a more leisurely look at these interesting times. There was, for example, the tension between liberals and conservatives in the administration as Mr. Nixon searched for a constituency that could support his policies and form an electoral majority. There was Nixon's own disposition to judicialize presidential decision-making, a process that featured the orderly presentation of alternatives to the President who would then withdraw, ponder in private, and emerge with a decision. This process placed a heavy burden on the White House staff, which was responsible not only for the formulation and presentation of alternatives and for seeing to the eventual execution of the policy chosen, but also for the protection of the President's time and energy during critical decision-making periods, when the pressure on the President's attention from concerned interest groups inside and outside the governmental bureaucracies was bound to be very high. One conse-

---

attribute the increase of "closed politics" in national security affairs to explicit choices by President Johnson.

[77] And also, as it now appears, on its rewriting, if we can judge from the series of retrospective television broadcasts which Mr. Johnson undertook. Cf. Frankel, *op. cit.*

[78] For a near miss, see James David Barber, "Analyzing Presidents: From Passive-Positive Taft to Active-Negative Nixon," *The Washington Monthly*, vol. 1 (October, 1969), pp. 33–54, especially pp. 50–54. Other articles establishing a canonical interpretation of the Nixon Presidency are Robert B. Semple, Jr., "Nixon's Style as Boss Combines Desires for Order and Solitude," *The New York Times* (January 12, 1970); John Pierson, "The Nixon Style: President Seeks Order in his Decision-making but Events Intrude," *The Wall Street Journal* (July 7, 1969); Don Oberdorfer, "The Presidency: Still Very Private after First Year," *The Washington Post* (January 18, 1970); and Richard F. Janssen, "Turmoil at the Top: An Inaccessible Nixon Stirs Anger and Despair within Administration," *The Wall Street Journal* (May 8, 1970).

quence of this process was a good deal of friction between the White House and persons of high responsibility in other parts of the government who were not themselves close to the President.

Mr. Nixon has had an unusual career. An early, undistinguished start in Congress was followed by eight years as Eisenhower's youthful, well-publicized, but politically powerless Vice President and then by another eight years of private life punctuated by abortive attempts to reemerge politically. He came to the Presidency with virtually no public record on most of the major issues of politics-in-government, with no concrete accomplishments in public policy. Thus a Nixon Presidency was bound to be a voyage of discovery, not only for the men who watch Presidents day by day, but also, perhaps, for President Nixon himself.

PROBLEMS IN EVALUATING PRESIDENTS

Some Presidents, fortunate in their instincts, their advisors, and their opportunities, have been great goal setters. Harry Truman and John Kennedy shared the distinction of bringing forth exciting policies and plans. Other Presidents have had superb executive talents. Lyndon Johnson seems sure eventually to be regarded as one of these, as were Coolidge and Hoover—two quite different men—in their time. And, of course, Franklin Roosevelt's performance on both counts is universally accounted as exceptional. In any event, the President's job must partake of both. The fundamental problems involved are two—deciding what to do and seeing that it is done. A man, or an administration, may be good at one and not the other. And a failure at one task, may sometimes—as I think was the case with President Eisenhower—help to explain failure at the other.

It may be that in inspecting the criteria by which Presidents are judged we shall learn more about judges of Presidents than about Presidents themselves. But the risk is worth taking. The Presidency is, after all, a role. Like other roles, it develops in response to identifications, demands, and expectations that impinge on it from outside. And some of these expectations are recorded in the form of evaluations of presidential performanace.

Two Theories of the Presidency. The first and most significant problem in evaluating a President is to decide how to weigh his own theory of his proper place in the American political system. Some Presidents did less than they might have because they believed that this was their proper role in the constitutional order. One President who has written eloquently in defense of this point of view is William Howard Taft. He said:

> The true view of the Executive function is, as I conceive it, that the President can exercise no power which cannot be fairly and reasonably traced to some specific grant of power or justly implied and included within such express grant as proper and necessary to its exercise. Such specific grant must be either in the Federal Constitution or in an act of

Congress passed in pursuance thereof. There is no undefined residuum of power which he can exercise because it seems to him to be in the public interest. . . .[79]

An alternative view was held by Theodore Roosevelt:

> I declined to adopt the view that what was imperatively necessary for the Nation could not be done by the President unless he could find some specific authorization to do it. My belief was that it was not only his right but his duty to do anything that the needs of the Nation demanded unless such action was forbidden by the Constitution or by the laws. Under this interpretation of executive power I did and caused to be done many things not previously done by the President and the heads of the departments. I did not usurp power, but I did greatly broaden the use of executive power. In other words, I acted for the public welfare, I acted for the common well-being of all our people, whenever and in whatever manner was necessary, unless prevented by direct constitutional or legislative prohibition. . . .[80]

The beginnings of this conflict in constitutional interpretation and practice have been traced back to the founding of the Republic. In those early years, Leonard White found:

> The Federalists emphasized the necessity for power in government and for energy in the executive branch. The Republicans emphasized the liberties of the citizen and the primacy of representative assemblies. The latter accused their opponents of sympathy to monarchy and hostility to republican institutions. . . . Hamilton . . . insisted on the necessity for executive leadership of an otherwise drifting legislature; Jefferson thought the people's representatives would readily find their way if left alone to educate each other by free discussion and compromise. . . . By 1792 Jefferson thought the executive power had swallowed up the legislative branch; in 1798 Hamilton thought the legislative branch had so curtailed executive power that an able man could find no useful place in the government.[81]

[79] William Howard Taft, *Our Chief Magistrate and His Powers* (New York: Columbia, 1916), pp. 138ff. Reprinted in J. P. Roche and L. W. Levy (eds.), *The Presidency* (New York: Harcourt, Brace & World, 1964), p. 23.

Oddly enough, Taft favored a relatively activist Supreme Court and was himself later a vigorously busy and highly political Chief Justice. See Walter F. Murphy, "In His Own Image: Mr. Chief Justice Taft and Supreme Court Appointments," *The Supreme Court and the Constitution*, Philip Kurland, ed., (Chicago: University of Chicago Press, 1965, pp. 123–157.

[80] From Arthur B. Tourtellot, *Presidents on the Presidency* (Garden City, N.Y.: Doubleday, 1964), p. 55–56.

[81] Leonard D. White, *The Federalists: A Study in Administrative History* (New York: Macmillan, 1948), p. 89. For a continuous account of the contrast between these two theories of presidential power in American administrative history, see also White's *The Jeffersonians* (New York: Macmillan, 1951), esp. pp. 29ff, and *The Jacksonians* (New York: Macmillan, 1954), esp. pp. 56ff.

Contemporary evaluations are likely to favor an activist view of the Presidency. "Mediocre" presidents, according to Arthur M. Schlesinger, Sr., "believed in negative government, in self-subordination to the legislative power."[82] Presidents such as Hoover and Eisenhower, who believed they should not seize power at the expense of Congress, have been downgraded for their performance in office.

Occasionally, evaluations of Presidents based on their theory of the Presidency mask disagreement over substantive policy. Passive Presidents serve the demands of the presidential coalition less well than active Presidents. Thus, constitutional theories have important impacts on specific policies and on the chances that the needs and desires of masses of citizens will be met. Unavoidably, therefore, preferences with respect to public policy enter into evaluations of presidential behavior by the back door of constitutional disputation.

Three Arenas of Performance. There are additional criteria in evaluating presidential performance apart from the appropriateness of the role a particular President chooses to play and its impact on public policy. It is quite common to speak of performance in foreign affairs, in administering the business of the executive branch, and in getting a program through Congress. Each of these arenas presents great difficulties to the evaluator.

The extent to which a President succeeds with Congress, for example, may hinge on simple good fortune in the makeup of the House and Senate—or even of certain key committees of Congress. Or it may depend on the sorts of things he asks them to do and the aid he receives from outside events in convincing them of the need for action. Still, congressional box scores are kept, showing how well the President's program is doing. Comparisons between programs that are relatively modest and those that are relatively ambitious, between presidential successes in times of crisis and in times of relaxation are almost meaningless but are made.

It is hard to imagine a great President during an era of good feeling in foreign affairs. International crises and winning battles provide the ideal setting for presidential leadership. Invariably, the short-run popular response to a President during an international crisis is favorable, regardless of the wisdom of the policies he pursues. Table 1 illustrates the point. Four fiascoes from the standpoint of American policy and three crises in which presidential action had happier outcomes produced quite similar transformations of public sentiment. So also with the longer view of historians. Presidents who have mobilized the energies of the nation against specific external threats have been rated high.[83]

[82] Schlesinger, "Our Presidents," op cit., p. 12. See also Thomas A. Bailey, Presidential Greatness: The Image and the Man from George Washington to the Present (New York: Appleton-Century-Crofts, 1966).

[83] Sudden crisis involving external threat and vigorous presidential activity seem best designed to provoke this response, at least in the short run. John E. Mueller's "Presidential Popularity from Truman to Johnson," American Political Science Review, vol. 64 (March, 1970), pp. 18–34, emphasizes that these benefits are visible only in the short run; however, he does document the presence of the phenomenon. Mueller argues that the war in Vietnam does not follow the same pattern, but his finding on this point may be contaminated

Table 1   Popularity of President in Foreign Crisis

Before Crisis		After Crisis
June, 1950		July, 1950
37 pro/45 anti	United States enters Korean War (Truman)	46 pro/37 anti
August, 1956	British, Israeli, French attack Suez; U.S.	December, 1956
67 pro/20 anti	refuses to aid them (Eisenhower)	75 pro/15 anti
July, 1958	U.S. sends Marines to Lebanon	August, 1958
52 pro/32 anti	(Eisenhower)	58 pro/27 anti
May, 1960	U-2 incident, summit meetings collapse	Early June, 1960
62 pro/22 anti	(Eisenhower)	68 pro/21 anti
March, 1961		April, 1961
73 pro/7 anti	Bay of Pigs, Cuba (Kennedy)	83 pro/5 anti
October, 1961		December, 1961
61 pro/24 anti	Missile Crisis, Cuba (Kennedy)	74 pro/15 anti
Late July, 1964	Gulf of Tonkin incident (Johnson)	Early August, 1964
59 pro/		65 pro/

Sources: Hazel Gaudet Erskine (ed.), "A Revival: Reports from the Polls," *Public Opinion Quarterly,* vol. 25 (Spring, 1961), pp. 135–137; and AIPO releases for indicated periods.

Perhaps the arena in which it is hardest to gather data is the purely administrative. Both Grant and Harding are treated severely in the history books because of the large-scale scandals that marked their administrations. Nowadays, internal and legal controls on the bureaucracy have been greatly strengthened, but even so the sheer size of the executive branch precludes presidential supervision of petty graft or corruption far down the line. Closer to the top of the executive branch, the main problem is normally not overt stealing but favoritism stemming from a conflict of interest. This sort of thing is extremely difficult to identify. Administrative discretion is wide, compelling substantive arguments may exist for a decision, and in some cases movement in any direction may be susceptible to interpretation as favoritism. Even so, scandals of a sort have occasionally developed in recent administrations. Several of President Truman's advisors were accused of influence peddling and one was convicted of income tax evasion. President Eisenhower's top White House aide was forced to resign over charges of improper use of his office.

Absence of widespread or widely publicized scandal is one mark of suc-

---

by other, stronger factors contributing to President Johnson's unpopularity. For further discussion of this point, see Kenneth N. Waltz, "Electoral Punishment and Foreign Policy Crises," in James N. Rosenau (ed.), *Domestic Sources of Foreign Policy* (New York: Free Press, 1967), pp. 263–293.

The Korean war hurt Mr. Truman with public opinion in the long run. See Angus Campbell et al., *The American Voter* (New York: Wiley, 1960), pp. 48–50. But perhaps the main reason the Korean war was unpopular was because Mr. Truman decided to limit the war and called for a *partial* rather than an all-out mobilization. See Samuel P. Huntington, *The Soldier and the State* (New York: Random House Vintage Books, 1964), pp. 387–391. For a general discussion of Vietnam and public opinion, see Richard A. Brody, "How the Vietnam War May Affect the Election," *Trans-action,* vol. 5 (October, 1968), pp. 16–23; and Sidney Verba et al., "Public Opinion and the War in Vietnam," *American Political Science Review,* vol. 61 (June, 1967), pp. 317–333.

cessful administration. Another, equally tenuous, is a reputation for being on top of the job. Presidents are watched closely by their subordinates, by congressmen and senators, by lobbyists, newsmen, the embassies of foreign governments, and so on. Sooner or later, these diverse President-watchers begin to develop a shared, composite picture of each President and the way he operates. A President's reputation with this community suffers if he does not do his homework (i.e., read a high percentage of the reports that are sent across his desk), if he fails to grasp the substance of issues as they are presented to him, if he restricts unduly the range of his acquaintance and his exposure to information. In these circumstances, a President is regarded as unreachable, as rigid, and as administratively weak.

Luck. Finally, however, we cannot rule out the tremendous role that luck plays in establishing a presidential reputation. So many circumstances that impinge mightily on the fate of nations are beyond the realm of presidential discretion. If things turn out well, we praise the President; if badly, we blame him. But we can only guess at the differences he and his policies have made.

Thus when we evaluate a President, we may be making a variety of judgments. We may be expressing agreement or disagreement with his theory of the proper role of the Presidency in the political system. Or we may be responding favorably or unfavorably to the circumstances in which he found himself, regardless of his best efforts.

MACHINERY OF PRESIDENTIAL POWER

The Presidency has always been a big job. It could be argued that at one point in history, it was a big job for a single man. Today, a huge executive establishment "takes care that the laws are executed"; and at the head of this establishment sits not a single man, but a superbureaucracy, the Executive Office of the President. In turn, at the apex of this conglomeration of agencies, is the President himself.

The many jobs or roles or "hats" of the President have often been enumerated—Chief of State, Chief Executive, Supreme Commander of the Armed Forces, Chief Diplomat, Chief Legislator, Chief of Party, Voice of the People, Protector of the Peace, Manager of Prosperity, World Leader. An impressive list.[84] But the main point about it is, as Richard Neustadt says, that the President must wear all the hats at once.[85] Perforce, some hats sit more precariously on that single head than others. The President is only one man, and he is subject to severe constraints on that account. He can only be at one place at a time. There are only twenty-four hours in his day. He has only two arms, two legs, two ears, two eyes. He is subject to illness, to fatigue, to deadlines, to conflicting demands, and to a glut of information. The job of the agencies in the Executive Office is to give the President the extra arms, hands,

[84] This list is Clinton Rossiter's. *The American Presidency*, rev. ed. (New York: Harcourt, Brace & World, 1960), chap. 1.

[85] Richard Neustadt, "The Presidency at Midcentury," *Law and Contemporary Problems*, vol. 21, (Autumn, 1956), p. 610.

brains, and time that he needs to make decisions, to keep his hats from falling off, to make policy, and to see that it is carried out. As these agencies have taken shape, they have developed characteristics and problems of their own. These have to be understood if we are to understand the contemporary Presidency.

The White House Office. Closest to the President is, of course, the group of aides and assistants he gathers around him in the White House. Even Roosevelt, who liked to keep job assignments flexible, had an appointment secretary and a press secretary, both of whom worked pretty much full-time at their specialties. Later on, especially under Eisenhower, further functions were differentiated, including, most significantly, an office of legislative liaison. In addition to these officials, the White House commonly houses a number of people who undertake specific tasks as they arise—looking into an explosive Latin-American situation, let us say, or mounting a campaign for a reciprocal trade bill. Others may spend their time writing speeches for the President. And still others may look after specific policy areas. The organization of this office is entirely up to the President; it exists entirely to serve his interests, as he defines them.

The Office of Management and Budget. The largest permanent presidential agency is the Office of Management and Budget (incorporating the activities of the former Bureau of the Budget), which has a variety of tasks defined by law. This is the agency that has routine charge of the "program of the President." As we shall see in a later chapter, bills introduced in Congress are routinely referred to agencies in the executive branch for opinions. These opinions are cleared through the Office of Management and Budget, which makes sure that they are in accord with policies laid down by the President. The Office also allocates funds to the executive branch in three-month installments and, in a complicated process described in Chapter 6, has major responsibility for the preparation and clearance of all requests for money made to Congress by all Federal agencies. The Office also undertakes administrative surveys of various kinds in the executive agencies at the President's request.

Special Expertise Agencies. The Council of Economic Advisors and the Office of Science and Technology are designed to offer the President continuing advice and counsel on the state of the economy and on scientific and technological developments. Both agencies are relatively new, dating from 1946 and 1962, respectively. They reflect the shrinking of our world, where developments in one sector rapidly affect outcomes in another. Nowadays, the state of the economy must be of continuous concern to the President. Actions by the government can do much to change the economic picture; the President must have a flow of information and advice always at hand to help anticipate these changes plus changes caused by outside events that may have impact on governmental policy. Increasingly, the Council also provides information and policy advice designed to assist Presidents in their active concern, developed in recent years, with using governmental power to affect economic growth, prices, wages, and levels of employment throughout the domestic economy and the balance of payments abroad.

Scientific advice at the presidential level is now also regarded as a critical necessity. In 1939, before this was regularly provided for, Albert Einstein wrote a cautious letter to President Roosevelt, calling to his attention "recent work" that "would . . . lead to the construction of bombs, and it is conceivable–though much less certain—that extremely powerful bombs of a new type may thus be constructed."[86] Since that time, the findings of pure science have intruded on national policy-making at an ever-increasing rate. Now, government is the principal support of and customer for science of all sorts— pure and applied, physical, biological, and even social. Not only must Presidents react promptly to scientific news, they must also make choices—increasing Federal support here and cutting it back there—that help determine what the scientific news is going to be. The Office of Science and Technology, manned by scientists and scientific administrators who are in touch with the various scientific communities, is designed to help with this task.

The Cabinet. Tradition decrees that the presidential Cabinet shall consist of the operating heads of the main departments of government.[87] Presidents have had great leeway in deciding how this group of top-level administrators is chosen and the extent to which it is used as a collective entity, either to thrash out interdepartmental problems or to advise the President. President Eisenhower's practice was, as I have mentioned, to use an expanded and augmented Cabinet quite extensively as a sounding board and policy-making group.[88] Eisenhower's three successors, on the other hand, have preferred to deal directly with those Cabinet members involved in a particular problem and have avoided large-scale formal meetings.

The National Security Council. The National Security Council is a Cabinet-like group, by statute consisting of the President, the Vice President, the Secretaries of State and Defense, and the Director of the Office of Emergency Preparedness. The Chairman of the Joint Chiefs of Staff and the Director of the Central Intelligence Agency are statutory advisors to the Council. This group meets to make formal determinations of policy in areas affecting foreign and defense policy. The politics of its inner workings have not been much explored, although, once again, there are indications that Presidents Eisenhower and Kennedy treated the Council in much the same ways that they treated their Cabinets—Eisenhower tending to open up meetings to a large

---

[86] My source for this often-quoted passage is Laura Fermi's charming memoir, *Atoms in the Family* (Chicago: University of Chicago Press, 1954), pp. 165–166.

[87] These are, in order of the seniority of their posts, the Secretaries of State, Treasury, Defense (as successor to the Secretary of War in Washington's Cabinet); Attorney General; Postmaster General; Secretaries of Interior, Agriculture, Commerce, Labor, Health, Education and Welfare, Housing and Urban Development, and Transportation. Others may be invited to Cabinet meetings at the discretion of the President.

[88] See Donovan, *op. cit.* The best general treatment of Presidents and their Cabinets is Richard F. Fenno, Jr., *The President's Cabinet* (New York: Random House Vintage Books, 1959). On Cabinet and sub-Cabinet appointment processes, see Dean E. Mann and Jameson Doig, *The Assistant Secretaries* (Washington, D.C.: Brookings, 1965).

number of formal participants, Kennedy tending to create working task forces to deal with specific problems.[89] Under President Nixon, the staff of the NSC has been greatly expanded and has become the core of "the central machinery in the process of policymaking for national security. . . ."[90] A report by President Nixon says:

> The National Security Council itself met 37 times in 1969, and considered over a score of different major problems of national security. Each Council meeting was the culmination of an interagency process of systematic and comprehensive review.
>
> This is how the process works: I assign an issue to an Interdepartmental Group—chaired by an Assistant Secretary of State—for intensive study, asking it to formulate the policy choices and to analyze the pros and cons of the different courses of action. This group's report is examined by an interagency Review Group of senior officials—chaired by the Assistant to the President for National Security Affairs—to insure that the issues, options, and views are presented fully and fairly. The paper is then presented to me and the full National Security Council.[91]

This system, which operates under presidential aide Henry Kissinger, was the earliest organizational innovation of the Nixon White House. Nixon copied its main features to create a Domestic Affairs Council under his assistant John Erlichman, but, traditionally, domestic affairs are much harder to manage within the government and it is too early to tell how this innovation will work out in practice.

Ephemeral Agencies. Some agencies have floated in and out of the purview of the Executive Office, gathering the prestige of close proximity to the Presidency before they were lodged somewhere else in the executive branch. Such was the case with the Disarmament Agency, once a special project of White House aide Harold Stassen and now a special agency housed in the State Department. The Office of Civil Defense, now in the Pentagon, had a similar history.

Other presidential agencies expand and contract with the demands of the times. During World War II, the Director of the Office of War Mobilization and Reconversion, in the White House, was virtually President in domestic affairs.[92] But after the war, the agency was cut back. Vestiges of the agency

[89] On the NSC under Eisenhower, see Paul Y. Hammond, *Organizing for Defense* (Princeton, N.J.: Princeton, 1961), esp. pp. 353–363; and Dillon Anderson, "The President and National Security," *The Atlantic* (January, 1956), pp. 42–46. On the NSC under Kennedy, see, for example, the account of the Cuban missile crisis given by *The New York Times* "Cuban Crisis: A Step by Step Review" (November 3, 1962); and Abel, *op. cit.*

See also, in general, the following documents of the U.S. Senate Subcommittee on National Policy Machinery: "Organizational History of the National Security Council," Committee Print, 86th Cong., 2d Sess. (1960); and "Organizing for National Security: The National Security Council," *Hearings, May 10 and 24, 1960*, Part IV (1960).

[90] Henry A. Kissinger, "The National Security Council," *Report of the Senate Subcommittee on National Security and International Operations, Committee on Government Operations*, 91st Cong., 2d Sess. (March 3, 1970) pp. 1–2.

[91] *Ibid.*, p. 5.

[92] See Herman M. Somers, *Presidential Agency* (Cambridge, Mass.: Harvard, 1950).

now remain in the White House as the Office of Emergency Preparedness. Under President Johnson, the director of this office (which was then called the Office of Emergency Planning) was used primarily as a liaison with governors and as a clearinghouse to help solve administrative problems between Federal and state executive agencies.[93]

Presumably, all these presidential aides can perform a variety of functions. They can protect their chief from burdensome irrelevancies. They can tell him what is going on, in the government and in the world. They can ascertain whether people in the executive agencies and in Congress are doing what the President wants them to do. And they can help the President to decide what he wants to do in the future and to anticipate difficulties and opportunities. How well or how badly they do these jobs depends on many things—on the difficulty of the circumstances that confront them, on the willingness or the ability of the Chief Executive to use their services, and on their own skill and diligence.

ARE PRESIDENTIAL POWERS GREAT OR SMALL?

Let us conclude this preliminary, general treatment of the Presidency by asking if presidential powers are great or small. We know they are many. As we shall see, the President is the initiator of much legislation. And his veto can be overriden only by a two-thirds majority in each house of Congress. He provides a coherent legislative program, party leadership, a budget coordinated with tax revenues. His appointees staff the executive branch and, as vacancies occur, the judiciary. He may decide which programs to emphasize, which to supervise perfunctorily, which to change, which to ignore.

On the other hand, there are many practical limitations to the President's powers. Deadlines must be met. Routine business hems him in. Although very little legislation can pass over his veto, well-placed and determined groups in Congress can thwart his desires as surely as he can thwart theirs.

In addition, many of the problems he faces are intractable, if not insuperable. The President must make decisions even when there is no way of knowing what decisions ought to be made. He must deal with allies who are sometimes petulant and enemies who are sometimes hostile and often devious.

Measured against the opportunities, the responsibilities, and the resources of others in our political system and in other nations, the powers of the Presidency are enormous. It is only when we measure these same powers against the problems of our age that they seem puny and inadequate.

[93] See "New Name Is Given U.S. Planning Office," *The New York Times* (December 14, 1968).

CHAPTER THREE

THE SENATE

Although vast powers are vested in the presidential office, the Chief Executive is much like other executives. He shares dilemmas of leadership common to many others in and out of government. Congress, on the other hand, is a unique institution. The analogies to parliaments that predominate in intelligent conversation about Congress do the powers of our national legislature less than justice. For unlike parliaments the world around, the American Congress dissolves neither itself nor the government when it has a serious disagreement with its Executive. Moreover, Congress does not meet briefly and hurriedly, as do so many of our state legislatures. Rather, it continues to function and to wield substantial power in season and out, quite independently of the preferences of the other branches of government.

To examine Congress closely, it is necessary to look at each house separately. The Senate and the House of Representatives share many characteristics, but they also differ significantly. The Senate, with only 100 members, is smaller. It also has more prestige; members of the House regularly resign voluntarily to run for the Senate, but no one in modern times has voluntarily done the reverse. Until 1913, each state legislature elected two senators for six-year-terms.[1] Since then, under the provisions of the Seventeenth Amendment, senators are popularly elected; but they still are chosen from statewide constituencies, and each state, regardless of population, has two senators. The Senate is a continuing body in the sense that at each biennial congressional election, only one-third of its members stands for reelection, thus giving senators greater job security than congressmen, who must run for office every two years.

[1] Actually, by 1911, twenty-nine of the forty-six states were holding direct elections for the United States Senate, to which their legislatures gave *pro forma* assent. See George E. Mowry, *The Era of Theodore Roosevelt and the Birth of Modern America* (New York: Harper & Row Torchbooks, 1958), pp. 80, 264.

THE DISTRIBUTION OF POWER:
IS THERE AN INNER CLUB?

Much ink has been spilled in recent years describing the inner workings of senatorial politics. The general feeling has been that the formal structure of the Senate has been less revealing of the actual distribution of power within the institution than is usually the case with political organizations. Therefore, writers have attempted to capture and codify "folkways"—informal prescriptions of behavior—an understanding of which is supposed to help in disentangling the mysteries of senatorial power and influence.

The Senate, it has been argued, is really run by a clique of interacting senators, an "inner club," small in number and not necessarily the most senior in rank, who are emotionally in tune with one another, who follow the folkways, and who are widely recognized as "Senate types." It is said that senators, if they aspire to this inner club, must adapt their behavior to fit the following composite description:

> [He is] a prudent man, who serves a long apprenticeship before trying to assert himself, and talks infrequently even then. He is courteous to a fault in his relations with his colleagues, not allowing political disagreements to affect his personal feelings. He is always ready to help another Senator when he can, and he expects to be repaid in kind. More than anything else, he is a Senate man, proud of the institution and ready to defend its traditions and perquisites against all outsiders. He is a legislative workhorse who specializes in one or two policy areas. . . . He has a deep respect for the rights of others . . . making his institution the last citadel of individualism. . . . He is a man of accommodation who knows that "you have to go along to get along"; he is a conservative, institutional man, slow to change what he has mastered at the expense of so much time and patience.[2]

The picture of senatorial life that this description gives has some historical validity. However, in some particulars, it may be extremely misleading. In order to see why, it is necessary to examine the following questions:

First, what are the folkways, as described in the books, magazines, and journals, on which real senatorial leadership is supposed to be based?

Second, who are the members of the inner club?

Third, in what sense do men of power in the Senate actually follow the folkways?

[2] This composite description was drawn by Ralph K. Huitt, "The Outsider in the Senate: An Alternate Role." *American Political Science Review*, vol. 55 (September, 1961), pp. 566–567, principally from work by William S. White, *Citadel* (New York: Harper & Row, 1956), and Donald Matthews, *U.S. Senators and Their World* (Chapel Hill, N.C.: University of North Carolina Press, 1960). The inner-club hypothesis has many proponents. See, for example, Joseph Kraft, "King of the U.S. Senate," *Saturday Evening Post* (January 5, 1963), pp. 26–27; Senator Joseph Clark, "The Senate Establishment," *Congressional Record*, daily edition (February 18–28, 1963), pp. 2413–2426, 2524–2531, 2703–2707, 2763, 2764, 2766, 2771, 2773; Allan Nevins, *Herbert H. Lehman and His Era* (New York: Scribner, 1963), especially pp. 369–370.

Finally, what does this suggest to us about the distribution of power in the Senate and about the roles available to senators who wish a significant share in the power of the institution?

The Senate's folkways have been described most succinctly by Donald Matthews in an article that has achieved wide currency and acceptance.[3] They consist of:

1. Practices of the Senate that grant individual senators few or no opportunities for deviation. Examples include the operations of the seniority system and the rules of comity governing floor debate.

2. Prescriptions of "good" behavior that apply to freshman senators only. During the period of apprenticeship—which lasts until the next class arrives two years later—the freshman senator is expected to perform many thankless tasks cheerfully, such as presiding over floor debate. He should seek advice from senior senators, make no speeches or remarks on the floor unless specifically invited, and take the initiative in getting acquainted with other senators.

3. Prescriptions of "good" behavior that apply to all senators in their relations with one another. Examples include the following commandments: make speeches only on subjects on which you are expert or that concern your committee or your state; do not seek publicity at the expense of less glamorous legislative work; do favors for other senators; address your colleagues in a friendly manner; speak well of the Senate as an institution; keep your word when you make an agreement.

In truth, these folkways provide little help to senators who seek to unravel the secrets of the inner club. Freshmen are apparently not the only senators excluded, and nonfreshmen who conformed as freshmen are not necessarily "in."

Who is in? Who, specifically, are the Senate men who in the last few years are supposed to have dominated this institution? "They [are] men of the type and character," said Dean Acheson, "who, in a quiet way, are apt to dominate any male organization. The main ingredients of such men are force, likeableness and trustworthiness. Alben Barkley, Walter George and Arthur Vandenberg were, perhaps, the *beaux ideals*."[4]

Perhaps not. William S. White, while granting Barkley and George entrance to the inner club, said, "The late Senator Arthur Vandenberg . . . for all his influence upon foreign relations . . . was never in his career a true Senate type, no matter how formidable he was as a public man."[5] For White, Senate types display "tolerance toward [their] fellows, intolerance toward any who would in any real way change the Senate," and commitment to the Senate as "a career in itself, a life in itself and an end in itself."[6] Yet certified Senate

[3] Donald Matthews, "The Folkways of the U.S. Senate," originally in *American Political Science Review*, vol. 53 (December, 1959), pp. 1064–1089; reprinted in Bobbs-Merrill Reprint Series, PS 189; in Joseph Fiszman (ed.), *The American Political Arena* (Boston: Little, Brown, 1962), pp. 199–210; in S. Sidney Ulmer (ed.), *Introductory Readings in Political Behavior* (Chicago: Rand McNally, 1961), pp. 94–104; and, no doubt, elsewhere. It also appears in Matthews, *U.S. Senators and Their World*, pp. 92–117.

[4] Dean Acheson, *Sketches from Life of Men I have Known* (New York: Harper & Row, 1961), p. 132.

[5] White, *op. cit.*, p. 87.

[6] *Ibid.*, pp. 84, 92.

types, White noted, such as Senators Taft or Russell (and he might have added Kerr, Humphrey, and Johnson) have often run for President. White's argument that they do this, not because the Presidency is a higher or more preferable office, but because it is "another" ambition of theirs is unconvincing.[7]

Other Senate insiders can be observed tampering with the decor of the institution in a variety of ways. The reformist agitations of insider Hubert Humphrey (later Majority Whip) abated only slightly after his celebrated speech suggesting the abolition of insider Senator Harry Byrd's Committee on Reduction of Nonessential Expenditures in the Executive Department.[8] Perhaps more significant was the then–Majority Leader Lyndon Johnson's successful reform of the committee assignment process on the Democratic side of the aisle. This change of real and undeniable significance, which took power away from senior senators and vested it in more junior ones, was effected by a man widely recognized as the most inside of insiders. As Ralph Huitt says, "One of [Johnson's] most successful political acts was his decision in 1953 to put all Democratic senators, even new ones, on at least one important committee."[9] Johnson was also a participant in a human drama of some poignance a few years later, when the elderly Senator Theodore Francis Green of Rhode Island, "a member of the very hierarchy of the Club,"[10] was persuaded to relinquish the chairmanship of the blue-ribbon Foreign Relations Committee to the next-ranking J. William Fulbright of Arkansas, who is, White said, "not . . . quite a Senate type."[11]

On the matter of tolerance, it is hard to judge senators from a distance. But if, as White seems to suggest, the practice of tolerance separates members of the inner club from those outside, we must assume that he is implying that the late Senator Walter George of Georgia, for example, was a more tolerant man than, say, the late Senator Herbert Lehman of New York, whom White places outside the inner sanctum.[12] It is instructive in this connection to recall the anecdote with which Mr. White introduces us to Senator George and to the Senate type.

No skin in all the world is more easily abraded than senatorial skin. Once, for an illustration, the Attorney General of the United States, Her-

[7] *Ibid.*, p. 85.

[8] *Ibid.*, pp. 75–76. See also Michael Amrine, *This is Humphrey* (Garden City, N.Y.: Doubleday, 1960), pp. 147–148. In an article published while he was Whip, Humphrey said, among other things, "the legislative branch has not been performing its functions with the order and effectiveness the nation deserves . . . the rules and traditions of Capitol Hill are not sacred. . . ." and offered seven concrete proposals for reform. "To Move Congress Out of Its Ruts," *The New York Times Magazine* (April 7, 1963), pp. 89ff.

[9] Ralph Huitt, "Democratic Party Leadership in the Senate," *American Political Science Review*, vol. 55 (June, 1961), p. 338. Both parties make committee assignments through their steering committees, subject to the general rule that a senator is entitled to keep whatever assignments he already has. Thus these committees handle transfers as vacancies occur and place freshman members. Republicans generally proceed strictly according to seniority for all vacancies. Democrats under the Johnson rule gave themselves more leeway. This has, however, led to charges that committee placements are now subject to manipulation designed to affect policy outcomes. See Clark, *op. cit.*

[10] White, *op cit.*, p. 92.

[11] *Ibid.*, p. 91.

[12] *Ibid.*, p. 83; Nevins, *op cit.*, pp. 369–370.

bert Brownell, Jr., was condemned to the pit of Senatorial displeasure for daring to permit his department to prepare a memorandum raising certain questions about a . . . proposed Amendment to the Constitution. . . . The incident struck the then Dean of the Senate, Mr. George of Georgia as [Mr. White's choice of words is exquisite] intolerable. It was his conclusion, expressed in the tragically wounded tones of which his majestic voice was capable, that Brownell was "a very *odd* Attorney General," and worse still, that his offensive paper had undoubtedly been written by "some cloik" [clerk] in the Justice Department.[13]

Tolerance, lack of presidential ambition, undeviating acceptance of the institutional status quo—all on closer inspection fail to differentiate members of the inner club from those who languish outside. What about the more diffuse folkways that seem to reward agreeable men who manage their interactions with their fellows smoothly? Is there, perhaps, an identifiable personality type that foreordains membership in the inner club?

It is difficult, without an exhaustive set of identifications from those in the know, to say who is and who is not in the inner club at any given time,[14] but I think we can reasonably assume that those men who over the last decade or so have been elevated by their fellows to high party posts within the Senate can be regarded as Senate types. This leaves aside the great number of self-selected leaders whose interest in particular policies might make them important in the Senate and that group of men who may be "in" by virtue of seniority. Both groups, because of the method of their selection, would be likely to display personal characteristics less compatible with the folkways than senators formally selected to leadership by fellow senators.

But even in this latter group, the variation in personal characteristics is quite striking. Over the last decade observers have noted the gregariousness of the former Democratic Whip Hubert Humphrey and the diffidence of his predecessor and current Majority Leader Mike Mansfield; the geniality of Alben Barkley and the brusqueness of Robert A. Taft; the adroitness of the late Everett Dirksen and the hamhandedness of Kenneth Wherry; the humorlessness of William Knowland and the wit of Eugene Millikan; the secretiveness of Styles Bridges and the openness of Arthur Vandenberg; the self-effacement of Ernest McFarland and the flamboyance of Lyndon Johnson; the steadiness of Thomas Kuchel and the unpredictability of Russell Long.[15] The list could

---

[13] White, *op cit.*, p. 10.

[14] To my knowledge the only exhaustive list of inner-club members ever compiled is Clayton Fritchey's, "Who Belongs to the Senate's Inner Club?" *Harper's* (May, 1967). Fritchey listed fifty-three members and provisional members, more than a majority. Eight others, being freshmen, were ineligible.

[15] On McFarland, see David B. Truman, *The Congressional Party* (New York: Wiley, 1959), pp. 113, 303–304; on Knowland, see Rowland Evans and Robert Novak, "Inside Report: Knowland's Return," *The Washington Post* (June 28, 1963), p. A19; on Wherry, see White, *op. cit.*, p. 106, and Acheson, *op. cit.*; on Humphrey, see Amrine, *op. cit.*, and "Merry Candidate," *Newsweek* (April 4, 1960), pp. 30–32; on Mansfield, see Douglass Cater, "The Contentious Lords of the Senate," *The Reporter* (August 16, 1962), p. 28; on Barkley, see White, *op cit.*, pp. 105–106; on Taft, see Matthews, *op. cit.*, p. 130; on Dirksen, see William Barry Furlong, "The Senate's Wizard of Ooze: Dirksen of Illinois," *Harper's* (December, 1959), pp. 44–49, Murray Kempton, "Dirksen Delivers the Souls," *New Republic*

undoubtedly be expanded indefinitely, but the point would remain the same —no clear standards of eligibility for membership in the inner club, if there is one, seem likely to emerge from an examination of personality characteristics of senators.

We must pause to ask: Is there an inner club at all? Or is power distributed in the Senate more widely? It is worthwhile to remember that there are only 100 United States senators. Each one enjoys high social status, great visibility, a large staff, and substantial powers in his own right. Each one has the right, by the rules of the Senate, to speak on the floor of the Senate on any subject for as long as he desires to do so. Where a tremendous amount of business must be transacted by unanimous consent, any single senator can, if he chooses, effectively stall and harass the machinery of government. But these are ultimate sanctions, rarely employed by an individual senator, though more frequently by groups of senators. In any event, settled Senate practice is to take account of the wishes of every interested senator with respect to the convenient scheduling and disposition of most Senate business. Senator Richard Russell has described this practice in debate on the floor:

> I have heard questions asked [the Senate majority and minority leaders] for 30 years—Senators come up to them and say, "What time are we going to vote? What time are we going to vote?" Of course neither the majority leader nor the minority leader knows any more about the time the Senate is going to vote than does the Senator asking the question, but he is supposed to have some pleasant and reasonable answer. Another day a Senator will say, "Well, I cannot be here Thursday, so you cannot vote on such and such a bill on Thursday." Likely as not, the majority leader or the minority leader had agreed with the author of the bill to have it acted on on Thursday. That is only one instance of perhaps 10,000 different commitments that they make.[16]

Ralph Huitt described a striking example of the way an individual senator can have a decisive impact on legislative outcomes. His subject was William Proxmire, then a freshman senator from Wisconsin.

> The provocation was a bill to allow the Metropolitan Sanitary District of Chicago to increase the amount of water it may withdraw from Lake Michigan by a thousand cubic feet per second for a three year test period. Similar bills had been passed by both houses twice before (by the Senate in the closing hours of a session with scant debate) only to be vetoed by the President because of objections raised by Canada. Once more it appeared that the bill would come up in the flood of last minute legislation, and with committee and leadership support, it seemed

---

(May 2, 1964), and Meg Greenfield, "Everett Dirksen's Newest Role," *The Reporter* (January 16, 1964); on Millikan, see Beverly Smith, "The Senate's Big Brain," *Saturday Evening Post* (July 4, 1953), p. 76; on Bridges, see "The Congress," *Time* (December 8, 1961), p. 25; on Vandenberg, see Richard H. Rovere, *The American Establishment* (New York: Harcourt, Brace & World, 1946), pp. 189–191; and on Johnson, see "A Man Who Takes His Time," *Time* (April 25, 1960), pp. 20–24.

[16] *Congressional Record*, daily edition (February 19, 1963), p. 2399.

sure to slide through the tired Senate. Moreover, because the Canadian position was now ambiguous, the President might sign the bill. But the pressure for adjournment which was the greatest factor in favor of the bill's passage could also be its doom—if its opponents had sufficient nerve. Their hope was to stall consideration as long as possible, then make it clear that the cost of passage was extended debate. It was a simple, time-proven strategy, but not one designed to make friends. Proxmire was by no means the only man fighting the bill—there was a militant bipartisan coalition on each side—but he was probably the most determined and certainly the most conspicuous. It was he who blocked unanimous consent to allow any deviation from the rules in handling the bill. Thus he objected to a meeting of the Public Works Committee while the Senate sat, and to the bill's being reported to the Senate after the expiration of the morning hour—tactics which brought sharp rebukes from two senior members but delayed the bill a day. And it was he who held the floor from nine till midnight the last night of the session, until the water diversion bill was put aside for other business; and he who sat through the early morning hours, armed with a score of amendments and great piles of materials, ready to resume the debate. When the session ended at 4:11 in the morning the unfinished business of the Senate was a Proxmire amendment to the water diversion bill.[17]

Or consider the following excerpt from a recent news analysis:

> When, at last, the Senate had voted on final passage of the battered foreign aid bill, Majority Leader Mansfield wore his habitual expression of martyred resignation. Chairman Fulbright of the Foreign Relations Committee appeared grateful to be alive.
>
> Only Senator Morse, Democrat of Oregon, was triumphant.
>
> The bill passed, but with $500 million less than its backers had hoped. It was largely due to Senator Morse's exertions and the exhaustion of the other Senators. Nobody wanted to take him on.
>
> The foreign aid bill did nothing for anybody else in Washington. The Senate leadership was flouted. Secretary of State Rusk protested in vain. The President pleaded too late. The President's men in the Senate . . . were too tired to fight—at least with Wayne Morse.
>
> Senator Morse alone came out of the tedious battle with something like prestige.
>
> His domination of the debate does not make him a leader. His forces were a motley group of defecting liberals and soured Southerners who may never march under the same banner again.
>
> Besides he is a lone wolf. . . . Senator Morse combines qualities of exceptional ability, supreme egotism, self-righteousness and vindictiveness that do not make a man a favorite with his fellows. . . .
>
> But if he is disliked, he can no longer be discounted as a power in the Senate. He is getting mail from all over the country, hailing his attacks on foreign aid.
>
> Presidential blandishments were of no avail. Invited to the White House, the Senator sat down with the Chief Executive for 45 minutes and went over the program.

[17] Huitt, "The Outsider in the Senate: An Alternate Role," *op. cit.*, pp. 569–570.

"Then I came back up here," he told his friends with a wolfish grin, "and put in a couple of more amendments." . . .

He threatened the Whip with a country-by-country review of the whole foreign aid. Senator Humphrey hastily withdrew his amendment. . . .

Senator Morse was satisfied. . . .

He went on to threaten "further debate of great length" if the Senate conferees on the foreign aid bill came back with a conference report that undid any of his work. . . .

It was one time when the Senate was content to have the Senator disposing of all problems, great and small, in what the President this week called "an untidy world." The leadership was out trying to cope with Senator Mundt's sticky and inopportune amendment on the wheat sale to Russia.

So Senator Morse had a perfect day. Even the passage of the bill, against which he voted, of course, could not mar his self-satisfaction. He had left his mark on foreign aid for all the world to see.[18]

It is clear that individual senators can, according to the rules and customs of the Senate, play a powerful hand in the disposition of legislation reaching the floor, even without the immensely useful fortifications of seniority, membership on a relevant substantive committee, a committee chairmanship, or a position of formal leadership. But nevertheless let us inquire into the distribution of these prizes, for much that happens off the floor, where so many legislative outcomes are actually settled, depends on the strategic locations of friends or foes of bills and their diligence and skill in shaping results to suit their preferences. There are a number of strategic locations, as a sampling of commentary on the contemporary Senate will rapidly reveal:

[Senator Robert S.] Kerr [Democrat, of Oklahoma] was correctly rated the most powerful member of the Senate, though not one of its nominal leaders, in the last (87th) Congress. . . . The base of Kerr's power was never his major committees. Rather, it was his chairmanship of the Rivers and Harbors Subcommittee of the Public Works Committee, an obscure post that makes few national headlines, but much political hay. Kerr not only used it to consolidate his position in Oklahoma by festooning the state with public works but placed practically all Senators under obligation to him by promoting their pet home projects. He never hesitated to collect on these obligations later, when the votes were needed.[19]

[In the 87th Congress] there is a class of 21 preferred Senators, who are permitted to hold positions on more than two major committees. . . . [20]

The office of Democratic Leader, it is true, combines all the most important elective positions—Chairman of the Conference, of the Steering Committee, of the Policy Committee (the Republicans fill these posi-

---

[18] Mary McGrory, "Morse Tackles an 'Untidy World,' " *Washington Evening Star* (November 17, 1963).

[19] Kenneth Crawford, "The Senate's Ways," *Newsweek* (January 14, 1963), p. 27.

[20] Senator Joseph S. Clark, *Congressional Record*, daily edition (February 21, 1963), p. 2704.

tions with four different men). Each position adds something to his influence and to the professional staff he controls. The Steering Committee handles committee transfers and assignment of new members. . . . As Chairman of the Policy Committee he has substantial control over legislative scheduling (in close collaboration with the Minority Leader) which gives him not only the power to help and hinder but an unequalled knowledge of legislation on the calendar and who [wants] what and why. A tactical power of importance [is] . . . the right of the Majority Leader to be recognized first when he wants the floor [which can be exploited to] initiate a legislative fight when and on the terms he [wants].[21]

It is probably not possible to identify *all* the institutional nooks and crannies that can provide a base of power for a United States senator. In any event the same base is often used differently by different men. For example, whereas Lyndon Johnson as Majority Leader pretty much ran his own show, his successor, Mike Mansfield, was more comfortable sharing substantial power when his assistant was Hubert Humphrey; this was less true during the tenure of Russell Long, who replaced Humphrey as Whip in 1965. But Mansfield continued to share power with his party's Policy and Steering Committees.[22] It may be useful, just the same, to see how the more obvious strategic positions were distributed among senators in the Ninety-first Congress. Among these positions, one might include elective leadership posts, memberships on party policy (agenda) and steering (committee-assignment) committees, committee chairmanships (or, in the case of the minority, shadow chairmanships), chairmanships of subcommittees, memberships on more than two regular legislative committees, and memberships on the Appropriations Committee.

Although there are considerable inequalities in the distribution of these prizes, virtually no senator in the Ninety-first Congress, save a sprinkling of freshmen, was without some institutional base that guaranteed him a disproportionate say, either in some substantive area of public policy or in the behind-the-scenes management of Senate business. Of fifty-seven Democrats, forty-six were chairmen of committees or subcommittees. A Capitol Hill veteran told a reporter: "If you're walking down the hall and you pass a member [of Congress] always say 'Good morning, Mr. Chairman.' If it isn't so, you won't offend him, but chances are it will be true."[23] Obviously, a senator such as Richard Russell of Georgia, member of four committees, chairman of one, subcommittee chairman of another, and member of the Democratic Steering *and* Policy Committees was in an institutional position more formidable than a senator such as Everett Jordan of North Carolina, who in the Ninety-first Congress sat on two relatively unimportant committees, chairing one subcommittee of each. But these disparities are easily exaggerated, for Senator Russell could not hope to accomplish his legislative ends without the help of men

[21] Huitt, "Democratic Party Leadership in the Senate," *op. cit.*, pp. 337–338.

[22] See, e.g., "Mansfield's Ideas on Leadership," *Washington Sunday Star* (November 17, 1963).

[23] Arlen J. Large, "Capitol Traffic Jam," *The Wall Street Journal* (February 18, 1969).

like Senator Jordan, and vice versa. The need for cooperative effort and uncertainty about the precise composition of any particular winning coalition make senatorial bargaining necessary, dilutes the power of the most entrenched, and enhances tremendously the powers of all senators, however low on the totem pole.

Senators, moreover, do not agree unanimously about the relative desirability of different institutional positions. Although at the extremes it is possible to rank committees according to their apparent desirability, there are some gray areas. This can be illustrated by comparing two attempts to rank Senate committees in the order of their attractiveness to senators. In the first column, committees are ranked according to the average seniority of the senators newly appointed to each committee from the Eightieth through the Eighty-fourth Congresses.[24] The reasoning here is that the committees attracting the senior men would be more desirable, first, because senior men would be likeliest to know which committees were most important and, second, because their seniority would make it possible for them to win appointment, even though competition were keen for vacant seats. In the second column, committees are ranked by their net gain or loss of members due to transfers of senators from the Eighty-first through the Eighty-fifth Congresses, corrected for the overall size of committees.[25] The reasoning behind this tabulation is quite similar to the first—presumably senators migrate toward desirable committees and away from undesirable ones.

[24] Matthews, *U.S. Senators and Their World, op. cit.*, p. 153.
[25] George Goodwin, "The Seniority System in Congress," *American Political Science Review*, vol. 53 (June, 1959), p. 433.

Table 2   **Senate Committees Ranked According to Two Criteria of Desirability**[a]

I	II
1. Foreign Relations	1. Foreign Relations
2. Appropriations	2. Finance
3. Finance	3. Commerce
4. Agriculture	4. Judiciary
5. Armed Services	5. Appropriations
6. Judiciary	6. Armed Services
7. Commerce	7. Agriculture
8. Banking	8. Interior
9. Rules	9. Banking
10. Interior	10. Labor and Public Welfare
11. Post Office	11. Public Works
12. Public Works	12. Government Operations
13. Government Operations	13. Rules
14. District of Columbia	14. Post Office
15. Labor and Public Welfare	15. District of Columbia

[a] Space Committee, created 1958, omitted.

Part of the dissimilarities in the two lists can be explained away by the narrowness of differences in the raw data on which the rankings are based. But it is interesting to reflect that committees low on both lists—Government Operations, Labor and Public Welfare, and Public Works—have in the past provided major sources of power for senators as disparate as Robert Kerr and Patrick McNamara, Joseph McCarthy and John McClellan, John Kennedy and Lister Hill. There are, in other words, several ways in which a post can come to be desirable.

When a senator brings unusual skill, resourcefulness, or luck to seemingly minor posts in the institution, sometimes he is remarkably and disproportionately rewarded. Senators Joseph McCarthy and Estes Kefauver, on strikingly different missions, catapulted themselves to national prominence (which they preferred to popularity within the Senate) by imaginative use of minor subcommittees to which they fell heir rather early in their senatorial careers. Brian McMahon, Thomas Hennings, and Henry Jackson carved out unlikely empires, small but significant, by making themselves specialists in atomic energy, constitutional rights, and national-policy machinery respectively.[26]

The division of labor in the Senate has a curiously ad-hoc quality, in which roles within the Senate are as much adopted by senators when it suits their interests as they are doled out by institutional forces beyond the control of individuals. There are two senses in which the term *role* may be used. In one sense, roles are job descriptions; the Senate has men who primarily investigate the executive branch, men who speak to the society at large, men who specialize in a wide variety of substantive policy areas, men who seek primarily to deliver Federal funds to their home state, men who engage mostly in backstage politicking and legislative coalition-building, and so on. Roles also refer to the stable expectations that develop around the ways people fit into the informal society of group life; the Senate has its sages, its clowns, its mavericks, its fools. The number of senators who are distinctively placed in job roles is almost certainly quite high; the number who are distinctively located in the informal social life of the Senate is almost certainly quite low. All groups of any substantial size have their deviant members, but the existence of mavericks does not necessarily demonstrate the existence of an inner club.

MAVERICKS

Mavericks attract unusual attention to themselves in the press, and the fact that there are always a few of these "outsiders" in the Senate is sometimes cited as lending plausibility to the inner-club hypothesis, because the presence of outsiders attests to the existence of some norms that define the limits of permissible behavior. Mavericks in the United States Senate, however, have often been far from powerless, and even if they were, they are so few in num-

[26] On Jackson's role in establishing a rationale for a strong State Department in the Kennedy administration, see Roger Hilsman, *To Move a Nation* (Garden City, N.Y.: Doubleday, 1967), pp. 22, 555–556.

ber at any one time that in order to validate the inner-club hypothesis it would be necessary to show that many non-maverick senators also were powerless.

What are mavericks like? Is there such a thing as a typical maverick? Probably not; senatorial mavericks at one time or another have exhibited a variety of behavior patterns and these have proceeded from a variety of causes. Some behavior that is regarded as deviant in the United States Senate would undoubtedly be regarded as deviant anywhere—excessive drinking is one obvious example. In general, however, senators regard themselves as part of a working body rather than a social club. For this reason, they may take notice of behavior that impairs the functioning of the legislative process but ignore behavior that might be regarded as extremely deviant in the society at large or in a purely social organization. One famous example is the Senate's treatment of the late Senator Joseph McCarthy, of Wisconsin. White says:

> The whole history of the Institution shows this general view of Sena-torial conduct: First a strong disinclination to proceed at all against *any* Senator. . . . It was this tradition that lay at the bottom of the Senate's long hesitation before it dealt with Senator Joseph R. McCarthy of Wisconsin. . . . When . . . he was at length condemned . . . it was for purely *Senatorial* offenses. . . .[27]

Repeatedly attacking the leadership of one's own party in the Senate, failing to keep one's bargains, extreme intractability or stubbornness or un-cooperativeness, unwillingness to "listen to reason," conducting interminable one-man campaigns in behalf of hobbyhorse projects—these may be regarded as deviant behavior patterns by senators within the context of the network of informal clearances, courtesies, obligations, and loyalties that facilitate the work of the institution. Senators who frequently exhibit one or more of them may come to be regarded as mavericks. They may be mavericks because of their psychological needs and predispositions, their political principles, the expectations of meaningful segments of their constituencies, or for any combination of reasons. But the result is that they engage in behavior thought to be inappropriate for the conduct of business or disruptive of relationships regarded by most members as necessary, stable, and enduring.

A keen understanding of the accommodative nature of legislative activity, where, after all, a majority of senators must be marshaled in order to pass legislation, is widespread in the Senate. Senators also understand the general run of pressures—of time, of obligation, and so on—that is their common lot. Inattention to these facts of political life is quite understandably regarded as deviant. An example of such deviance is illustrated in a recent case study:

> The hearings became what it would be fair to call tedious. A contri-bution to tedium was Senator Malone (R-Nevada); nearly three-fifths of

---

[27] White, *op. cit.*, p. 126. For accounts of Senator McCarthy's deviant behavior, see Richard A. Rovere, *Senator Joe McCarthy* (New York: Harcourt, Brace & World, 1959); and, especially, Michael Straight, *Trial by Television* (Boston: Beacon Press, 1954).

the record—that is, 1,200 pages of testimony—resulted from his questions and statements. [Witnesses were largely] confined to saying in answer to these statements, "That is right," and Malone through his remarks made the bulk of the record. Frequently the chairman urged Malone to speed up, but to no avail. Evening sessions were conducted, at which it appears that frequently Senator Malone alone was present to interrogate witnesses and hear testimony. . . . Even his colleagues became irritated with him; his most acrimonious run-ins were with two [likely allies].

[On the final vote, the side he favored] was the victim of Malone's own intransigence. He was against reciprocal trade for "Three years, two years, one year or three minutes". The ethos of a parliamentary body was lost on him. Like most laymen outside the Capitol, he saw the issue as a bipolar one. . . . Malone was the sort of man—laudable in the public arena but indigestible in a negotiatory decision-making body— whose decision rule on voting was simple. He voted for what he believed in and against what he opposed [but in this case causing his own side to lose].[28]

In the main, and as this example illustrates, most of the harm that comes to mavericks in the Senate—if, indeed, any harm comes to them—is self-inflicted. Ralph Huitt has demonstrated that the Senate is an extremely hospitable place, which perforce tolerates a wide range of personal styles rather comfortably and which permits senators to respond in whatever way they think best to the multiplicity of demands their variegated constituencies place upon them.[29] In the modern Senate, it is only when an unusual senator meets an unusual political situation that trouble develops. Thus former Senator Wayne Morse of Oregon ran afoul of a hairline party split when, in a most unusual act, he left the Republican party and became an Independent. He was not reappointed to his old committees. "The Republican leadership denied any wish to discipline Morse. What they wanted was to control the Senate. As Taft pointed out, the Republican margin was paper-thin; with Morse an Independent the Senate division stood at 48–47–1."[30] Morse was dropped from his committees by the Republicans because otherwise they could not have controlled majorities on those committees under the terms of the Legislative Reorganization Act, which apportions committee assignments according to the overall party ratio in the Senate. So Morse was left places on what were regarded that year as the two least important committees, Public Works and District of Columbia. These assignments did Morse no permanent harm, however. "Wayne Morse received better committee assignments from the Democrats [two years later] in 1955, just before he joined their party, than he had lost two years earlier."[31]

---

[28] Raymond Bauer, Ithiel de Sola Pool, and Lewis Anthony Dexter, *American Business and Public Policy* (New York: Atherton, 1963), pp. 66–68.

[29] See Huitt, "The Outsider in the Senate," *op. cit.*, especially pp. 574–575.

[30] Ralph K. Huitt, "The Morse Committee Assignment Controversy: A Study in Senate Norms," *American Political Science Review*, vol. 51 (June, 1957), p. 317.

[31] *Ibid.*, p. 329. Huitt concludes from this study of party bolting in the Senate that this form of extreme deviance is rarely punished, and, when punished, the consequences are

PARTY LEADERSHIP: LYNDON JOHNSON'S
SECRETS OF SUCCESS

The wide and generous distribution of power in the Senate and the relative geniality with which deviants are tolerated suggests that devices for coordinating the work of the institution are weak indeed. In some respects they are weak, but they exist, and in dedicated and capable hands they can be made to yield impressive results.

Many devices for coordinating the Senate are the product of tacit bargains, mutual adjustments, individual clearances, and other piecemeal accommodations among senators. These are necesary because the division of labor parcels out power over such a variety of substantive problems in so many different directions. A second source of coordination for senatorial behavior arises out of the party loyalties and partisan (and sometimes ideological) identifications that most senators, as intensely political men, bring to the institution. If unanimous or nearly unanimous sentiment fails to coordinate voting, party loyalty of a voluntary kind has a major impact.

Beyond these tacit and institutional factors and in spite of the wide diffusion of senatorial power, one office—that of Majority Leader—is, or can be, preeminent. The Majority Leader is in charge of getting a legislative program —usually the President's—through the Senate. The powers to stall, amend, modify, and block legislation—in short, *negative* powers—are widely distributed in the Senate. The power and the responsibility to get things done— especially big things—is predominantly in the hands of party leaders. Other senators recognize that their leaders, who are elected by their respective senatorial party caucuses, have this responsibility. Yet the specific tools they place in the Majority Leader's hands to help him do this job are not overly impressive. A variety of tasks that must be routinely performed in the Senate, such as placing senators on committees or making up an agenda for floor action, provide the main strategic opportunities for the party leadership. This is particularly true when these routine functions are used to put together legislative proposals that are satisfactory to a majority coalition or when they are used to round up hard-to-find but necessary votes.

The Republican and Democratic parties in the Senate handle their routine functions somewhat differently. This has consequences for the powers of the party floor leaders. The Republicans traditionally spread their formal powers more thinly about: one man acts as floor leader; another acts as his assistant; a third chairs the Policy Committee, which acts as a reasonably coherent party voice on the legislative agenda; a fourth man heads the Republican Committee on Committees; a fifth has the honor of chairing the caucus of all Republican senators; and a sixth acts as chairman of the Republican Senatorial Campaign Committee. On the Democratic side, the floor leader chairs the

---

rarely lasting. See also A. Robert Smith, *The Tiger in the Senate* (Garden City, N.Y.: Doubleday, 1962), especially pp. 179–201; and Clarence E. Berdahl, "Party Membership in Congress," *American Political Science Review* (April, June, August, 1949), pp. 309–321, 492– 508, 721–734.

caucus, the Policy Committee (on agenda), and the Steering Committee (on committee assignments). He has an assistant, also known as the Whip, and there is a secretary to the caucus, also nominally a leadership position. The Campaign Committee is also run somewhat independently.[32]

By common consent, the most effective Majority Leader to serve in recent times was Lyndon Johnson, Democrat of Texas, who led the Senate from 1953 to 1960. An examination of his success in this job will be helpful in understanding the Senate, the legislative process, and, more generally, the process of government in the United States.

It is possible to explain at least part of Johnson's formidable reputation historically. He was Majority Leader under quite unusual and, on the whole, quite favorable circumstances. President Eisenhower, whose term of office coincided with Johnson's period as Democratic leader, wanted very little in the way of new legislation from the Senate, and, being of the opposing party, Eisenhower was entitled to only a modicum of cooperation from the Democratic majorities of 1954 to 1960. This left Johnson free to set his own priorities and pursue goals comfortably within reach. There was no necessity to do what a Majority Leader of a President's own party must do—extend his energies and spend his influence in behalf of a schedule of priorities and demands that are not his own and that could be strategically more difficult to accomplish. The Speaker of the House was Johnson's old friend, mentor, and fellow Texan, Sam Rayburn. Sometimes legislative proposals that would have created difficulties for the Senate Majority Leader could be effectively bottled up in the House. And, finally, just by chance, William S. White, another fellow Texan, good friend, and strong partisan of Johnson's, was during Johnson's stewardship covering the Senate for *The New York Times*. This gave the Majority Leader handsome and timely recognition, something rarely accorded legislative leaders in the predominantly President-oriented news media of America. Thus moderate external demands and an exceptional array of coincidental extrasenatorial resources helped Johnson achieve preeminence as a senatorial leader.

It would be incorrect to suggest, however, that on this account Johnson's reputation was unmerited. A variety of political skills and abilities made it possible for him to use his advantages and his resources with great success. Among these resources were his phenomenal energy, which he used, quite consciously, to maintain daily communication with almost every Democratic senator. Many social psychologists and some political scientists define leadership as centrality in a communications network.[33] Johnson, in effect, made himself the leader by putting himself at the center of an enormous number of bargains in the Senate—especially bargains concerning the allocation of time in the chamber and the division of labor. These bargains, in turn, ramified in several directions. Notably, they gave Johnson a tremendous head start at being at the center of bargains over policy. He was in a position to

---

[32] See Hugh A. Bone, "Introduction to Senate Policy Committees," *American Political Science Review*, vol. 50 (June, 1956), pp. 339–359; and "Some Notes on Congressional Campaign Committees," *Western Political Quarterly*, vol. 9 (March, 1956), pp. 116–137.

[33] See, e.g., Truman, *op. cit.*, pp. 293–294.

know more about the relative intensities of senators' positions on a variety of issues; in this way, he could create coalitions of senators who would never have thought to get together on their own but who, under Johnson's guidance, could be brought together to help one another on projects important to them. In return, they would give Johnson support on items that for them mattered less.

Any leader who performs this brokerage function for a while is bound to become reasonably skilled at it, and Johnson profited enormously from his on-the-job training in legislative maneuvering. At the same time, he built up a deposit of good will for favors done in the past. This, in turn, could be invested to produce bigger and better results for senators who then would feel obligated to help with the "tough ones," and so it went. Johnson himself was not unaware of the process. He once described how he worked to Arthur Schlesinger, Jr.:

> The Treatment began immediately: a brilliant, capsule characterization of every Democratic Senator: his strengths and failings, where he fit into the political spectrum; how far he could be pushed, how far pulled; his hates, his loves. And who (he asked Schlesinger) must oversee all these prima donnas, put them to work, knit them together, know when to tickle this one's vanity, inquire of that one's health, remember this one's five o'clock nip of Scotch, that one's nagging wife? Who must find the hidden legislative path between the South and the North, the public power men and the private power men, the farmers' men and the unions' men, the bomber-boys and the peace-lovers, the eggheads and the fatheads?[34]

Another quality of Johnson's that seems to have contributed to his success as Majority Leader was a relative indifference to most policy outcomes coupled with an interest in finding constructive legislative solutions even in the face of considerable disagreement among his colleagues on the substance of policy. To Senator Johnson, public policy evidently was an inexhaustibly bargainable product. Few issues incited him to intransigence, and thus he could arrange for solutions and compromises that would have been unimaginable to an equally constructive but a more committed man. Having few strong policy preferences, Johnson could also expedite the inevitable without regret. This gave him a reputation for being on the winning side, which was another resource at his command, because he could sometimes use this reputation as a bluff and get away with it.

Party leaders in the Senate are not without inducements—a coveted committee assignment, perhaps, or an appointment to an honorific commission whose meetings will be held in Paris or Bermuda, a pet bill rescued from oblivion or an accommodation in the schedule. The Senate is, after all, an ongoing institution that meets continuously. There are many routine ways in which senators can make one another's lives pleasant or inconvenient if they

---

[34] Rowland Evans and Robert Novak, *Lyndon B. Johnson: The Exercise of Power* (N.Y.: New American Library, 1966), pp. 104–105.

choose to do so, and these opportunities generally come more often to the party leaders, who are the custodians of Senate routine.

THE SENATE AS INCUBATOR
FOR POLICIES AND PRESIDENTS[35]

Whereas the House of Representatives is a firmly structured and highly articulated machine for processing bills and overseeing the executive branch, the modern Senate is, increasingly, a great forum, an echo chamber, a theater, where dramas—comedies and tragedies, soap operas and horse operas—are staged to enhance the careers of its members and to influence public policy by means of debate and public investigation. In both the House and the Senate a fundamental commandment to new members is "specialize."[36] But this means vastly different things in each house. "Specialize" to a representative means "tend to your knitting"—work hard on the committee to which you are assigned, pursue the interests of your state and region. In the Senate everyone has several committee assignments. Boundaries between committees are less strictly observed than in the House. Access to the floor is much less regulated. So the institution itself gives few clues and no compulsions to new senators wondering what they should specialize in. For senators, specialization seems increasingly to mean finding a subject and cultivating a nationwide constituency that has not been preempted by some more senior senator.

It is a cliché of academic political science that in legislative matters, it is the President who initiates policy and Congress that responds, amplifying and modifying and rearranging elements that are essentially originated in the executive branch. But where do innovations in policy come from *before* the President "initiates" them?

Old Washington hands know the answer. There is very little new under the sun. A great many newly enacted policies have been "in the air" for quite a while. In the heat of a presidential campaign or when a newly inaugurated President wants a "new" program, desk drawers fly open all over Washington. Pet schemes are fished out, dusted off, and tried out on the new political leaders. There is often a hiatus of years—sometimes decades—between the first proposal of a policy innovation and its appearance as a presidential "initiative"—much less a law. Commentators have greatly underestimated the role of the Senate in gestating these ideas, by providing a forum for speeches, hearings, and the introduction of bills going nowhere for the moment. This process of gestation accomplishes a number of things. It maintains a sense of community among far-flung interest groups that favor the innovation by

[35] I have elaborated on the argument that follows in several articles: "Goodbye to the Inner Club," *The Washington Monthly*, vol. 1 (August, 1969), pp. 30–34; "Policy Analysis and Congress," *Public Policy*, vol. 18 (September, 1969) pp. 61–74; and "Strengthening Congress in National Policy-Making," *Yale Review*, vol. 59 (June, 1970), pp. 481–497. The first and last of these are reprinted in Nelson W. Polsby (ed.), *Congressional Behavior* (N.Y.: Random House, 1971).

[36] For a more traditional formulation of the commandment to specialize and its meaning, see Matthews, *U.S. Senators, op. cit.*, pp. 95–97.

giving them occasional opportunities to come in and testify. It provides an incentive for persons favoring the innovation to keep information up-to-date on its prospective benefits and technical feasibility. And it accustoms the un-committed to a new idea. Thus the Senate is in some respects at a crucial nerve-end of the polity. It articulates, formulates, shapes, and publicizes de-mands and can serve as a hothouse for significant policy innovation, espe-cially in opposition to the President.

How long has this been going on? Certainly since World War II, there has been a general movement of political resources and public attention to-ward Washington and away from local and regional arenas.[37] This has been reinforced by the growth of national news media, especially television. The impact on the Presidency of this nationalization of public awareness has been frequently noted. But, to a lesser extent, the same effect can be noted for all national political institutions. Of these, only the Senate has taken full advan-tage of its increased visibility. The Supreme Court has remained aloof. Sam Rayburn, and John McCormack after him, refused to allow televised coverage of any official House function. The bureaucracies have been expected to leave the public formulation and defense of their programs to their political execu-tives—especially the President. Only the Senate has had no constraint placed on its availability for national publicity, except the ban on photographing or televising activity on the Senate floor itself.

As senatorial names—Kefauver, McCarthy, Kennedy, Goldwater—have become household words in the last two decades, most governors have slipped into relative obscurity. Where once a governor's control of a political "base," by virtue of his leadership of a state party organization, was the single overwhelming resource in deciding, at a national party convention, who was presidential timber, television and the nationalization of resources have eroded gubernatorial power. Proliferating Federal programs, financed by the lucrative Federal income tax, are being distributed among the states in part as senatorial patronage. Governors are by no means always ignored in this process, but their influence is on the whole much reduced. Meanwhile, at the state level, services have not kept pace with demands, and taxes are often inequitable and unproductive. Responsible governors of both parties have often tried to do something about this problem, but it has led to donny-brooks with state legislatures, great unpopularity, and, on some occasions, electoral defeat.[38]

But the decline of the influence of governors and the shift of public at-tention to national politics and national politicians are not quite enough to explain how the modern Senate became the incubator of policies and Presi-dential hopefuls. Historical accidents have also played a part. The first was Lyndon Johnson. Ambitious for the Presidency and immensely skilled, John-

[37] See E. E. Schattschneider, *The Semi-Sovereign People* (New York: Holt, 1960), pp. 78–96.

[38] Cf. Louis Harris, "Why the Odds Are Against a Governor's Becoming President," *Public Opinion Quarterly*, vol. 23 (Fall, 1959), pp. 361–370. J. Stephen Turett argues that the problems governors have had in recent years have not, however, increased the rate at which they have left office. See Turett's "The Vulnerability of American Governors, 1900–1969," *Midwest Journal of Political Science*, vol. 15 (February, 1971).

son sedulously perpetuated the myth of the inner club while destroying its substance.[39] Joseph Clark, newly elected to the Senate in 1957, described a lunch Majority Leader Johnson gave for freshman Democrats. "As we sat down . . . we found at our places copies of *Citadel* . . . autographed 'with all good wishes' not only by its author . . . but by the majority leader as well. During the course of the lunch . . . Senator Johnson encouraged us to consider Mr. White's book as a sort of McGuffey's *Reader* from which we could learn much about the 'greatest deliberative body in the world' and how to mold ourselves into its way of life."[40]

Yet if the essence of the *Citadel* was collegiality among the fellowship of the elect, the essence of Johnson's Senate operation was the progressive centralization of power in the hands of the Majority Leader. By the time Johnson left the Senate, after six years as Majority Leader, the inner club could command little of its old power. It had too long been merely a façade for Johnson's own activity, a polite explanation for the exercise of his own discretion in committee appointments, legislative priorities, and tactics. And under the loose rein of Mike Mansfield, the Senate has become a collegial body whose corporate work has been pretty much determined by presidential programs and priorities. It has never recaptured the sense of cohesion, community, and separateness that obtained "in the old days," before Johnson. Younger men have come in, and liberal majorities on legislation are by no means uncommon.

These younger man have pursued a style of senatorial service that in its search for national constituencies has little in common with that of the old Senate type. Nevertheless, these men are not regarded as mavericks.[41] Rather, they are national politicians, something that the mass media have made it increasingly possible for senators to be. They are following a style of service hit on by several postwar senators but most notably pioneered by Arthur Vandenberg of Michigan and, in the 1950s and 1960s, brought to full flower by Hubert Humphrey.

Much earlier than most members of his generation, Humphrey sensed the possibilities in the Senate for long-range political education. He spent the Eisenhower era incubating ideas that in a better climate could hatch into programs. In the late 1940s and early 1950s, a flood of Humphrey bills (many of them cosponsored by other liberal senators) on all aspects of civil rights, medicare, housing, aid to farm workers, food stamps, job corps, area redevelopment, disarmament, and so on died in the Senate. A little over a decade later, most of them were law, and Humphrey had in the meantime become a political leader of national consequence. The force of his example has not been lost on younger senators.

---

[39] See Evans and Novak, *op cit.*, esp. pp. 88–118.

[40] Joseph S. Clark, *Congress: The Sapless Branch* (New York: Harper & Row, 1964), p. 5.

[41] Fred Harris, Birch Bayh, Robert Griffin, Edward Kennedy, Walter Mondale, Charles Percy, and Charles Goodell are a few examples that come immediately to mind. Their success in senatorial politics can be contrasted with the relative isolation and ineffectiveness of similarly inclined senators in an earlier era. See, for example, Allan Drury's discussions of Senators Carl Hatch and Joseph Ball in *A Senate Journal 1943–1945* (New York: McGraw-Hill, 1963).

In recent years, it has proved much easier for senators to reconcile their ambitions for large public accomplishments with accommodation to Senate norms. The Senate is now a less insular body than it was in former times, and the fortunes of senators are correspondingly less tied to the smiles and frowns of their elders within the institution.

SUMMARY: COORDINATION AND DECENTRALIZATION

We can summarize our discussion of power and leadership in the Senate by noting resemblances between the Senate and any sizable group of human beings who meet and do business together fairly often. We can think of the Senate not as an institution controlled by a small group of powerful men surrounded by everyone else, but as a group that divides labor and power—unequally to be sure, but still significantly—among almost all its members. Some of its members are regarded as deviants and mavericks, and some of these enjoy less personal prestige, but even they are not necessarily powerless. The ties of party, regional interest, and policy preference are the ones that bind senators to one another in coalitions. Personal tastes and habits play a part, of course, as they do in shaping the ways senators do their jobs and approach their constituencies and the executive branch.

Despite a number of devices that party leaders have at their disposal to concentrate power in the Senate in their own hands, the forces making for decentralization of power in the Senate are even more striking. When partisan or factional lines are drawn closely, each senator's support on legislation becomes more valuable and can be quite difficult to obtain, if senators choose to make the lives of their leaders miserable.

Decentralization of power is also reflected in the committee system, which parcels out substantive legislation entirely to bipartisan committees, which are run almost exclusively according to seniority. Within their domains, the committees are quite beyond any but the most perfunctory control of the parent body. Senators are expected to specialize in their work—surely the only rational possibility in a time when issues are complex and require technical mastery as well as wisdom. These men are extremely busy and so not only specialize themselves in one or two subjects but also rely on fellow specialists in matters in which they are not competent. Reciprocity on substantive questions of public policy as well as in matters of housekeeping is regarded in the Senate as a necessary condition of life.

Coordination is accomplished mainly through party loyalty and party leadership. Party leaders depend especially on the cooperation of committee chairmen and the President. When they are in agreement, party leaders can exercise great power. They have control over the agenda and over the machinery for rounding up votes within the Senate. Rank-and-file senators recognize that party leaders may legitimately use this machinery in behalf of the program of the party and especially in behalf of measures high on the priority list of the President. Senate party leaders also exercise influence in the allocation of committee assignments, and they often have access to extrasenatorial sources of influence, such as those found in the executive agencies. Finally, changes in the Senate's position in the political system have made for decentralization. Senators now seek to cultivate national constituencies on their own, receive great amounts of publicity, and are more likely than heretofore to find independent advocacy more satisfying than coordinated legislative activity.

CHAPTER FOUR

THE HOUSE OF REPRESENTATIVES

On April 3, 1964, Everett G. Burkhalter, a Democratic representative in Congress from California, announced that he would not be a candidate for reelection. In an illuminating statement to the press, the California congressman explained why: "I could see I wasn't going to get any place. Nobody listens to what you have to say until you've been here 10 or 12 years. These old men have got everything so tied down you can't do anything. There are only about 40 out of the 435 members who call the shots. They're the committee chairmen and the ranking members and they're all around 70 or 80."[1] Mr. Burkhalter correctly saw that as a sixty-seven-year-old freshman in the House, the likelihood of his becoming a leader—or indeed of getting anywhere at all—was extremely slim.

His plight contrasts sharply with the position of a freshman senator. A newly elected senator enters immediately into the big whirl of Washington social and political life. He and his brethren sit four notches up the table from their House colleagues according to the strict protocol of Capitol society.[2] His comings and goings are likely to be chronicled by the society pages. The press releases prepared by his sizable staff often find their way into print. After holding his peace for a decorous period, he may join in the well-publicized debates on public policy that the Senate stages from time to

[1] John Beckler, "Men in Dotage Hamstringing House," *The Washington Post* (April 3, 1964); "House Freshman Raps 'Old Men,'" *Washington Star* (April 3, 1964).

[2] Carolyn Hagner Shaw, "Protocol, Address of Officials and Social Forms," *The Social List of Washington and Social Precedence in Washington* (Washington, D.C.: Shaw, 1963), pp. 10–14. Senators are outranked by the President, former Presidents and their widows, the Vice President, Speaker of the House, members and retired members of the Supreme Court, foreign ambassadors and ministers, the Cabinet, and a few other officers of the executive branch. Representatives are outranked by all of these and by the governors of states, acting heads of executive departments in the absence of the Cabinet member and former Vice Presidents.

time. He is a member of several committees and is consulted when the business of the Senate touches concerns of his own, as, for example, when a presidential appointment from his party and his state is scheduled for confirmation. If he wants to take the trouble to present a fairly convincing case, he can block the appointment by saying that the prospective appointee is personally unacceptable to him. This invokes "senatorial courtesy." His colleagues can be counted on to protect his position in the party politics of his home state by voting against the nominee.

The visibility and eminence of senators makes the Senate a less than cosy place to do business. Each senator is to a certain degree the product of his staff and what they do for him. He is exposed to public inspection both at home and in Washington, is quite often active in the politics of his home state, and, in short, is a public man with numerous, diverse, pressing public obligations and connections. In such circumstances, the norms of the Senate, powerful as it is as a social institution, cannot reach senators and shape their behavior in the same sense that the norms of the House can shape the behavior of the relatively anonymous individuals who labor there.

Compared with the Senate the House is a big institution, consisting of 435 members, allocated among the states according to their populations. Each member stands for election every two years, usually in a single-member district whose boundaries are established by the state legislature. Collectively, the House is quite as powerful as the Senate. Both houses share fully the power to legislate; bills must pass each house in order to become laws. The Senate alone has the power of confirmation, giving it the right to advise and consent to major presidential appointments. And the Senate alone ratifies treaties. But the House has other advantages. Under the Constitution, it originates all bills raising revenue—which means all tax bills, tariff bills, and bills pertaining to the social security system (in spite of the dubious revenue-raising aspect of the latter types of legislation). By an extension of this constitutional privilege, bills appropriating money to run the Federal government also start in the House. The mere privilege of initiating bills does not mean they cannot be changed in the Senate. But the power of initiation does set the terms of legislation, often suggesting limits beyond which the Senate cannot go if it wishes bills on a given subject to pass at all. The House enjoys another advantage. Because of its size, it can apportion work among more hands than can the Senate. One result is that the House has developed over the years a corps of members who are devoted subject-matter experts to a degree quite unusual in the Senate. Busy senators, due at three meetings at once, must rely to a much greater extent on their staffs. House members can dig into subject matter themselves. The mastery of subject matter on the House side of the Capitol is conspicuously displayed in the appropriations process (to be discussed in Chapter 6), but it also crops up on other matters. For example, Wilbur Mills, chairman of the House Ways and Means Committee, has no counterpart in the Senate in tax legislation. The late Francis E. Walter had no peer at unraveling the intricacies of the immigration law he codified. In housing, the recently retired Representative Albert Rains was the most expert person on Capitol Hill. And Representative Emilio Daddario of Connecticut did far more than any senator to educate himself—and his colleagues—on government policy toward scientific research.

On the whole, individual rank-and-file representatives must be regarded as somewhat less powerful than individual senators. Internally, power in the House is held by a small group, just as Representative Burkhalter said—perhaps no more than 10 or 20 percent of the total membership. But this group is seldom united, and its members generally concern themselves only with sharply limited areas of public policy. On such a matter as making up the schedule of activity on the floor, Senate Majority and Minority Leaders customarily touch bases with all senators who ask to be consulted on a given question. In the House, on the other hand, only those members who, because of their committee assignments, are legitimately concerned with a piece of legislation are normally consulted when the schedule for debate is arranged. We also may contrast the unlimited debate of the Senate with the sharply restricted debate in the House. In the House, the most senior committee members allocate among themselves and other members strictly limited segments of time, as suits their preferences and strategies, usually according to a formula dividing time equally between the parties, with driblets of time going to majority and minority members of the relevant committee. As far as the preferences of individual members are concerned, floor action resembles a car pool in the Senate, a bus line in the House. The Senate runs by unanimous consent; the House, by a codified set of rules.

THE SPEAKER

It would be foolish to conclude that the Senate is the more powerful body because the average senator is likely to have more powers than the average representative. Buses are, after all, capable of moving passengers as far and as fast as car pools. Hence it is necessary to inquiry into the identity of the driver. We look first to the Speaker of the House as a center of power. The Speaker, by tradition and practice the active leader of the majority party in the house, the "elect of the elect," second in succession to the Presidency, occupies an office of great prestige and importance in the Federal government. An examination of power in the House would naturally begin with him.

Woodrow Wilson wrote in 1884 about the impressive powers residing in the office of Speaker.

> The Speaker is expected to constitute the Committees in accordance with his own political views . . . [and he] generally uses his powers as freely and imperatively as he is expected to use them. He unhesitatingly acts as the legislative chief of his party, organizing the Committees in the interest of this or that policy, not covertly or on the sly, as one who does something of which he is ashamed, but openly and confidently, as one who does his duty. . . .[3]

[3] *Congressional Government* (New York: Meridian Books, Inc., 1956; 1st ed., 1884), pp. 85–86.

At that time, the Speaker also sat as chairman of the then five-man Rules Committee, which controls the flow of legislation to the floor of the House. But in 1885, once legislation reached the floor, the Speaker's control was severely diminished. This was largely due to the "disappearing quorum," a time-honored device that members used to delay or defeat legislation. Because a quorum consists of an absolute majority of the whole House of Representatives, any large minority could halt the business of the House indefinitely by suggesting the absence of a quorum and, though they were present in the chamber, simply not answering to their names when the roll was called. Normally, this was enough to stall business.

In 1890 Speaker Thomas Reed abolished the disappearing quorum. He called off to the tally clerk the names of those members he saw in the chamber who had not answered to a roll call. This tactic caused a huge uproar, but, after four days of battle, Reed was sustained by a vote that, in effect, went along party lines. Soon afterward, a new set of rules, composed by Reed, was adopted. It changed the quorum required for the Committee of the Whole from a majority of the House to 100 members, thus making it much easier to do business on the floor. In addition, all members present could be counted by the Speaker and the Speaker was given powers to declare motions as dilatory and hence out of order. Later, the constitutionality of these rules was upheld in the Supreme Court, and when the Democrats next controlled the House, in the following Congress, they themselves used the Republican Reed's rules.[4]

From the Fifty-first to the Sixty-first Congresses (1890–1910), the Speaker was clearly supreme in the House. Reed had added the effective control of floor action to the formidable arsenal of weapons off the floor that had previously been at the Speaker's disposal. But a Republican successor, Joseph Cannon (Speaker, 1905–1910) fell victim to the splits within the majority party that eventually led to the formation of the Bull Moose and Progressive parties. In 1910 the House of Representatives' experiment with strict majoritarianism and party discipline was terminated with a revolt against Speaker Cannon by a coalition of Democrats and Progressive Republicans led by George Norris.[5] A contemporary congressman and former parliamentarian of the House comments:

> The power of the Speakership in the halcyon days of Reed and [Joseph] Cannon lay principally in three rules: the appointment of the Committees of the House, chairmanship and control of the Committee on Rules, and the arbitrary powers of recognition. . . .
> The revision [of the rules] of 1911 was the most drastic since the

[4] See Barbara W. Tuchman, "Czar of the House," *American Heritage*, vol. 45 (December, 1962), pp. 33–35, 92–102; George Galloway, *History of the House of Representatives* (New York: Crowell, 1961), pp. 52–53; Samuel W. McCall, *The Life of Thomas Brackett Reed* (Boston: Houghton Mifflin, 1914), pp. 162–172; and Lewis Deschler (ed.), *Constitution, Jefferson's Manual, and Rules of the House of Representatives* (Washington, D.C.: Government Printing Office, 1961), sections 52 and 863.

[5] See Norris, *Fighting Liberal* (New York: Collier Books, 1961), pp. 121–132; Blair Bolles, *Tyrant From Illinois* (New York: Norton, 1951), pp. 200–224.

promulgation of Jefferson's Manual. The power to appoint committees was taken from the Speaker; he was made ineligible for membership on the Committee on Rules and the power of recognition was circumscribed by the Calendar Wednesday Rule, the Consent Calendar, the Discharge Calendar and restoration to the minority of the right to move to recommit.[6]

Curiously, the Reed rules were not a casualty of this episode; to this day the Speaker has substantial powers to monitor floor debate. Most of the weapons Reed gained have remained securely within the control of the Speaker, but the weapons Reed already *had* have passed from the Speaker's grasp.

Today, the Speaker is relatively weak, although this fact was obscured by the sixteen-year tenure in that office of Sam Rayburn, the "indestructible, imperishable and indomitable."[7] Rayburn was a man of enormous legislative skill, great rectitude, and earthy charm. He sat in the House for nearly fifty years, accumulating knowledge, friendships, and political debtors. Rayburn had no wife or family, only a career in the House, which he pursued with fierce concentration. He could gain legislative results because he was Rayburn, not only because he was Speaker. No successor of Rayburn's, not even John McCormack of Massachusetts, who had been a senior member of the House, a long-time majority leader, and an ally of Rayburn's, could have the chance to build the personal following that through luck, time, and his own peculiar genius made Rayburn a strong Speaker.

The Speaker today has many small weapons that he can use to influence the course of legislation. As chief executive of the House for its internal business, he can help his friends by allocating to them extra office space or recommending them favorably to the committee of his party that distributes minor patronage appointments on the Capitol grounds. He can provide access to executive agencies for members in behalf of their projects "back home" that might make a difference in a difficult election campaign. He can help members of his party improve their committee assignments by making his views known to the appropriate committee on committees. He can speed a member's private bill through the unanimous consent process or through suspension of the rules. He can enhance a member's prestige in the House by asking him to preside over the Committee of the Whole, and he can increase a member's political opportunities and contacts by appointing him to one or more of the various public boards, commissions, and delegations on which members of Congress serve—the annual delegation to the International Parliamentary Union, the board of the Woodrow Wilson Centennial Commission, and so on. These are not without their importance in a world where political careers and fortunes rise and fall as the result of unknown combinations of minor accidents and contingencies. Even so, the formal powers of the

---

[6] Remarks of Clarence Cannon, *The Leadership of Speaker Sam Rayburn: Collected Tributes of His Congressional Colleagues*, 87th Cong., 1st Sess., House Document 247 (Washington, D.C.: Government Printing Office, 1961), pp. 15, 16.
[7] Remarks of Carl Vinson, *ibid.*, p. 13.

Speaker today are not to be compared with the powers that previously went with the office.

THE COMMITTEE CHAIRMEN

In contrast, the chairmen of the twenty-one standing committees today are more powerful than were the chairmen of the forty-seven committees that existed in 1885. In January, 1947, under the Legislative Reorganization Act of 1946, the number of committees was drastically reduced and their legislative tasks clarified. This served to reduce materially the discretion of the Speaker in assigning bills to committees, because it did away with most of the shadow areas where two or more committees shared jurisdictions. Previously, the Speaker could kill bills by routing them to unfavorable committees and save bills by sending them to favorable committees, when more than one option existed.[8] The reorganization made this much more difficult. But at the same time, it strengthened the hand of committee chairmen. Most congressional committees have divided into many subcommittees since the reorganization of 1946, and these look less to the Speaker than to the chairmen of the full committees for leadership.

The chairmen of committees in the House are formally elected by the whole House, but since 1919 they have virtually always been those men of the majority party who are most senior in consecutive service on each committee.[9] Committee rank is counted by party and by committee service, not by service in the whole House. The chairmen are the executive officers of the committees. They hire and fire staff members, allocate the time and supervise the efforts of the staff, and substantially determine the business of the committee, as to both amount and content, subject only to informal consultation with and persuasion from their party leaders in the House, high officials of the executive branch, and, to a lesser extent, their own committee colleagues. As one congressman commented: "Committees are variously run, depending on the temperament of the chairman. He has the widest latitude, and he may play the Caesar role or not, as he sees fit."[10]

Of the twenty-one committees of the House, three outrank all others in importance: the Rules Committee, whose agenda-making function is treated in the next chapter; the Committee on Appropriations, discussed in Chapter 6; and the Committee on Ways and Means. The Ways and Means Committee originates all laws raising revenue, including tax laws; laws regulating foreign trade (because of their tariff aspect); and laws pertaining to the social security system (including medicare).[11] Because of the complexity of the bills this com-

[8] See, for example, Stephen K. Bailey, *Congress Makes a Law* (New York: Columbia, 1950), pp. 151–153.

[9] See Nelson W. Polsby, Miriam Gallaher, and Barry Spencer Rundquist, "The Growth of the Seniority System in the U.S. House of Representatives," *American Political Science Review*, vol. 63 (September, 1969), pp. 787–807.

[10] Clem Miller, in John W. Baker (ed.), *Member of the House* (New York: Scribner, 1962), p. 7.

[11] See John F. Manley, "The House Committee on Ways and Means: Conflict Management in a Congressional Committee," *American Political Science Review*, vol. 59 (December, 1965), pp. 927–939.

mittee writes and because of the temptation that exists for congressmen to add special exemptions and provisions to tax bills, legislation originating in the Ways and Means Committee normally comes before the House under rules of debate that forbid amendments. An additional increment to the committee's power comes from the fact that Democratic members of the committee also sit as their party's Committee on Committees.

The table on page 79 lists the names of the standing committees and their jurisdictions. House committees under the Reorganization Act of 1946 were consolidated to provide unified supervision of particular executive departments and agencies.[12] This is not an ironclad arrangement, but it holds in general. The prestige of House committees to a certain extent is tied to the size of the agencies they supervise—size measured in terms of employees or, more often, in terms of the share of the Federal budget they spend. The importance of committees thus changes over time. When the Committee on Science and Astronautics was started in 1958, it was anticipated that the committee would not be important.[13] Its members originally were a few senior men who elected to leave subordinate but high-ranked places on other committees and a large group of freshman members. In five brief years, the budget authorized by the Science Committee grew from 48 million to over 3.5 billion dollars, essentially all of which was actually appropriated. Subsequently, the original chairman, a congressman not highly regarded by the leaders of his party, died; his replacement was more willing to share power with young and vigorous subcommittee chairmen. As the prestige and importance of the committee grew, nonfreshman members of both parties (including the Majority Leader) asked to be transferred to the committee.

How can chairmen control the output of their committees? First, by their control over committee staffs—how many employees they hire, who they are, and what they do. Numerous, competent, and active staff members lead to a product quite different from the output of a corporal's guard of somnolent incompetents. Second, by manipulating the division of labor among committee members. Chairmen, by custom, decide if there will be subcommittees, whether subcommittees shall have explicit jurisdictions, the extent to which subcommittees shall have adequate or competent staff aid, and who shall chair and sit on subcommittees. These powers are not unlimited; custom also decrees that senior committee members shall be consulted in the process and that minority assignments shall be made by the "shadow" chairman—the ranking minority member.

It sometimes happens that men become chairmen of committees in areas where they are actually opposed to the enactment of legislation. In such a case, the powers of the chairman are used to obstruct, often with considerable success.[14] In other cases a chairman may be somewhat circumscribed

---

[12] See George Galloway, *The Legislative Process in Congress* (New York: Crowell, 1953), pp. 612ff.

[13] See Neil MacNeil, *Forge of Democracy* (New York: McKay, 1963), p. 159.

[14] See, for example, the discussion of the Rules Committee, under Chairman Howard W. Smith in *ibid.* See also H. Douglas Price, "Race, Religion, and the Rules Committee," in A. Westin (ed.), *The Uses of Power* (New York: Harcourt, Brace & World, 1962); and Miller, *op. cit., passim.*

Table 3 Committees of the House of Representatives, 91st Congress, 1969–1970

Committee	Number of Members	Jurisdiction
Agriculture	34	Agriculture generally, farm price supports, Department of Agriculture
Appropriations	51	The Federal budget and all other appropriations measures
Armed Services	40	Common defense generally, Department of Defense generally
Banking and Currency	36	Banking and currency generally, Federal Reserve System, housing and home finance, urban redevelopment
District of Columbia	25	Municipal affairs of District of Columbia
Education and Labor	35	Measures relating to education and labor generally, Labor Department
Foreign Affairs	38	Relations of U.S. with foreign nations generally, State Department, mutual security, foreign-aid authorizations
Government Operations	35	Budget and accounting measures other than appropriations, reorganization in executive and legislative branches of government, studying intergovernmental relations between U.S. and the states and municipalities, general legislative oversight of executive branch
House Administration	25	Employment of persons by the House, travel expenses of members of House, general "housekeeping"
Interior and Insular Affairs	33	Public lands, reclamation, natural resources
Internal Security (Formerly Un-American Activities)	9	Subversion in the U.S., propaganda efforts of subversive groups
Interstate and Foreign Commerce	37	Weather Bureau, public health, interstate and foreign commerce generally
Judiciary	35	Civil and criminal judicial proceedings, constitutional amendments, civil liberties, the courts, immigration
Merchant Marine and Fisheries	37	Navigation laws, merchant marine generally, coast guard, fisheries and wildlife
Post Office and Civil Service	26	Federal civil service, postal service, census
Public Works	33	Flood control and improvement of rivers and harbors, water power, highways, and public buildings
Rules	15	Rules and order of business in the House
Science and Astronautics	32	Astronautical research and development, NASA, Bureau of Standards, National Science Foundation
Standards of Official Conduct	12	Ethical standards of House members
Veterans' Affairs	25	Veterans' measures generally, Veterans' Administration
Ways and Means	25	Revenue measures generally, social security, tariffs and trade bills, medicare

(There are also several select committees, e.g., Small Business and Government Research; and joint committees, e.g., Atomic Energy and Internal Revenue Taxation.)

because a majority of his committee (including both Democrats and Republicans) is out of sympathy with his views. In such an instance the chairman must proceed with care, because it is only custom that permits him to run his committee without hindrance; more formally, the chairman is subject to majority rule within the committee. From time to time, chairmen see their committees "taken away from them" on one or another issue. At least one chairman, Graham Barden of the Education and Labor Committee, resigned from Congress after his committee was packed with new members who supported liberal legislation for education and labor, as he did not.[15]

COMMITTEE ASSIGNMENTS

The assignment of members to committees is one of the most significant activities—not only for members, who after all must live with the results, but also for legislative outcomes and public policy. The process of committee assignments differs between the parties and is quite complicated for each.[16]

The Republicans have a Committee on Committees, consisting of one representative from each state that sends a Republican to Congress. Each representative votes with the strength of his state delegation—one vote apiece for Wyoming or Vermont in the Ninety-first Congress, eighteen votes for Ohio, fifteen for New York. The real business of this committee is conducted by a subcommittee, consisting mostly of representatives of the large state delegations meeting with the party leader (the Minority Leader in the Ninety-first Congress). This subcommittee fills committee vacancies with freshmen and members who are requesting transfer; and they report back to the full committee, where their decisions are customarily ratified—because, after all, the subcommittee members have enough votes to win in the full committee. This process works to the disadvantage of Republicans from small state delegations. Nevertheless, it is usual to throw a few bones in the direction of the small states—one seat out of five minority seats on the present-day Rules Committee is customarily theirs, for example.

The qualifications of members are not irrelevant to the process. The Committee on Committees takes into account the career backgrounds of applicants, their district's interests, their seniority, and their reputation for "soundness"—which means, in some cases, willingness to do business equably and, in others, adherence to conservative policy positions. It is not at all unheard of for senior men on key committees to check into the public records and private views of members who aspire to their committees.

On the Republican side, each state delegation is formally represented in the committee assignment process. On the Democratic side, state delega-

---

[15] See Richard F. Fenno, Jr., "The House of Representatives and Federal Aid to Education," in R. L. Peabody and N. W. Polsby (eds.), *New Perspectives on the House of Representatives* (Chicago: Rand McNally, 1963). An excellent case study showing Barden at his most effective is John E. Moore, "Controlling Delinquency: Executive, Congressional and Juvenile, 1961–64," in Frederic N. Cleaveland and associates, *Congress and Urban Problems* (Washington, D.C.; Brookings, 1969), pp. 110–172.

[16] See Nicholas Masters, "Committee Assignments in the House of Representatives," *American Political Science Review*, vol. 55 (June, 1961), pp. 345–357.

tions and their spokesmen are also important but are less formally engaged in decision-making. The fifteen Democrats (ten when the Democrats are in the minority) on the Ways and Means Committee sit as their party's Committee on Committees, and each is assigned a zone consisting of one or a few states. Members requesting committee transfers and freshmen from each zone are expected to transmit their preferences to their zone representative on the committee; the zone representative, in turn, is charged with negotiating with the rest of the committee. Deans of state party delegations normally help their members in making a favorable case before the Committee on Committees.

State delegations are regarded as having title to certain committee posts by custom—Virginia, for example, long claimed two seats on the Agriculture Committee. When a valued seat on a committee falls vacant because of the death, defeat, or resignation of a member, all eyes automatically focus on the delegation of the departed member in the expectation that it will provide a suitable successor. Besides strict delegation succession, other criteria of suitability, including acceptability to party leaders—and to the rank and file, since assignments are ratified in the caucus—appropriate experience or training, and so on, are of course applied. Republican members' initial committee assignments are pretty much negotiated by the leadership, the heads of their delegations, ranking members of key committees, and the subcommittee of the Committee on Committees. Democratic members will confer with the party leadership, their state delegations, their zone representative on the Committee on Committees, and all other members of the Committee on Committees as well. In both parties it is usually necessary for members to "run" for committee posts. Only members of large state delegations that are "entitled" to specific vacant seats can afford not to; other members must make a case to receive the assignment they desire, except when there is no competition for an assignment.

The importance of state delegations cannot be overemphasized. Some of the larger state delegations systematically distribute their members among important committees. For example, under Speaker Rayburn, the large Texas delegation (twenty-one Democrats in the Eighty-seventh Congress) did especially well. In the Eighty-eighth Congress, their first without the Speaker, they had a man on Rules; one on Ways and Means; two very senior men on Appropriations; the chairmen of Veterans' Affairs, Banking and Currency, and House Administration; and other members strategically located. One small delegation, Arkansas, by virtue of good luck, long tenure (an advantage mostly accruing to one-party states), and, in several cases, the friendship of Mr. Rayburn, did nearly as well. Their four representatives in the Eighty-eighth Congress were the chairman of Ways and Means, the chairman of Commerce, a member of Rules, and the fourth-ranking member on Agriculture.

Another way of seeking advantage in committee assignments is represented by the Illinois Democratic delegation—an unusually cohesive bloc of fourteen votes in the Eighty-seventh Congress. This delegation was fortunate in having as its zone representative in charge of committee assignments the late Representative Tom O'Brien, who was an old friend of Speaker Rayburn's. Mr. O'Brien was reputed to have provided the Speaker in 1937 with the margin by which he won election as Majority Leader.[17] One of Mr. O'Brien's major legislative goals was placing members from his zone in the first place in any group newly assigned to a committee, thus making an Illinois member senior within the committee to men of equal seniority in the Congress. This device could be expected to pay dividends for the state of Illinois many years after Mr. O'Brien had passed from the scene.

With respect to committee seniority, the rules of the House say only that members are to be seated in the order in which they are presented to the floor in the resolution prepared by the party committees on committees. In the Eighty-sixth and Eighty-seventh Congresses, however, Illinois freshmen always came first on the list of newly assigned members regardless of alphabetical order, seniority on the Ways and Means Committee, or date of entry of members' states into the Union—all of which are given in *The Precedents* as methods for allocating committee seniority among men of equal seniority in the House.[18]

PARTY LEADERSHIP

Voting in the House, as in the Senate, is predominantly along party lines.[19] This is not simply because there are such sharp ideological divergences between all the members of each of the two parties. Rather, the act of voting is regarded as a public act, with ramifications that run beyond the confines of the House community. In roll-call votes, the parties in the House "make a record," and congressmen draw the overly simple lines that they carry back into their home districts to campaign with. Generally, the people back home have few ways of assessing a congressman's performance on the job other than taking note of his attendance at roll calls and keeping track of how he votes. As we will see in the next chapter, roll-call votes can be quite misleading because of the enormous number of less public opportunities open to a congressman to express himself on a bill. But roll calls are at any rate the public face that Congress wears, and they do determine the fate of legislation.

At voting time, party leaders are most in evidence. Each party in the House has a whip system, which operates not so much as a device to coerce or even persuade members as it does simply to inform the leadership of the dispositions of members toward legislation. Each party leader has a small staff that prepares summaries of the forthcoming week's legislative business for

---

[17] Mr. O'Brien's obituaries were most informative. For example, *The Washington Post*, April 15, 1964, told this anecdote: "Rep. O'Brien was a great friend of the late Speaker Sam Rayburn and regularly called on Rayburn a few days in advance of crucial House votes. On one such occasion, according to a Rayburn aide, Rep. O'Brien ambled into Rayburn's office and asked, 'How do you want them fellows to vote, Mr. Speaker?' Rayburn told him. 'They'll be there,' Mr. O'Brien replied."

[18] See Masters, *op. cit.; Cannon's Precedents 8*, section 2179, 2195; and Floyd M. Riddick, *The U.S. Congress: Organization and Procedure* (Manassas: National Capitol Publishers, 1949), pp. 164–168.

[19] See David Truman, *The Congressional Party* (New York: Wiley, 1959); Julius Turner, *Party and Constituency* (Baltimore: Johns Hopkins, 1951); and David R. Mayhew, *Party Loyalty among Congressmen: The Difference between Democrats and Republicans, 1947–1962* (Cambridge, Mass.: Harvard, 1966).

party members. In addition, approximately fifteen members of each party, drawn from geographic zones, act as deputy whips. They assist the assistant leaders, or Whips, in counting noses and bringing members to the floor to vote on non-roll-call matters, since the electric bell system for calling members to the floor is not used except for record roll calls or quorum calls.

A member recently described the job of the Whip in these terms:

> The whip is more the eyes and ears of the leadership than anything. On controversial matters, they like to know what the chances of success are. So the deputy whips count noses and the whip's job is to evaluate the count—especially to assess the doubtfuls. . . . A lot of these eastern guys have a Tuesday through Thursday club [which means that they spend the rest of the week in their home districts]. The whip takes the duty of telling them if the signals change so they can get back here if they're needed.[20]

Simply bringing members to the floor at the right time is often a substantial accomplishment. Congressmen are extremely busy, time is short, and the demands on them from every conceivable direction are tremendous. The late Congressman Clem Miller described the problem with great sensitivity:

> So much of what occurs on the Floor is routine. There are only rare occasions when circumstances *demand* one's presence. Thus, what is of overriding significance gives way to what is immediate. The competing interests, the endless details of congressional routine take hold. Members are called to the Floor for a quorum call as the afternoon's debate begins. Soon, nearly everyone arrives to answer his name. Most stay for a while, listening and chatting. Then inevitably the drift begins. Pages hurry up and down the aisles with sheaves of messages, calling a Congressman to argue with an executive department on behalf of a constituent, or to tell a garden club delegation why he favors the shasta daisy for the national flower.
>
> Or the member goes downstairs for lunch, or over to the Senate, or downtown to a conference. . . . Almost without volition, he finds himself back in his office trying to keep up with the mail, interviewing and being interviewed by a stream of callers. Now he is too far away to get back to the Floor for a teller vote.[21]
>
> Once away from the Chamber, he is far away. The urgency, the insistence is gone. A million words of testimony, the results of a thousand patient meetings may be going down the drain. But it is another world from the Congressional office.[22]

[20] Nelson W. Polsby, "Two Strategies of Influence in the House of Representatives: Choosing a Majority Leader, 1962," in Peabody and Polsby (eds.), *op. cit.*, p. 342.

[21] Four kinds of voting take place in the House—voice; standing; teller, where members march up the aisle to be counted; and roll-call. Roll-call and teller votes are announced by the electric bells in the House office buildings.

[22] Miller, *op cit.*, p. 52. A 1970 change in the rules makes it possible for the names of congressmen to be recorded on teller votes as well as on roll calls. This is expected to exert considerable pressure against the forces described in this quotation.

This, of course, is where the Whips come in. The Whips call the deputy whips; deputy whips or their secretaries call the secretaries of members trying to get votes to the floor—sometimes urgently, sometimes perfunctorily. As Miller said:

> The key to effective whip action is timing. The whip is on the Floor surveying the scene and weighing alternatives. He watches the [opposition] to observe whether they are present in force or are hiding in the cloak room awaiting a prearranged signal to descend on the Floor. He gauges the end of general debate and estimates the time when a vote is likely. If he puts out a call too soon, too urgently, many members will assemble, take a quick look, and then begin to fade until there is a critical deficiency when the vote is taken. Yet, he cannot defer too long, because a vote might come unexpectedly. . . .[23]

The third member of the majority party leadership team, along with the Speaker and the Whip, is the Majority Leader. His job in the House is to lead his party on the floor: he is the custodian of the weekly schedule; he makes *pro-forma* motions from the floor; and, if he desires, he leads his party in debate on substantive issues. Off the floor, he divides the duties and functions of leadership—negotiating with committee chairmen and the White House, informally persuading reluctant members to "go along" with the Speaker. Who does what, who consults whom are matters the incumbents of the offices work out for themselves.[24]

For a short time after the revolt against Cannonism and the rules changes weakening the Speaker, the majority party was run "from the floor" by a strong Majority Leader who operated through the caucus.[25] But Rayburn's long incumbency blurred somewhat the distinctive role of the Majority Leader. On the Republican side, there is a policy committee that through its pronouncements gives some guidance to members. A similar function on the Democratic side has been served by the incumbency of a Democratic President and his administration. Under a Republican administration, Democratic policy leadership is divided among several leaders, of course including the Speaker and the formal House leadership. The Democratic Study Group, an informal caucus of liberal Democrats, has been another major source of policy leadership within the House Democratic party but certainly not the only one. As we shall observe in later chapters, the program of the President

---

[23] *Ibid.*, p. 53.

[24] The Speaker, through his power of recognition on the floor, by tradition has exclusive control over the conditions under which legislation may be brought to the floor under suspension of the rules (by two-thirds vote). The Majority Leader, who normally clears his activities with the Speaker, has control over the conditions under which bills are brought up and passed by unanimous consent. Each party has a committee of three "objectors" who object to the passage of particular bills by unanimous consent if certain conditions are not met, e.g., if they authorize more than 1 million dollars of expenditure, if they fail to receive clearance from the executive, or if they are controversial between the parties. See Rep. Wayne Aspinall, "The Consent Calendar," *Congressional Records*, vol. 109 (February 4, 1963), part 2, pp. 1630–1631.

[25] See Polsby, Gallaher, and Rundquist, *op. cit.*, and MacNeil, *op. cit.*, p. 96.

and his executive departments constitutes a rallying point for members of the President's party, though it does not bind them.

PARTY CAUCUSES

The fundamental fact of political life in the House is party—the two parties are communities that elect their own leaders, have established policy positions, and determine committee assignments. Informal social groupings of Congressmen seldom cross party lines. The parties have separate cloakrooms, sit separately on the floor, and maintain separate clubs and meeting places outside the Capitol building. Increasingly in recent years, changes in the general composition of each congressional party have had considerable influence on policy outcomes and to a degree have changed the responsibilities of party leaders.

Although there are some floating and some overlapping Democrats who defy precise pigeonholing, for most purposes we can think of the Democratic party in the House as being composed of three loosely coordinated factions of almost equal size. First, there are the Southern Democrats, who vary from the most liberal to the most reactionary on social-welfare issues but who are all more or less constrained by the implacable sentiments of those who vote in their constituencies to oppose civil rights measures. This group is declining in importance as more Southern Republicans are elected to Congress, but in recent years, there have been about seventy-five Southern Democrats, including their full share of committee chairmen, in the House. The second faction is made up of city machine Democrats, who owe their nominations and elections to strong urban political parties. Often these congressmen come to the House late in life and do not work overly hard at legislative tasks. Consequently only a few machine Democrats have made a significant mark on the House as individuals, although collectively they account for a large number of votes for the programs of Democratic Presidents. In the past, machine Democrats have been unfailingly liberal on welfare and civil rights matters, but increasingly they have reflected the concerns over racial issues of the working-class neighborhoods they represent.

For most of the last thirty years, the vast preponderance of Democratic committee chairmen and party leaders in the House have been drawn from these two groups. These leaders shouldered the major responsibilities for dealing with House Republicans, Senate conference committees, interest groups, the White House, and, not infrequently, their own misgivings on legislative matters. Nowadays, they must reckon as well with a third group, larger and better organized than before. This group consists of programmatic liberal Democrats, who come from all sections of the country and have as their main interests the pursuit of programs reflecting traditional Democratic concerns with social welfare, civil liberties, and racial equality. These congressmen took the lead in the late 1950s in establishing the Democratic Study Group, which in recent years has pooled their information and concerted their tactics on a wide range of issues. The Study Group has pressed for reform of House rules, but it has not had great success on this issue except in the Eighty-ninth Congress, when its ranks were swollen by Democrats elected as a result of Barry Goldwater's disastrous campaign. However, the Study Group has had many notable victories. It has formed the nucleus in the House for an informal whip system to concert the maneuvers of House liberals on civil rights. In earlier years, tightly organized Southern Democrats ran rings around the somewhat more numerous but much less experienced House liberals on all manner of issues. The Study Group has brought those days to a close. On one occasion, they upset a committee-assignment arrangement favorable to conservatives; on another, they vastly strengthened the hand of the Speaker—against his own wishes—in controlling the legislative process.[26]

At the beginning of each Congress, all the members of each party in the House meet in caucus to select their leaders and ratify committee assignments. By organizing the largest bloc of Democrats in the caucus, the Democratic Study Group has gone far in stiffening the resolve of House Democratic leaders to represent the programmatic traditions of the national party even when the President is Republican.

The Republican conference, as its caucus is called, is by no means as ideologically diverse as the Democratic. The handful of Republican liberals from the Northeast and one or two other urban-suburban constituencies are not sufficiently numerous to make a dent in the course of Republican party policy in the House. The main concerns that in recent years have divided most House Republicans have had to do with the flexibility, constructiveness, and efficiency with which the Republican minority position has been pursued. Twice in recent years—in 1959 and 1965—the Republican conference has deposed its party leader, each time moving toward a younger, more vigorous man.[27] This reflects the main cleavage in the Republican party in the House —not between liberals and conservatives but between junior and senior con-

---

[26] Mark F. Ferber, *The Democratic Study Group: A Study of Intra-Party Organization in the House of Representatives*, unpublished Ph.D. dissertation (Los Angeles, Calif.: University of California, 1964); Kenneth Kofmehl, "Institutionalization of a Voting Bloc," *Western Political Quarterly*, vol. 17 (June, 1964), pp. 256–72; and Richard W. Bolling, "Defeating the Leadership's Nominee in the House Democratic Caucus," ICP #91 (Indianapolis: Bobbs-Merrill, 1970).

[27] Charles O. Jones, "Minority party and Policy-making in the House of Representatives," *American Political Science Review*, vol. 62 (June, 1968), pp. 481–93; and Robert L. Peabody, "The Ford-Halleck Minority Leadership Contest, 1965," Eagleton Institute Cases in Practical Politics, no. 40 (New York, 1966).

Table 4   **Members of Congress Serving Three Terms or Less**

Congress	Year Elected	Republicans	Democrats
87th	1960	37% (74/172)	31% (81/260)
88th	1962	47% (84/177)	36% (92/258)
89th	1964	47% (66/140)	43% (126/292)
90th	1966	51% (97/187)	34% (84/247)
91st	1968	46% (87/189)	30% (72/242)

gressmen. It is quite usual for congressmen without much seniority to complain about the management of the House, as Representative Burkhalter did. Junior Republicans have been in a position to do something about it, owing to their numerical strength within their caucus. As Table 4 shows, Republicans with six years of service or less in the House have over the last decade made up almost half the strength of the party caucus, whereas Democrats similarly situated have composed only one-third of their caucus, except in the Goldwater landslide year. In 1965, these young Republicans voted overwhelmingly to replace the aging Minority Leader, Charles Halleck, with Gerald Ford, the current holder of that office; they have also supported moves to broaden the base of leadership in the Republican congressional party. But because junior Republicans are on the average as conservative as senior Republicans, these changes have not had much impact on the course of public policy.

THE DISTRIBUTION OF INFORMATION

Life in any legislative body is bound to be difficult for its members. There is an enormous amount of routine business that has to be transacted but that involves only a few members. For everyone else, this business constitutes a distraction—yet it must be done. On the other hand, sometimes extremely controversial and important measures demand the close attention of all members for indeterminate periods of time—two days, three days, or even a week. Then they must put aside everything else in order to be available for voting on amendments and on final passage of a bill. Legislative life is often a matter of "hurry up and wait," where the schedules of congressmen for long periods of time are controlled by the strategic maneuverings of their party's leaders and the opposition.

Time pressures are expressed in other ways too, for example, by the two-year term. This means that many members are campaigning for office all the time. Attentiveness to the constituency is reflected in the frequent trips many members make back home—indeed, a few congressmen spend most of their time in their home districts even when Congress is in session. Most congressmen also devote the major portion of their staff (usually consisting of six or seven people) and much of their own time to what they call casework—complying with requests for help from constituents. This often involves helping constituents—individuals, firms, and local communities—make representations before agencies of the executive branch, for a favorable administrative ruling or for such things as a Small Business Administration loan or an Area Redevelopment Agency grant. The casework may involve submitting a private bill to admit an immigrant—and clearing the bill through the watchdog procedure that both parties in the House and, to a lesser extent, in the Senate, have set up to guard against unjustifiable exceptions to public laws. The number and variety of casework activities is great; they do not, in general, have very much directly to do with the congressman's strictly legislative work, but they help the congressman maintain a link with his constituents, and they also help him learn about the inner workings of the various executive agencies that are administering the laws he makes.

Obviously, it is not possible for most congressmen to learn a great deal about the provisions and consequences of most of the bills they vote on. Time is short; the bills are many and sometimes technically complex. Congressmen are busy, and their staffs are overloaded with work. As a result of these inexorable pressures, congressmen have worked out shortcuts to inform themselves on legislation. Like their constituents at election time, many of them use party loyalty to help decide how they will vote. Others are particularly alert to the preferences of their state delegations. Voting with the party or with one's state delegation is at the least a sound defensive maneuver; when a congressman votes against one or both, he is "sticking his neck out," laying himself open to criticism from people whose support he needs, either back home to be reelected or in the House to speed his private bills through or to obtain a coveted committee assignment.

A congressman may, of course, vote on the merits of bills if he can inform himself about their merits. This is a complicated process, however. Most public men realize that in practice bills often do not do what they are intended to do, that grants of wide discretion and latitude are commonly made to administrative agencies, that there are always numerous competing demands for Federal funds. Hence, in order really to understand the import of a bill, it is necessary to read the bill, the committee report that explains it, and perhaps the public testimony at hearings; and it may also be necessary to seek out committee staffmen who can explain the distribution of forces in society that have mobilized for and against the bill. Even then, the correct decision does not automatically present itself. Sometimes a bill a congressman favors is "watered down" in the legislative process, and he must decide whether he would rather take half a loaf now or hope for demands to build up behind the bill so that he can try for a full loaf later. There are times when a legislator would rather have the bill, other times when he would prefer to have the issue. Another dilemma is created when his party leaders in the Congress are urging him in one direction and local party leaders are urging him in another. He needs to inform himself not only about what the legislation is designed to do and about who is for it and who against it, but also what the consequences are for himself of choosing one course of action or another. He arrives at conclusions and votes even when there seem to be costs and benefits, advantages and disadvantages on both sides of a question. As Representative Jerry Voorhis wrote: "It would be a great deal easier if only one could answer, 'Fifty-five per cent aye,' or 'seventy per cent no,' or 'I vote aye but with the reservation that I do not like Section 3 of the bill,' or 'I vote no but God have mercy on my soul if I am wrong, as I may very well be.' "[28]

Normally, no congressman has the time to satisfy his uttermost curiosity on a large number of bills. He may ask a friend on the relevant committee: "Do you really think this will solve your problem?" or "How strong are the interest groups behind this bill?" or "What objections did the executive agency that will administer this raise?" From brief, cryptic, informal exchanges

[28] Jerry Voorhis, *Confessions of a Congressman* (Garden City, N.Y.: Doubleday, 1948), p. 233.

such as these (often made over the telephone, or as congressmen mill about on the floor to answer routinely to quorum calls), a representative's opinion on the merits of a bill may crystallize. In general, congressmen read very little material unconnected with their committee work. If they do, it is more likely to be newspapers and magazines than books. They rely on their colleagues, the news media, constituents, and lobbyists to tell them about pending legislation. They rely on the mail and visits back home to keep them abreast of constituent problems.[29]

In their area of specialization, determined almost entirely by their committee assignment, congressmen are much better able to get an intellectual grasp of the merits of legislation. Lobbyists may seek them out; executive agency people try to inform them; official committee trips and hearings fill in concrete details on public policies, how they are executed, and the attitudes of interest groups toward them. And congressmen may find themselves consulted by others, just as they ask their colleagues to inform them in areas outside their competence. Few congressmen serve on more than one major committee. This rule enforces specialization and encourages technical expertise in a small range of issues and reliance on shortcuts in most other areas. Senators who serve on two or more committees spread themselves more thinly.

SUMMARY

Whereas the Senate is exposed on every side to public acclaim and attention, the House, because of its size and intricacy, confuses casual observers; hence its members are relatively enclosed and insulated. Senatorial debate is long and voluminous; it attracts and holds the attention of the press, and of public-opinion makers. House debate is comparatively short, pointed and often technical. Senators are famous men, whose doings are noticed and whose sayings are celebrated; some of them use their office as a springboard for their presidential ambitions. House members (other than the Speaker) are anonymous, whether they want to be or not. There are too many of them. To busy Capitol Hill newsmen, they seem to come and go too fast. And so they are deprived of the limelight, even those whose decisions matter more than the deeds of any ten senators. Finally, the sheer number of members in the House has forced the growth of customary ways of doing things—incomprehensible rituals to outsiders but absolutely indispensable for the efficient conduct of business. The intricate rules governing debate or the customs concerning the allocation of committee seats are examples. The House is, much more than the Senate, both an oligarchy and a world all its own.

[29] See Lewis A. Dexter, "The Representative and His District" and "What Do Congressmen Hear?" both printed in revised and expanded forms from earlier publications in Nelson W. Polsby, Robert A. Dentler, and Paul A. Smith, *Politics and Social Life* (Boston: Houghton Mifflin, 1963), pp. 485–512.

CHAPTER FIVE

NATIONAL POLICY-MAKING I

The Legislative Labyrinth

The task of the student of Congress and the Presidency would be greatly simplified if there were a typical process by which a bill becomes a law, that is to say, a process typical in some sense other than the narrowly formalistic. But most bills do not become laws; they are introduced, referred to committees, and there languish and die. So even to speak of a bill's actually becoming a law is to speak of an atypical event. The figures for the Ninetieth Congress (1967–1968) are shown in Table 5.

Furthermore, bills have all shapes and sizes. Some propose to authorize the expenditure of billions of dollars; others tinker with existing laws, expanding or contracting the powers of executive agencies; still others provide for the relief of individual citizens. Bills may be short and straightforward or long and technical. They may deal with a handful of Federal employees—as a bill to equalize the salaries of judges of the Court of Military Appeals with those of other judges of comparable jurisdiction. Or they may deal with many people, including vast numbers of private citizens—as a bill setting rates at which Federal income taxes are levied. A bill may excite great concern—or none at all—among interest groups, newsmen, executive agencies, and electorates. All the different kinds of bills are exposed to different political

Table 5

	House	Senate
Bills introduced and referred to committee	20,587	4,199 (total, 24,786)
Bills reported by committee	1,319	1,403
Bills enacted into law	1,133	1,286 (total, 2,419)

contingencies, different parliamentary pitfalls, different strategies and tactics. No single case study can do these various contingencies justice. On the other hand, neither can a summary statement, such as that which will be attempted here.

THE ORIGIN OF BILLS

Bills begin their formal existence by being dropped into a hopper by a representative in the House and by being sent to the desk by a senator in the Senate. The process is separate for the House of Representatives and the Senate, but since no bill can become law without being passed in identical form by both Houses, some coordination is necessary. This can take place in a variety of ways. Perhaps the most usual is for identical bills to be introduced at about the same time in each house of Congress, for their provisions to be remolded in somewhat divergent ways in separate houses, and then for their differences to be reconciled for joint action at the last stage, in the conference committee.[1]

Where do bills come from? The President's preeminence as legislative leader is most obvious in this first stage of the process. The Constitution requires that the President "from time to time give to the Congress information of the State of the Union."[2] In recent years this message has been delivered at the opening of each session of Congress and has been used by Presidents as an opportunity to announce their legislative programs. Specific messages embodying the President's legislative recommendations follow on the heels of the State of the Union message. Friendly senior congressmen and senators from the various committees—usually the chairmen—are consulted and asked to introduce in their respective houses bills prepared by the executive agencies. These bills are referred in a semiautomatic process to the appropriate committees for study.

Not all bills introduced in Congress are inspired by the executive departments or included in the presidential program. Some embody a congressman's or a senator's own ideas, and some are offered at the request of an interest group or a constituent.

REFERENCE TO COMMITTEES

There is an art to drafting bills. In part, bills are written so as to be sent to committees that will act on them favorably. But this is not always so easy as it sounds. Here is a sample dilemma. In the present-day House of Representatives, it is reasonably easy to get bills in support of labor or education passed out favorably by the Committee on Education and Labor—but not with the bipartisan support of the committee. This, in turn, jeopardizes the chances for the bill to clear the Rules Committee and reach the floor, and it also

[1] The most important set of exceptions are, of course, taxing and spending bills, which must begin in the House. Measures for spending money will be considered at length in the next chapter.
[2] Article II, Section 2.

means that a coalition of Republicans and conservative Southern Democrats might defeat the bill even though a majority of Democrats (presently the majority party in the House) supported it. But let us suppose that the bill is on a subject that permits its proponents some room to maneuver, that it provides, say, for medical education. Instead of placing the program in the hands of the U.S. Office of Education, which is mistrusted by conservative congressmen, and routing it through the Committee on Education and Labor, the bill can be written so that the program comes under the aegis of the Surgeon General of the United States, who is the head of the Public Health Service. In that case the bill would be referred to the Commerce Committee, whose jurisdiction includes public-health legislation. If this committee reports the bill, its chances of survival are greater, but the chances that it would be as strong or as liberal a bill as one from the Education and Labor Committee are slim; indeed, the more conservative Commerce Committee would be less likely to report any bill at all. Or consider civil rights. Suppose that supporters of civil rights wanted to write a bill pertaining to racial discrimination in commercial practices and that the two committees to which the bill might be sent, depending on how it was titled and written, were the Commerce Committee and the Judiciary Committee. Suppose also that the committees were chaired as shown in Table 6. In order to avoid having the civil rights bill bottled up in committee, it must be written a bit differently for each chamber and referred to the Judiciary Committee in the House and the Commerce Committee in the Senate.

Thus strategic maneuvering designed to keep a bill alive begins while it is being written and certainly before it is introduced. Sometimes it is possible to word bills ambiguously and hope for a favorable referral.[3] But the committees guard their jurisdictions; the parliamentarians (who do the actual referring of bills under the direction of the Speaker in the House and the Majority Leader in the Senate) know the precedents, and only a case of genuine ambiguity gives the Speaker or the Majority Leader any real option in referral.

Still, occasions do arise. In 1962, an interstate water compact for New England rivers was reported out of the House Public Works Committee, which deals with water-resource management. A closely similar bill for the Dela-

---

[3] For an extremely complex recent example, involving maneuvers between rival agencies of the executive branch as well as presidential ambitions and party rivalry, see E. W. Kenworthy, "Ocean-Dumping Bill by Muskie Appears to Outmaneuver Nixon," *The New York Times* (November 18, 1970).

Table 6

	House	Senate
Commerce	Oren Harris, Ark.	Warren Magnuson, Wash.
Judiciary	Emanuel Celler, N.Y.	James O. Eastland, Miss.

ware River Valley came out of the Judiciary Committee, which deals with Federal-state compacts. When quizzed on the apparent discrepancy in the handling of the two bills, the chairman of the public works subcommittee pointed out, in somewhat resigned tones, that the ranking Democrat on the Judiciary Committee, Francis E. Walter, was from the Delaware Valley and was "mighty interested" in the bill and that it therefore had "just gravitated" to the Judiciary Committee.

IN COMMITTEE

Once in committee, automatic processes carry bills no farther. From this point onward they must be carefully and assiduously nurtured or they die. Needless to say, those bills in which the committee chairman is personally interested are given the most prompt attention,[4] but even for a chairman it is futile to promote legislation that cannot command widespread support, at least from the leadership of his own party or from a vast majority of his colleagues on the floor.

In every session of Congress, each committee has a great many bills referred to it—more bills than it can possibly attend to. The committee chairmen play a strategic role in selecting the bills that committees will take up, but in this decision the preferences of the White House and the chairman's own legislative party leaders weigh heavily. Chairmen pride themselves on their success in obtaining passage of legislation reported favorably out of their committees. The chances of success are enormously enhanced if the full weight of the party leadership is behind a measure. If party leaders are indifferent, the entire burden of assembling a majority on the floor falls on the chairman; if party leaders are opposed, it will probably be very difficult to build this majority.

Chairmen who oppose White House measures may delay taking up the offending bill or may seek to water it down or substitute legislation on the same subject more satisfactory to themselves. A firm and intense majority on the committee may successfully oppose a chairman who wishes to do this, but such majorities are rare for several reasons. Avoidance of conflict within committees is so much easier for all concerned. Committee chairmen may take an active hand in assigning new members to their committee and in shaping the size and jurisdiction of future subcommittees. Chairmen can reward their friends by giving them the sponsorship of bills or taking up legislation they may want or need. And, finally, the chairman who opposes his party leadership and the President may in fact have a reasonably accurate sense of which provisions in a bill will actually attract a legislative majority.

In the House, there is a provision—the discharge petition—by which the signatures of a majority of members of the whole House (218) can force any bill out of committee—even if the committee has voted it down—after

---

[4] Tabulations demonstrating this point for the Senate in the field of foreign affairs are contained in James A. Robinson, *Congress and Foreign Policy-Making* (Homewood, Ill.: Dorsey, 1962), pp. 99–100.

it has been held there for thirty days. In the Senate, committees can be by-passed by amending legislation on the floor with the provisions of bills bottled up in committee. This was the method—permitted under loose senatorial rules of germaneness—by which medicare was brought to a vote in 1962. However, neither of these devices is much used. Senators and representatives are loath to play fast and loose with their own procedures. Many fear the wrath of powerful committee chairmen thus affronted. And many feel a responsibility to work according to the regular order, even at the sacrifice of policies they favor. One liberal congressman commented, "Members are reluctant to sign a discharge petition. It could be construed as a vote of no confidence—as an attack upon the committee system or on the integrity of the members of the committee. . . . As long as we have the committee system we need to try to make it work, but what about the public interest? It is heart-rending to see how slow. . . ."[5]

Each major committee seldom aims at producing more than one bill of substantial scope in a session of Congress, and this bill is usually on a subject selected by the President in consultation with the relevant executive departments. Minor bills, favored by executive agencies, interest groups, and/or individual congressmen, may flow through the committees at a brisk or slow pace, depending on the habits and inclinations of the chairman and his instructions to the staff.

On all bills that the chairman decides to take up, it is usual for him to begin by instructing the staff to solicit comments from the executive agency that will be charged with administering the bill's provisions if it becomes law. This is routinely cleared through the Bureau of the Budget (now the Office of Management and Budget), which takes care that the agency's comments are not inconsistent with the presidential program.[6] A negative response from the agency usually dooms a bill unless its congressional sponsor is especially vehement, resourceful, and influential. A favorable executive response may move a minor bill swiftly toward the floor; if the bill authorizes an expenditure of less than a million dollars and appears to be noncontroversial, it can be sent rapidly out of committee. In the House it is placed on the consent calendar and will probably be passed *pro forma* when this calendar is called, as it is on the average of twice a month. In the Senate, similarly, the Majority Leader asks periodically for unanimous consent to pass noncontroversial bills.

On major legislation or controversial legislation, the committee deliberates more slowly. If the chairman favors the bill in question, he will undoubtedly choose to become its sponsor and will schedule the bill for early consideration by the committee. Or he may send the bill to a subcommittee.

Few congressional committees are merely holding companies for subcommittees; the subcommittees are very much the creature of the committee and its chairman. But some committees have built up over the years traditions of decentralization and subject-matter specialization that have led them to spin off major responsibilities to subcommittees. It is quite common for the

[5] Interview by the author, March 25, 1963.
[6] See Richard E. Neustadt, "Presidency and Legislation: the Growth of Central Clearance," *American Political Science Review*, vol. 48 (September, 1954), pp. 641–671.

relations between subcommittees and the full committee to be in flux. For example, observers noted a tendency for Chairman Carl Vinson of the House Armed Services Committee in the latter years of his long chairmanship to allow greater autonomy to his subcommittees and their chairmen. Likewise, subcommittees seemed to be growing in importance as the House Science and Astronautics Committee gained in stature and responsibility. On the other hand, neither the House Rules Committee nor the Ways and Means Committee uses subcommittees on a regular basis. They prefer to work in the full committee. The House Appropriations Committee, as we shall see, depends heavily on subcommittees, but the membership, size, and jurisdictions of these are controlled closely by the chairman of the full committee.

Although the peculiarities of subcommittee-committee relations can also affect the outcome of legislation, for the sake of simplicity, let us examine the process when, as sometimes happens, the committee chairman refers a bill to a subcommittee of which he is also chairman. The staff solicits and receives material backing the bill from the appropriate executive agency, and the chairman instructs the staff to arrange for hearings.

HEARINGS

Hearings serve a variety of functions. Ideally, they are an effective research device—a way of focusing the attention of congressmen on the substantive merits of a proposed bill and its possible pitfalls. In an ideal world, of course, issues are raised *de novo*, and legislators' minds are clean slates. In the real world, however, the subjects of major legislative proposals are familiar to committee members long before they reach the stage of hearings. Sometimes these proposals have been the subject of protracted partisan debate, and interest groups often exist on all sides of the issue. So it is not uncommon for hearings to become rather perfunctory, with spokesmen for the various points of view coming before the committee and delivering speeches that the members have heard many times before. As one congressman said, "I get so bored with those repetitious hearings. We've been listening to the same witnesses saying the same things the same way for ten years."[7] Still, all this is necessary —to make a record, to demonstrate good faith to leaders and members of the House, to provide a background of demonstrated need for the bill, to show how experts anticipate that the bill's provisions will operate, to allay fears, and to gather support from the wavering. Not only does it tell congressmen what the technical arguments for and against a bill are, but, even more important, it tells them *who*—which interests and which groups—are for and against bills and how strongly they feel about them.

The committee staff at the direction of the chairman can manipulate the roster of witnesses before the committee and can ask witnesses unfriendly to the bill to file statements rather than appear in person. Here is a recent account of the strategic use of hearings:

[7] Lewis A. Dexter, "What Do Congressmen Hear?" in Nelson W. Polsby, Robert A. Dentler, and Paul A. Smith (eds.), *Politics and Social Life* (Boston: Houghton Mifflin, 1963), p. 492.

Senator McClellan is known as the most adroit committee chairman on the Hill when it comes to generating publicity for something that he is concerned about, or that he wants to appear to be concerned about. A former rural prosecutor of the jury-rail–thumping variety, he has always made great use of simplicity in conducting Senate hearings. Characteristically, he has stuck to the main point and one side of that point—his. In this case his point was the same one that he had been making all along—that decisions of the Supreme Court endangered the nation's stability. But he also said "I want to get the other side of it and see what can be presented in opposition to these bills." To accomplish this, he invited fifty-odd witnesses to testify, only half a dozen of whom opposed his viewpoint, and he inserted in the record scores of letters, editorials, and statements favorable to his position, with only a handful opposed.[8]

But committee chairmen often play scrupulously fair with all interested parties and allow everyone to speak his piece. The timing and length of hearings is of course strategically important. Sometimes it is desirable from the chairman's point of view to drag hearings out perhaps until the other body can act. Often, leaders on the House side of the Capitol who desire to pass a bill find that pressure for it builds up if the more liberal Senate can be allowed to act first. Therefore, a chairman may drag House hearings on until the Senate acts favorably. On the other hand, House leaders may wish to move quickly, because if the Senate passes a very liberal bill before the House acts, then opponents of the bill in the House will be galvanized at once into opposition. Opponents of a measure realize that when a conservative House bill and an extremely liberal Senate bill go into conference, the combined result may be too liberal for them. Conference committees have great leeway, and the House conferees may be drawn from senior members of the substantive committee reporting the bill, who are proponents of the bill.[9] Unless formally instructed to the contrary by a vote of the House or Senate, conferees can agree to delete provisions of the bill that passed their chamber; when the conference report returns to the House and Senate floors for a vote, no amendments are in order, and opponents of some of a bill's provisions can only vote yes or no on the whole package. On issues where there is an overwhelming consensus that *some* legislation is necessary, opponents of a conference report are at a great disadvantage. And so House committee chairmen sometimes try to keep one step ahead of possible opposition by hastening bills through hearings.

The format for the hearings varies with the committee and the circumstances. At each hearing the ground rules may change ever so slightly, but in general it works as follows. Witnesses from the executive agencies, first of all, are invited to appear, in order to describe how they anticipate the bill will operate and in order to record their support for the bill. After the govern-

---

[8] Richard Harris, "Annals of Legislation: The Turning Point," *The New Yorker* (Dec. 14, 1968), p. 84.

[9] When this is not the case and senior committee members oppose the bill, the chances are that the House will report no bill in the first place or that the chairman will pursue some strategy other than the one suggested here to hasten hearings.

ment witnesses and interested congressmen and senators appear, it is customary for witnesses from interest groups to testify for and against the bill. Usually each witness makes a prepared statement and then is questioned by members of the committee in order of seniority, starting with the chairman, then the ranking minority member, and so on, alternating back and forth between the parties. Ordinarily, time is limited and so it is quite unusual for very junior members of the committee on either side to get a chance to question witnesses.

Committees vary in the opportunity they give to their more junior members. One of the ways in which congressmen tell whether a committee is being run democratically is the extent to which opportunities are provided for newer members to interact with witnesses at hearings. Those committees that place a time limit, say five or ten minutes, on questions from any one member are usually the committees that are most solicitous of junior members. Many committees, however, allow senior members to preempt most or all of their question time.

Not all hearings are organized to consider specific legislation. Sometimes committee chairmen will ask that hearings be organized simply to furnish general information to the members or in order to investigate the execution of laws by an executive department. Committees differ in the extent to which they hold investigatory hearings without a specific legislative purpose. The House Committee on Internal Security (formerly HUAC) is, of course, the committee that is most active in holding hearings that do not especially pertain to any specific legislation before it. Even when there is no particular bill before a committee, however, the general legislative purpose of inquiring whether present laws within the committee's jurisdiction are adequate is legally sufficient to justify holding hearings.

Some committees, less famous by far than HUAC or the subcommittee on investigations of the Senate Government Operations Committee, have used hearings quite consciously as a device for the general education of members. In recent years the Jackson subcommittee on national policy machinery of Government Operations in the Senate has conducted what amounts to a high-level seminar for senators.

THE MARK-UP

At the conclusion of hearings, the subcommittee may meet and consider the bill. At this point its meetings are not public. The bill will be read line by line, and the various members will voice their approval or objections to its provisions. It is at this point, the mark-up, where the bill is amended and rewritten so as to gather the necessary support in the committee to make it possible for the bill to survive its subsequent trip through the Congress. If the bill can be written here so as to receive substantial support, its chances of survival later are immensely improved. If, on the other hand, the provisions of the bill are such as to divide the committee, the chances of the bill's survival are much less. Representative Clem Miller has described the mark-up process:

The committee staff has a proprietary interest in our bill. The bill we went to hearing with was probably its creature to begin with. Its details were worked out in conferences with the executive department "downtown." The staff knows every byway in the bill, has hedged against every technical problem. . . .

What we are seeking is maximum majority support at mark-up time. The hostility of the [subcommittee] chairman is almost fatal and division between the Majority members almost equally so. . . .

After hearings, to be sure of some unity, the subcommittee chairman calls a meeting of Majority members to look over some possible changes in the bill. The Chairman insists on informality. It is a "discussion." Nothing is to be "final." Your "ideas" are sought. One member wants a much tougher section in one part of the bill. There is a chance of agreement. The staff had anticipated this with some appropriate language. Another member, not primed by a staff man, throws out an innocent suggestion which it turns out the Chairman is most opposed to. The "suggestion" is permanently shelved.

Quickly the friction points are reviewed, and assent is secured for our Majority position. We are now ready for the executive session of the full subcommittee, the marking-up with a united front. . . .

The Minority function at the subcommittee mark-up is to test every major segment of the bill, looking for weakness. One member leads off with a challenge to the whole bill. He has a substitute which is disposed of in a second. Then the bill is read, line by line. At the appropriate places, the Majority amendments are offered. There is some discussion. Staff members hover behind members, counselling in whispers. A vote is taken and the clerk reads on.

At step after step the Minority amendments are offered. The attitude is offhand and perfunctory. If a glimmer of interest or a shade of response is elicited from the Majority side, the proposal is pressed. One amendment does seem reasonable. A word or two is said in its behalf. The chairman stirs about unhappily, seeing an opening wedge in Majority unity. It is disposed of, but the restlessness is noted for future exploitation by the Minority in full committee and on the Floor. Finally, the bill has been read. The disagreements—first among Democrats, then between Democrats and Republicans—have resulted in much new language, changing the shape of the bill accommodating to our needs.[10]

Perhaps the most important factor in determining whether or not a bill emerges at all is the extent to which there is a widespread belief, at least among the majority, that there should be some legislation or other on the subject being considered. If even a medium-sized minority feels that there is really no use or necessity for the contemplated legislation, the number and variety of objections they can raise is quite staggering. If, on the other hand, everyone believes that some legislation is desirable or inevitable, the chances that a bill will emerge are much greater. Under these circumstances, both

[10] Clem Miller, in J. W. Baker (ed.), *Member of the House* (New York: Scribner, 1962), pp. 13, 14, 15.

majority and minority are willing to compromise at least sufficiently to provide for some kind of legislation.

After a suitable amount of bargaining, the subcommittee may take a vote on the bill and report to the full committee. In some cases, the full committee provides only a perfunctory review of subcommittee action. In other cases, however, amendments that failed to be adopted in the subcommittee may be in order in the full committee, if their proponents wish to bring them forward. On some committees this is regarded as bad form. On others it is regarded as perfectly acceptable to sustain subcommittee conflict within the full committee.

Customarily, by this time the chairman has instructed the staff to prepare a report. The report is an explanation of the bill from both a substantive and a political standpoint. The purpose of the report is to explain the bill and its contemplated effects to members of Congress and also, on occasion, to the courts, who later, in the course of litigation, may look at reports to ascertain legislative intent. The report may include minority views. It is a point of pride with committee chairmen to bring their minority along with them as much as possible. The long-time chairman of the House Armed Services Committee, Carl Vinson, prided himself on the fact that the bills he brought to the floor were nearly always unanimously recommended by his committee. In committee, at any rate, the process is very similar to that in the subcommittee. Once the bill is marked up and the report written, it may be voted out of committee. It then goes on the calendars of the respective houses.

THE CALENDARS

In the Senate there is only one legislative calendar; from it the Majority Leader, in consultation with the Minority Leader, the President, committee chairmen, and interested senators, select bills for floor action. The method and timing of introduction may be manipulated at the discretion of the Majority Leader to his strategic advantage.

In the House there are five calendars. One, the consent calendar, has already been mentioned.[11] A second calendar is for bills introduced for the relief or benefit of named individuals or groups. A third, rarely used, is the calendar for bills discharged by petition from committees. The other two calendars are for public bills of some importance; bills are listed on them on a first-come (from any committee), first-served basis. This method of setting priorities has been found to be unacceptable, and so these calendars are never called. Rather, substitute methods for placing bills on the agenda are used. Some committees are granted privileged use of the floor—most notably the Appropriations Committee, which can bring its bills to the floor whenever it is ready to report them and suitable arrangements for their consideration

[11] An alternative method of bringing bills to the floor, similar to unanimous consent, is by suspension of the rules, which is accomplished by a two-thirds vote and always with the cooperation of the Speaker. It is clearly unsuited for the passage of most controversial legislation.

can be made with the Speaker and Majority Leader. The Rules Committee is also privileged to bring to the floor special orders making it possible for the House to consider specific bills. These special orders are voted by the Rules Committee and brought to the floor at the request of leaders of the various committees of the House. And so, normally, when a bill is voted out of a House committee and is entered on a calendar, the next step is for the chairman to request the Rules Committee for a special order taking the bill from the calendar and placing it before the House. The Rules Committee chairman may be quick or slow in responding to this request. Normally, however, he will respond with reasonable promptness and schedule a hearing at which the managers of the bill from the substantive committee and its opponents can appear before the Rules Committee and state the case for and against the granting of a special order.

THE RULES COMMITTEE

On the appointed day, the Rules Committee convenes its hearing in a room on the floor above the House chamber in the Capitol; the room is small and cluttered by congressional standards but ornately decorated. In the center is a long table, covered with blue felt and surrounded by fifteen leather upholstered swivel chairs. At each member's place on the table there is a silver nameplate. On one end there is a low lectern for the chairman; at the other, a chair for witnesses, who are chairmen of the other congressional committees and other members of Congress. Meetings are open to the public, but no official stenographic record is taken. There are chairs for perhaps twenty spectators and witnesses awaiting their turn. At the side, a table marked "Press Only" contains copies of bills and reports to be considered that day. Two of the committee's three employees bring in messages to congressmen and help visitors find their seats; the third, the clerk, perches on a chair behind the chairman. The atmosphere is intimate, even cozy. Only two or three newsmen appear regularly; a handful of observers from executive departments and an especially knowing tourist or two may also be in attendance. From ten to ten-thirty in the morning, members of the committee drift in; they greet one another cordially and chat briefly with their congressional colleagues who have come to appear as witnesses or retire to an anteroom to answer the telephone. At ten-thirty, or shortly thereafter, most of the members are in their chairs. The chairman calls the committee to order.

By the time a bill gets to the Rules Committee, political lines on it are drawn fairly clearly. The Rules Committee is not a perfunctory procedural hurdle; its members consider bills on their merits and on the basis of party strategies. On most issues, however, the voting behavior of factions within the committee is quite predictable.

There are three major factions within the committee, as there are within the House generally. Republicans regularly vote against reporting to the floor legislation, both foreign and domestic, on which there is any substantial partisan division in the substantive committee or on which Democratic Presidents place high priority. They are in alliance with conservative Southern Democrats, who also oppose Democratic presidential programs for expanding the welfare activities of the government, increasing the size of governmental bureaucracies, intervening in the economy, or sending aid abroad. The third faction consists of Northern Democrats, who are allied with a few Southern liberals and moderates. They normally unite to back programs sponsored by the House Democratic leadership and Democratic Presidents.

On some issues, especially when the Presidency is in Republican hands, these patterns of alliance break down. Civil rights is a conspicuous example. The usual strategy is for Democrats in the Judiciary Committee (from which civil rights legislation normally comes in the House) to accede, during the mark-up, to some Republican suggestions. The idea is to gain the support of a body of Republicans sizable enough to make possible a coalition between Northern Democrats and Republicans on the Rules Committee. Meanwhile, normally liberal Democrats from the South ally with their conservative Southern brethren. But the Southerners do not have enough votes to defeat Northern Democrats and Republicans on the granting of a rule.

The main weapon of the South in the Rules Committee over most of the last three decades has been the shrewdness of its senior members, such as Eugene Cox of Georgia and Judge Howard Worth Smith of Virginia, who from the Eighty-fourth to the Eighty-ninth Congress was chairman of the committee. A colleague of Judge Smith's described his political skill (and, in a sense, the political skill of all legislative craftsmen inside the House) in the following terms:

> One of the interesting things is to watch the way he plays all these different things the way a great conductor conducts an orchestra. It's really fascinating. If he sees he's going to be overrun here, unless it be in the civil rights field . . . but on an economic issue, or a welfare issue . . . let's say there are five or six of them, he'll play them as carefully as he can and very skillfully to kill as many as possible, but if he has to knuckle under in order to get "X" by going along with "A" he will. It's really magnificent skill.[12]

The devices Judge Smith used to discourage legislation he opposed were many and various. The committee had no regular meeting time but rather convened at the call of the chairman.[13] So when legislation obnoxious to the Judge was pending, it was not unknown for him to delay—sometimes for long periods of time—convening his committee.

> In August, 1957, he vanished from Washington, leaving his committee without the power to call itself to order, while the civil rights bill gathered dust in its files. Word seeped back from Virginia that Judge Smith had gone to inspect a barn that had burned on his near-by dairy farm.

[12] Congressman Richard Bolling, "The Keeper of the Rules: Congressman Smith and the New Frontier," "CBS Reports" (January 19, 1961).
[13] In 1967, liberal Democratic committee members finally overran Judge Smith's successor as chairman (William Colmer, of Mississippi) and forced through a few token changes in committee procedure. Among the changes was the establishment of a regular meeting time—which under House rules all committees are supposed to have anyway.

"I knew Howard Smith would do most anything to block a civil rights bill, but I never suspected he would resort to arson," Speaker Rayburn quipped, somewhat wryly.[14]

Or he could stall by piling up other bills ahead of the one he wanted to bury. When at last the bill he disliked was reached, it was possible to hear a long parade of witnesses against it and have lengthy and searching questions waiting for its proponents. Both these tactics would consume days—perhaps until the Rules Committee members who were key proponents of the bill had to be out of town; then he could abruptly call for a vote. Alternatively, gentlemanly fair play required further delay while the Judge's colleagues met their other obligations.

Thus hamstrung, the managers of a bill often tried to strike a bargain with the Judge and his conservative allies, amending one section or removing another in return for prompt action, in fear that there would be no action at all. It was this bargaining process that the Judge referred to when he once spoke on the floor of the powers of his committee.

> You know, it so happens that the Rules Committee has a little something to do about when these bills come to the floor. I want to assure you that if there is any . . . deal going on or has gone on, I am going to use what little finagling and delaying, and so forth, that I can bring to pass on this situation to see that that does not happen. . . . You know, we southern boys are pretty good old horse traders. I was raised to be a pretty good horse trader myself. . . .[15]

Much of this is now in the past. Neither Judge Smith nor his successor, the equally conservative William Colmer of Mississippi, could control Democratic committee assignments to the committee, and the composition of the committee has been changed over the years to approximate the will of the majority of the majority party. Before 1959, the committee was composed of twelve members divided in a two-to-one ratio between the parties, reflecting the House tradition that the majority party should have control over and responsibility for the agenda. However, the defection of two conservative Democrats (Smith and Colmer) could and did tie the committee up and prevent legislation favored by the majority party to reach the floor. One liberal Democrat ticked off the score in the Eighty-seventh Congress:

> For example, the area redevelopment bill passed the Senate in 1959, but the [Rules] Committee refused to report the House version. Through the almost forgotten procedures of Calendar Wednesday, the bill finally reached the floor in May, 1960, and passed after many procedural roll

---

[14] Tom Wicker, "Again That Roadblock in Congress," *New York Times Magazine* (August 7, 1960). Incidentally, the committee did, in fact, have the power to call itself to order, but the process is laborious and would have been extremely insulting to Judge Smith. See Lewis Deschler, *Constitution, Jefferson's Manual and Rules of the House of Representatives* (Washington, D.C.: Government Printing Office, 1961), Section 734.

[15] *Congressional Record*, daily edition (July 25, 1963), p. 12621.

calls. In June, 1960, a discharge petition was used to circumvent the Committee and bring the Federal pay-raise bill to the floor for approval. . . . The threat of a discharge petition finally forced committee action on the 1960 civil rights bill. The threat of Calendar Wednesday prodded the Committee into clearing the school construction bill, although the Republican–Southern Democratic alliance within the Committee ultimately blocked the bill by refusing to report a resolution sending it to conference.[16]

A Rules Committee deadlocked on most matters of domestic policy was tolerable to liberal Democrats in Congresses gripped by problems of World War II or in Congresses whose major accomplishments were in foreign affairs, as they were under President Truman, or even, as from 1952 to 1960, when a Republican was in the White House. But with the advent in 1961 of a Democratic President, who would need the assistance of his party in bringing his program to the House floor, it became clear to Democrats in the House that something drastic had to be done about the Rules Committee. Something was; after a very intense and protracted struggle between mainstream Democrats and liberals on one side and conservative Democrats, mostly Southern, and the vast majority of House Republicans on the other, the size of the committee was expanded by three—two Democrats and one Republican. Sam Rayburn saw to it that the Democrats who were appointed were party loyalists, and since that time no other sort of Democrat has been appointed to the committee. In consequence, the Rules Committee, which at one time captured nationwide attention by its capacity—and willingness—to say "no" to the best-laid plans of Presidents, Speakers of the House, and committee chairmen, now has all the fascination of an open valve.

At the conclusion of hearings before this committee, the committee customarily clears the room and goes directly into executive session to vote whether or not to grant a special rule making in order floor debate on the bill that has just come before them. If the vote is affirmative, the chairman and the ranking minority member each appoint a member of the committee from his side of the table to take the rule to the floor.

FLOOR ACTION IN THE HOUSE

When a special order is granted by the Rules Committee, this fact is rapidly communicated to the House leadership—the Speaker and the Majority Leader —who schedule the bill for debate. They have some flexibility in this process and may wait for strategic reasons or reasons of convenience. On the scheduled day, two members of the Rules Committee, one each from the majority and the minority, appear on the floor of the House and report the committee resolution setting the terms of debate on the bill. This resolution is itself debatable, and sometimes debate on the resolution provides a hint of the controversy that will ensue when the bill is debated directly. Only in rare in-

---

[16] Richard Bolling, "The House Committee on Rules," speech delivered at the Midwest Conference of Political Scientists, Columbia, Missouri (May 11, 1961), p. 6.

stances is the resolution from the Rules Committee not adopted, after which the House customarily resolves itself into the Committee of the Whole.

The membership of the Committee of the Whole House is identical to that of the House of Representatives itself, but parliamentary rules in the committee are somewhat relaxed. Proponents and opponents of the bill from the substantive committee—customarily senior men from the majority and minority sides—move up to long tables on either side of the center aisle in the House. [17] They will manage the time for debate, make split-second decisions whether to support or oppose amendments, and keep a weather eye on the attendance of friends, waverers, and foes.

In the Committee of the Whole there are no record votes, only voting by voice, standing, or by tellers, when members walk down the aisle and are counted for and against. The quorum is 100, not a majority of the House as in regular proceedings. This smaller quorum and the absence of roll-call voting makes it more difficult to halt proceedings to bring supporters to the floor.[18] And as the bill is read, amendments may come up unexpectedly. An observer says:

> In Committee of the Whole a premium is placed on effective organization and on the sense of commitment that will hold members on the floor hour after hour. Thus, early in 1961, administration supporters were caught off guard on a controversial minimum wage vote, which was lost 186 to 185 (with a dozen or more "supporters" skulking in the cloakrooms, or House barbershop).[19]

At the conclusion of debate in the Committee of the Whole, the committee rises and reports the bill back to the whole House with such amendments as may have been agreed to. At that point the bill is read by title, and amendments that passed in the Committee of the Whole may be voted on once more. Then the entire bill as amended is put to a final vote. This time, if one-fifth of the members so desire, a roll-call vote on each amendment and on the bill may be taken. If the bill is passed, it is sent to the Speaker for his signature. It is then sent to the Senate.

FLOOR ACTION IN THE SENATE

The Senate may or may not have been waiting for the House bill. It is not uncommon for the Senate committees to undertake hearings on their own bill on a subject. Senate committees hear bills and mark them up in a process very similar to that in the House. But these committees are much smaller than

---

[17] The House, unlike the Senate, does not provide a desk for each member in the chamber in which they meet; it has only banks of seats. These tables are the only working surfaces available to members.

[18] In 1970, the rules were changed to permit the taking of names on teller votes in the Committee of the Whole. This was expected to help party leaders keep members, who dislike being recorded as absent, on the floor during the consideration of amendments.

[19] H. Douglas Price, "The Congress: Race, Religion and the Rules Committee," in A. F. Westin (ed.), *The Uses of Power* (New York: Harcourt, Brace & World, 1962), p. 60.

House committees; thus individual senators have greater opportunities to question witnesses and participate in the mark-up. On the other hand, senators have many more committee assignments than representatives, so unless the bill is within a senator's area of special interest or attracts his attention for some reason, he is likely to depend heavily on staff members. Senate committees may permit television to cover their proceedings; House committees were forbidden this option by Speaker Rayburn, and although this rule has come under attack, it has not been reversed. In any event, ordinary committee hearings of the Senate rarely attract the interest of the television networks. The networks usually ask to cover only investigative hearings, which are more likely to provoke a sensation. When a bill is reported out of a Senate committee, it goes on a single calendar, from which it may be taken at any time by the Majority Leader and presented as the order of business before the Senate.

Senate debate is less restricted than debate in the House as to both time and substance. In the House there is a strict rule of germaneness, but in the Senate germaneness is required only for short periods of time. Senate debate is normally more keyed to the needs of the news media than is House debate; it is certainly more voluminous. This can easily be seen by comparing the number of hours the House and the Senate are in session. Whereas the House managed to get its business done in the Ninetieth Congress in 1,594 hours and 52 minutes, the Senate took 1,960 hours and 59 minutes (thirty more legislative days) in which to accomplish virtually the same tasks.

A famous feature of senatorial debate is the filibuster. This refers to the occasions when senators, by prolonging their talk, tie up the Senate for days (sometimes weeks) at a time and stall the legislative machinery so as to win concessions on the substance of the legislation being debated. A filibuster, which can be halted only by a vote of two-thirds of those present and voting in the Senate, may be undertaken for a variety of purposes. Proponents claim that this is a valid way of bringing sharply to the attention of the country the imminent passage of laws that they feel are unjust or unwise. Opponents regard filibusters as inimical to the rule of the majority.

The conditions under which a successful filibuster may be launched are fairly well understood. First, it should take place as far toward the end of the legislative session as possible, because its main effect is to stall legislative machinery. If the wheels of progress can be stalled long enough, some bills strongly preferred by nonfilibustering senators will be lost in the end-of-session shuffle. When enough bills are jeopardized, their proponents presumably will become willing to withdraw their support of the measures being filibustered and will agree to scuttle the issue for that session of Congress. Thus the closer to the end of the session the filibuster takes place, the greater its chances of success.

A second condition for successful filibusters is that numerous senators participate. At least one-fifth of the Senate seems to be necessary to carry on a full-scale filibuster. Normally one of the major techniques of the leadership when attempting to defeat a filibuster is to call for round-the-clock sessions. This tactic is employed in order to exhaust marathon speakers. But the speakers may retaliate by suggesting the absence of a quorum throughout the night hours, thus necessitating the physical presence in the chamber of all senators, not merely those filibustering. For if a quorum cannot be mustered, Senate business is stalled without the expenditure of extra energy by filibusterers. When tactics such as these are employed, as they occasionally are, the Senate takes on the appearance of a besieged fortress. Cots are set up in hallways. Senators wander bleary-eyed around the Capitol, awaiting a call to the floor. As few as twenty senators can provoke this kind of situation for some time before they are exhausted. But a smaller number can probably not sustain a filibuster, because it is so much easier to muster the two-thirds majority against them that is necessary to close off debate.

Perhaps the most important characteristic of filibusters is that they are exceedingly rare. Generally, senators do not undertake to waste their time and that of their colleagues in such a fashion unless they are prompted by strong external stimulus. In the case of Southern senators, for example, such a stimulus would be the extreme position of their constituencies with respect to civil rights legislation, which almost makes it mandatory for them to make a fuss that is easily audible back home.

If a bill evades the severe controversy implied by the filibuster, it can be debated and voted on promptly in the Senate. Normally, however, the Senate and the House pass bills that are not identical in every particular. And so either house may ask for a conference in which their differences are resolved.[20]

THE CONFERENCE

Conference committees are appointed, for the House, by the Speaker and, for the Senate, by the Vice President, on the recommendation of the chairmen of the substantive committees handling the legislation. The conference committees normally consist of senior members from the substantive committees or subcommittees that had the most to do with managing the bill, with the majority usually outnumbering the minority two to one. The entire delegation from each house votes as a unit in conference committees. Occasionally it is possible to pack a delegation by varying its size, but this normally requires cooperation between the committee chairman and the presiding officer of his house.[21] These *ad hoc* committees meet in private and attempt to reconcile the differences between the House and the Senate bills. They are generally given great latitude in reporting a consolidated bill back to their respective houses. Sophisticated liberal members of the House, realizing that the House of Representatives tends to be more conservative than the

[20] Technically, the house "possessed of the papers" asks for a conference, which means that the house dealing with the issue last initiates the conference. A motion in the House of Representatives to go to conference is usually granted by unanimous consent. If unanimous consent fails, however, a motion to go to conference is scheduled like most other business, that is, via the Rules Committee.

[21] See Bertram Gross, *The Legislative Struggle* (New York: McGraw-Hill, 1953), pp. 320–322; and Stephen K. Bailey and Howard D. Samuel, *Congress at Work* (New York: Holt, 1952), p. 267.

Senate, often make no attempt to insert liberal provisions into House measures initially but may arrange for them to be put into the Senate version of the bill. In this way they avoid the strong possibility that the House of Representatives will explicitly reject provisions they are interested in. Once there is such an explicit rejection in the House, it is very difficult to pass any conference report that includes the offending language, because conservative House members will make much of the fact that the House has already rejected the provisions of the bill. Thus the technique is to see that the liberal provisions are introduced on the Senate side and then make every effort to assure that the combined bill that comes out of the conference has predominantly Senate provisions in it. But conferees may also put new matter into the bill by a broad interpretation of their powers. Reports of conference committees are privileged business in both Houses. Furthermore, no amendments may be made to these reports in either House. They may, however, be voted down or returned to conference with instructions in the House or without instructions in the Senate. Thus Senate conferees have somewhat greater leeway; House members may fear being bound by instructions if they stray too far from the provisions of the bill passed by the House. And leaders of the opposition to a bill sometimes extract informal commitments from House conferees as the price for not objecting to the unanimous consent motion that allows the bill to go to conference. House conference-committee members are thus constrained in a variety of ways from acquiescing too thoroughly to liberal Senate provisions.

Close observers have often noted differences between House and Senate members of conference committees. Conference-committee behavior often reflects greater degrees of technical specialization by House members and preoccupation with matters other than the business at hand by senators. This is strikingly illustrated in one case by the conference committee that met on the Securities Act of 1933.

> The rules of a Conference Committee are apparently not unlike those rules that govern collective bargaining negotiations. . . . Senator Fletcher was the chairman of the Senate group and Sam Rayburn [then chairman of the House Commerce Committee] headed the House delegation. . . . On the Senate side, there were such distinguished names as Carter Glass of Virginia, James Couzens of Michigan and Hiram Johnson of California. Senator Robert Wagner of New York was also a member of this Conference Committee. Although he signed its final report I cannot recall his appearance at any of the sessions. . . . The House, on the other hand, had no such distinguished personalities except for Sam Rayburn, although each of its members was far better acquainted with the subject matter at hand than the representatives of the Senate.
>
> Jockeying occurred at the beginning as to the procedures that should be adopted. In its midst, Senator Glass, who had been rapidly scanning the House bill, broke out into a tirade to the effect that he was the proponent of legislation dealing with banks and their relationships to the sale of securities and that he wanted no interference with his handling of these issues. We pointed out to him that the House bill had carefully

excluded from its operations all securities issued by banks. . . . He growled, thumbed the bill for any further references to banks, found none, and shortly thereafter left the committee never to reappear.

Senator Fletcher, with the courteousness that always characterized him, suggested to Rayburn that he should accept the chairmanship of the committee at least for the first meeting. Rayburn agreed and shortly thereafter suggested that the first business was to come to a determination of which bill should become the basic working draft of the Committee. Rayburn quietly asked Senator Fletcher if he did not desire to make a motion on this matter. The Senator replied by moving that the Senate bill should be made the working draft. Rayburn took a vote on this motion and, finding that all the Senators voted for the motion and all the members of the House voted against the motion, applied the unit rule and declared that since the vote was a tie the motion failed of adoption and consequently the House bill would become the basic draft. That was the last we heard of the unit rule and the last of Title I of the Senate bill. . . .

Work moved reasonably smoothly thereafter and Title I was completed by Friday. Senator Fletcher never requested to alternate the chairmanship, and, absent any request from him, Rayburn continued to guide the proceedings. The Committee met daily. Its sessions carried on throughout the mornings. . . . The representatives of the House were assiduous in their attendance, the Senate members less so. . . .[22]

THE PRESIDENT ACTS

Once a consolidated bill is agreed on in conference and passed in identical form by both houses, it goes to the President for his signature. If the President fails to sign the bill within ten days of the time he receives it (Sundays excepted), the bill becomes law unless Congress has adjourned. If Congress has adjourned, the President's failure to act constitutes a pocket veto and the bill fails of enactment. The pocket veto seems like a technicality of minor significance, but it is not, because the final days of a congressional session are hectic, and a great deal of legislation is passed under the pressure of adjournment. Congress, too, is constrained by the calendar—every two years they must adjourn long enough for House members and at least one-third of the Senate to go home and campaign for reelection. Understandably also, in years when there is no election, members of Congress are under some pressure to adjourn at least long enough to snatch a Christmas vacation with their families.

More formidable than the pocket veto is, of course, the veto. Under the Constitution, the President may return a bill to the House that originated it with his objections. The bill then may be reconsidered but must pass both houses of Congress in identical form by two-thirds majorities in order to become law. This means, in effect, that one-third of the votes plus one vote in either house constitutes a presidential majority, at least for the purpose of

---

[22] James M. Landis, "The Legislative History of the Securities Act of 1933," *George Washington Law Review*, vol. 28 (October, 1959), pp. 29–49. Quoted passage, pp. 43–45.

preventing the passage of legislation. The President may employ the threat of veto to discourage the consideration of legislative alternatives earlier in the process. This threat must normally be taken seriously, because it is a rare issue on which a President cannot find sufficient allies in the House or Senate to prevent passage over his veto.[23]

SUMMARY AND REVIEW:
POWER IN THE PROCESS

The mere chronicle of the complicated and tortuous passage of bills through the legislative process should give some concrete meaning to the notion that there are many points in the American political system where it is possible for interest groups and interested parties to advance their cause. The considerable powers of committee chairmen and committee staffs, of the House Rules Committee, of the Speaker, of the Senate Majority Leader, and of the President and the executive agencies in the legislative process is nowhere more apparent than in the massive artistic production that is involved in producing a legislative product of any substantial significance. Even so, most of the dispersed powers in the process are essentially negative—legislation can be stalled or defeated in so many different ways, by so many different people. The powers to create formulas acceptable to successive majorities in committees and on the floors of both houses of Congress, formulas that are technically workable and politically feasible—these powers are more concentrated. They rest most heavily with the President and his congressional agents, with the majority leadership in House and Senate, and with the men who manage the bills in House and Senate committees and on the floor.

[23] From 1913 to 1968 there were 1,270 vetoes, including 524 pocket vetoes. Only 37 vetoes were overridden.

NATIONAL POLICY-MAKING II

The Budgetary Process

In our political system, both Congress and the President shape national policy-making. It is, as one observer correctly noted, "a system of separated institutions *sharing* powers";[1] and probably the most significant set of national policies over which both Congress and the President share powers is the Federal budget.

The budget, according to David E. Bell, President Kennedy's first Director of the Bureau of the Budget, is

> . . . a major means for unifying and setting forth an over-all executive program. . . . [It] reflects [the President's] judgment of the relative priority of different Federal activities. Thus, the President's budget necessarily reflects his policy judgments and the Congress in acting on the President's budget necessarily reviews these policy judgments as to the relative importance of alternative uses of national resources. . . .
>
> The essential idea of the budget process is to permit a systematic consideration of our Government's program requirements in the light of available resources; to identify marginal choices and the judgment factors that bear on them; to balance competing requirements against each other; and, finally, to enable the President to decide upon priorities and present them to the Congress in the form of a coherent work program and financial plan.[2]

One of the Eisenhower administration's major financial officials agreed: "The American system of government provides no good alternative to reliance on

---

[1] Richard E. Neustadt, *Presidential Power* (New York: Wiley, 1960), p. 33.
[2] Statement of Hon. David E. Bell, "Organizing for National Security. The Budget and the Policy Process," *Hearings before the Subcommittee on National Policy Machinery*, part 8 (Washington, 1961), pp. 1134–1135.

110

the budget process as a means of coordinating and reviewing the activities of the departments and raising periodically for Presidential decision and review their effectiveness in actual performance."[3]

The budget is an enormous document, formulated annually. Until 1967, it reflected only the administrative expenditures of the government and excluded the rather sizable payments made by trust funds held by various governmental agencies, such as Old Age and Survivors Insurance and the Federal Unemployment Trust Fund. The inexorable growth of the American economy and population made it clear that 1966 was going to be the last year in which the administrative budget would be under 100 billion dollars. For President Johnson, this figure was politically a magic number; in 1964 he had opened a sizable credibility gap with the press by broadly hinting that the budget would go over 100 billion dollars, so that the eventual figure, which he knew would be less, would be publicized as a great exercise in governmental self-denial and frugality.[4]

When the administrative budget finally cracked President Johnson's magic ceiling, the time seemed ripe to consolidate it with trust-fund expenditures, a move that had long been recommended by experts in this recondite field. The budget documents were written so as to permit accurate comparisons with previous years. Thus, the retrospective addition of trust-fund expenditures produced an illusion that the 100-billion-dollar mark had been passed long since.

The budget must be enacted into law, pursuant to the provision of the Constitution that "no money shall be drawn from the Treasury, but in consequence of Appropriations made by law."[5] This means that appropriations bills must be enacted annually before the wheels of government can turn and that these bills must come from Congress.[6]

But the budget, as a document, is in the first instance the President's. It is the President who must decide whether to retrench, expand, or hold the line in program planning, whether to risk a deficit, accumulate a surplus, or balance the budget. He must decide where and how to cut back existing programs and where and by how much other programs are to be encouraged to grow. And, early each year, it is the President who submits the detailed

---

[3] Statement of Hon. Wilfred J. McNeil, in *ibid.*, pp. 1060–1061.

[4] See Rowland Evans and Robert Novak, *Lyndon B. Johnson: The Exercise of Power* (New York: New American Library, 1966), pp. 368–376; and James Deakin, *Lyndon Johnson's Credibility Gap* (Washington, D.C.: Public Affairs Press, 1968), p. 50: "To reporters keeping vigil in Austin late in December 1966, the word was passed by one of those ubiquitous 'high administration sources' that the new federal budget would be $135 billion to $140 billion. . . . Reporters recalled the great budget hoax of 1964, when the President protested mournfully that it would be practically impossible to keep spending under $100 billion, then sandbagged them with a $97.7 billion total."

[5] Art. I, Sec. 9, paragraph 7.

[6] One of the most confusing features of congressional procedure is the fact that the appropriations process parallels the regular legislative process. When a bill becomes a law, it may *authorize* the expenditure of money for stipulated purposes. But this does not mean that the amount of money will actually be *appropriated* to this end. How much money is appropriated depends on the process I am about to describe. Normally, to initiate a program, it is necessary to go through the legislative process to receive authorization and then the budgetary process to be financed.

document to Congress. In February, 1970, the budget called for the expenditure of 200.8 billion dollars.

Formulating and enacting the Federal budget is not merely a matter of bookkeeping; it is an intensely political procedure. The budgetary process determines to a great extent in any given year what activities the Federal government will undertake and to what extent it will undertake them. And so it is not surprising that the process by which a budget is born should call forth responses from the various parts of our political and governmental system and reflect in microcosm some of the major forces in national policy-making.

The fiscal year of the Federal government begins on July 1. For convenience, we can divide the budgetary process into four stages, beginning in March of the calendar year before the money is to be spent, that is, fifteen months before the start of the fiscal year.

PRESIDENTIAL PLANNING: MARCH–JUNE

Negotiations on the shape of the budget begin at a theoretical level. Economists in the Executive Office of the President, working for the Council of Economic Advisors (CEA) and the Office of Management and Budget (OMB), meet with economists from the Treasury Department and attempt to arrive at a mutually satisfactory forecast of levels of Federal revenue and expenditure for the year beginning two Julys hence. In the executive branch, some attempt is made to keep the budget in a known relationship with the expected income of the Federal government. Some Presidents have expressed strong desires for "balanced" budgets, in which expenditures never exceed income. But it is very difficult to bring a Federal budget into precise balance, primarily because Federal revenues depend in large measure on the state of the economy as a whole. When domestic production and consumption are high and unemployment low, the government takes in more money. The income of the government is largely pegged to domestic prosperity. When businesses and private individuals make more, they pay more in taxes, swelling the government's coffers and permitting a higher level of Federal expenditure within a balanced budget.

If a recession occurs, production falls and unemployment increases, so individual and business incomes decline and the government takes in fewer tax dollars. This means that the government can finance fewer of its activities from current income. If the President is determined to balance the budget under these circumstances, he must cut back on Federal expenditures. It is more likely, however, that he will seek ways to stimulate the economy, which will eventually increase the flow of governmental income, although, in the short run, it further unbalances the budget.

The so-called automatic stabilizers of the economy, Federal payments that alleviate recessions, then come into operation as required by law. One such stabilizer is the payments by the unemployment insurance program, which increase as the number of unemployed increases. The graduated Federal income tax is another major automatic stabilizer, because tax payments to the Federal government decrease as income decreases. In addition, the

Federal government may, at the discretion of the President, accelerate the pace at which expenditures that are going to be made anyway are disbursed, as when the timetable on new defense contracts is advanced so that work can commence more rapidly.

These and many other activities of the Federal government affect corporate and private decisions to invest and consume. The cumulative impact of all these decisions determines the level of the economy, and so it is no mean trick to forecast Federal income from six to eighteen months ahead.[7]

In order to forecast Federal expenditures for this period, it is necessary to get some idea of the demands Federal agencies will be making for funds. The OMB has in hand estimates that the agencies had made in the past of their needs for the fiscal year they are considering, but the larger agencies are asked to review these estimates and to project their probable needs for as long as five years ahead. As these estimates are reported to the OMB, they are examined and discussed with the agencies.

Meanwhile, the President discusses the preliminary forecasts with Cabinet members. At this point, discussions are being shaped toward two key decisions, both of which are made by the President and his top-level economic advisors. The first decision relates to the fiscal policy the government will follow for the year. The President must decide whether to try to balance the budget, accumulate a surplus, or agree to deficit spending, which is spending at a higher rate than current income permits. This involves selling government bonds either to banks or to the public and increasing the so-called national debt, which is the amount in dollars of all outstanding marketable obligations of the government. This first decision sets a policy that will ultimately govern how much money all the various agencies of the government will be able to plan on spending in the year ahead.

The second major decision is what the government will try to buy with the money available. The President and the OMB Director go over the main items of the budget, and the President sets policy guidelines in which the extent and direction of new programs are decided in the light of expected demands and expected resources. Expected resources are estimated by the revenue forecasts and fiscal decisions I have already described. Forecasts of expected demands are equally difficult to determine. In the case of expected revenues, the most useful information to forecast the state of the economy next year is the state of the economy now. So also for demands—the basic datum of overriding importance in determining next year's expenditure level is this year's budget. Naturally, there will be changes. But looked at in large, the changes are marginal. This can be seen by examining Table 7, which gives the annual percentage of increase or decrease in appropriations for thirty-seven agencies (all concerned with domestic policy) over a twelve-year period.

[7] Table 10 shows the extent to which Federal budgets predict actual Federal expenditures. Inaccurate predictions of receipts appear to account for the major source of error in dollar terms. Bear in mind, however, that political leaders may demand that estimates of income be given optimistically in budget forecasting, because this permits them to ask for a larger budget without incurring a predicted deficit—and all the political (or at least propaganda) disadvantages that go with it.

In general, barring mobilization crises, there is a similar picture even for defense spending. Consider Table 8, which gives the percentage of the gross national product (GNP) and the percentage of the national budget spent on defense from 1950 to 1969. Table 9, which compares the federal budget with

Table 7   Range of Variation in Annual Appropriations for Thirty-seven Agencies over a Twelve-Year Period

Percentage change from previous year	0–5	6–10	11–20	31–40	41–50	51–100	101+
Cases (one agency per year = 1 case)	149	84	93	21	15	24	7
Total cases: 444							

Source: Aaron B. Wildavsky, *The Politics of the Budgetary Process* (Boston: Little, Brown, 1964), p. 14. Data from Richard F. Fenno, Jr., *The Power of the Purse* (Boston, Little, Brown, 1966).

Table 8   Percentage of GNP and of National Budget Spent on Defense, 1950–1969

	Defense budget as a % of total budget	Defense budget as a % of GNP
1950	32.8	5.0 ← Korean War begins
1951	50.6	10.3
1952	67.2	13.4
1953	67.8	13.5 ← Korean War cease fire
1954	69.2	11.3
1955	62.9	9.8
1956	61.1	9.6
1957	62.3	10.0
1958	61.4	10.1
1959	57.5	9.5
1960	59.1	9.0
1961	48.4	9.4
1962	47.8	9.4
1963	46.9	9.1
1964	45.2	8.8
1965	41.9	7.6
1966	42.2	7.9
1967	44.3	9.1
1968	44.9	9.8
1969	44.0	9.1

Source: Samuel P. Huntington, *The Common Defense* (New York: Columbia, 1961), pp. 282, 283. Since 1961, U.S. Bureau of the Budget, *The Budget in Brief* (Washington, D.C.: U.S. Government Printing Office, annually).

Table 9   Federal Budget and GNP compared

	Federal budget as a % of GNP
1956	15.8
1957	15.5
1958	16.0
1959	16.6
1960	15.2
1961	16.0
1962	15.8
1963	16.1
1964	19.4
1965	18.1
1966	18.7
1967	20.7
1968	21.7
1969 (est.)	20.6

Source: *The Budget of the U.S. Government, 1965* (Washington, D.C.: U.S. Government Printing Office, 1964), p. 464; *Economic Report of the President* (Washington, D.C.: U.S. Government Printing Office, 1964), p. 207; and *The Budget in Brief—Fiscal Year 1970* (Washington, D.C.: U.S. Government Printing Office, 1969).

the gross national product, reveals essentially the same thing—that changes in the budget are marginal from year to year.

PRESIDENTIAL "CEILINGS" AND AGENCY ESTIMATES: JUNE–NOVEMBER

When the President has made basic decisions on the size of the budget, its role in the economy, and its general allocation pattern, the OMB Director notifies the heads of the bureaus and departments of these preliminary decisions. He does this by means of a letter to the bureau heads asking for firm estimates of their agency's needs for the coming year and informing them of presidential budget policy—"ceilings" for each agency and guidelines about the proposal of new programs. It is difficult to describe precisely what presidential "ceilings" consist of and what they are used for. Maurice Stans, Director of the Bureau of the Budget[8] under President Eisenhower, was once asked whether there was an overall "ceiling" for the 1961 budget. He replied:

[8] Bureau of the Budget is the former name of the Office of Management and Budget. The name was changed by the Nixon administration in 1970. The Nixon administration also gave the OMB a greater political role. One observer has commented: "The assistant directors for the budget have been removed from the Civil Service and their jobs made more political. . . . [They] have phones plugged into the White House switchboard and they now act as 'desk men' for the departments and agencies; when a Cabinet officer has a problem, he's expected to call them first." John Pierson, "Who's in Charge? Coming Cabinet Moves Point Up the Big Decline of Secretaries' Role," *The Wall Street Journal* (November 20, 1970).

I have not fixed a ceiling this year and did not fix one last year.

I do think that it is important, in considering a budget of this size, to take a look at it at various levels. By that I mean I think the Department of Defense should determine what kind of defense it can provide for $40 billion.

If this is done and everything is given its proper ranking in priority, then it can be determined whether or not it provides an adequate program, which items are next in rank of priority that should be considered, and which items are marginal or least essential. This does not mean I think that the defense of the country can unquestionably be satisfied for $40 billion. It means that as a matter of method I think the Department should start with a figure of that general magnitude and see what kind of a budget it can prepare at that level, and what, if anything, is then left out that is still sufficiently important that it has to be added.

That, in my opinion, is not a ceiling at all and it is not a target either. It is a method of procedure that I think is a desirable one to follow.[9]

David Bell described ceilings in these words:

There are cases . . . in which . . . the President would give some kind of preliminary planning dollar figure to an agency . . . [on] July 1 or thereabouts. In such cases, however, we would not regard this, nor would the President regard this as a ceiling in the literal sense. We would regard it as a preliminary planning figure. The agency head would be expected to submit to the President a budget which would show what could be done for that figure, but he would also be expected to submit to the President any additions, any changes in that figure, which he regarded as necessary to carry out the agency's mission.

The President would not expect to end up with the figure that he started with. He would expect that after considering the detailed figures, the detailed budget, and the agency heads' opinion of the changes that would be desirable, the President would make a different and final judgment in the fall of the year.[10]

There is, in other words, a process going on in which successive approximations of a final figure are being made. The presidential ceiling is one such approximation, but it is open to negotiation and to appeal from agencies and is subject to modification.

At this point, the major focus of activity shifts to the agencies and bureaus within the executive branch, at a subdepartmental level. The chart on page 117 gives a simplified view of the organization for one department; it will help in visualizing the types of organizations in which budgetary activity at this stage is taking place. Bureau chiefs, receiving the letter from the OMB setting out presidential guidelines for their estimates, proceed to call for budget estimates from their offices and divisions. This call gives policies and priorities to be observed within the bureau.

[9] Statement of Hon. Maurice Stans, in *Hearings, op. cit.,* p. 1096.
[10] Bell, in *ibid.,* pp. 1142–1143.

DEPARTMENT OF LABOR

Secretary of Labor

Undersecretary of Labor

Office of Information, Publications, and Reports

Office of Legislative Liaison

Department Level

Bureau and Agency Level

Assistant Secretary for Employment and Manpower
- Office of Manpower Automation and Training
- Bureau of Employment Security
- Bureau of Apprenticeship and Training

Assistant Secretary for International Affairs
- Bureau of International Labor Affairs

Assistant Secretary for Labor Standards
- Bureau of Labor Standards
- Bureau of Employees' Compensation
- Employees' Compensation Appeals Board
- Women's Bureau

- Bureau of Labor Statistics
- Regional Staff Committees

Administrative Assistant Secretary
- Personnel Administration
- Program and Budget Evaluation
- Management Analysis and Development
- Administrative Management
- Accounting and Financial Procedures
- Library

Solicitor

Assistant Secretary for Labor-Management Relations
- Office of Welfare and Pension Plans
- Bureau Labor-Management Reports
- Wage and Hour and Public Contracts Division
- Bureau of Veterans Reemployment Rights

These estimates and the justifications that accompany them will serve many purposes. Within the executive branch they will be the basis on which claims for a larger allocation are made, either in support of or as an appeal from presidential guidelines. It is here that agency executives show that it is necessary to expand the scope of their activities in order to do their job under the law or that it is necessary to spend more in order to maintain their current level of service. The same sorts of justifications will have to be presented first at the departmental level, where agencies within a department may have to compete for funds, then at the presidential level, at hearings conducted by examiners of the OMB, and still again before the appropriations subcommittees of Congress.

Under President Johnson a concerted attempt was made to reorganize the traditional methods for justifying budgetary demands so that expenditures could be more directly related to the missions and programs of agencies and to the results these programs were supposed to achieve. The Planning, Programming Budgeting System (PPBS) was modeled on Secretary McNamara's efforts in the Defense Department to assert control over strategic planning and procurement.

Although McNamara brought civilian control of the gigantic Defense Department to new heights of efficiency, the strategic missions and expected benefits attributable to the activities of other departments have not always proved easy to codify. In most agencies, budgetary justification by means of PPBS has not advanced far. It has meant, however, a greater involvement by department-level and Office of Management and Budget officials in examining bureau estimates before the OMB letter establishing departmental guidelines goes to the department.[11]

Estimates from the offices and divisions are put together in detail at the bureau level and submitted to scrutiny at the department level, usually by a departmental budget committee, which may include budget officers from the various agencies, the departmental budget officer, and the assistant secretary for administration of the department. The task of this group is to bring budget requests from the agencies into line with departmental policy, as laid down by the Secretary, with presidential policy, as expressed through the OMB, and with congressional sentiment, as expressed in years past at appropriations subcommittee hearings and through informal contacts between departmental and bureau congressional liaison and budget officers, on the one hand, and congressmen, senators, and Appropriations Committee staff, on the other hand.

The process of harmonizing a departmental budget with the various demands and policies of these different groups is not mechanical, but political. Departmental policy-makers must calculate whether the time is right to forge ahead with a particular program, and if so, how far ahead. They must count the costs of cutting back another program in terms of the interest

---

[11] See two symposia on the PPBS appearing in the *Public Administration Review* in December, 1966, and March/April, 1969; David Novick, *Program Budgeting* (Cambridge, Mass.: Harvard, 1965); and Charles L. Schultze, *The Politics and Economics of Public Spending* (Washington, D.C.: Brookings, 1968).

groups affected and their access to key congressmen. The major decisions, and especially cases of disagreement, are settled by the departmental Secretary.

PRESIDENTIAL OVERSIGHT: SEPTEMBER–DECEMBER

Before the Budget and Accounting Act of 1921, the process on the executive side had less presidential participation and ended at this point, with the departmental estimate. Budgetary requests from individual departments were assembled at the Treasury Department and transmitted in a single document without alteration; the rest was up to Congress. In 1921, the Bureau of the Budget was created in the Treasury Department as an agency through which departmental requests could be filtered. When the Bureau was moved to the Executive Office of the President in 1939, the budget became a major device for presidential control of the executive bureaucracies.[12]

At this stage of the process, departmental budget requests are submitted to the OMB, which goes over them with some care. OMB agency specialists discuss requests informally with departmental representatives and hold hearings at which agency budget and operating officials make formal presentations in defense of their requests. Here, once again, major attention is devoted to deviations from expectations, to changes in requests from last year, to justifications for new programs, to performance statistics, such as those reporting workloads of employees, and to deviations from presidential guidelines.

When these hearings are completed, the OMB puts together a final recommendation to the President, who has a final opportunity to go over the results and to propose last-minute adjustments. As soon as his final decisions are made, letters are prepared and sent to the agencies informing them of the budgetary requests the President intends to send to Congress in their behalf. There is then a short period in which emergency appeals from top executives of bureaus and departments may be entertained, but by this time, the calendar is crowding in on all participants in the process. The budget must be printed, proofread, and submitted to Congress in early January.

The budget has been described as a vast network of bargains. The President has his ceiling to protect and certain programatic interests. Agencies want to give service to their clientele and often want to expand their programs. Interest groups served by agencies maintain a keen interest in the capacity of agencies to serve them. Through the continuous participation of the OMB in the process of budget-making, the President bargains with the executive agencies. When he sends his final letter to departments and bureaus, the President seals the bargain and adopts as his program the various programs of the agencies for which money has been requested. It is still incumbent on each department and bureau to make its case before Congress;

---

[12] See Edward H. Hobbs, *Behind the President* (Washington, D.C.: Public Affairs Press, 1954), Chap. 2; and Louis Brownlow, *A Passion for Anonymity* (Chicago: University of Chicago Press, 1958), Part III.

but now the President is at least formally on their side of the bargaining table, not across the table as heretofore.[13]

Some agencies may still feel slighted or shortchanged by the outcome of this process. Their part of the bargain entails defending their part of the President's budget before Congress. Bureau chiefs may not volunteer their disagreements with the final figures, but they may, and often do, respond to direct questions in congressional appropriations hearings with "personal opinions" at variance with official budget requests. Appropriations subcommittee hearings often contain examples of this.

> *Official*: If I go into those questions my personal opinions might conflict with the Budget Report. . . . But I want to make it clear to the committee that I have acquiesced in the limiting figure of the Budget.
>
> *Congressman*: You want this committee not to increase the amount of this budget?
>
> *Official*: Oh, no; I recognize in Congress the power to do what it wants with this Budget.
>
> *Congressman*: Do you feel that it [library service] is adequate? . . .
>
> *Official*: It is all I am permitted to come here and ask you for.
>
> *Congressman*: How much would you like to ask for?
>
> *Official*: Oh, 50 per cent more.
>
> *Congressman*: What did you ask the Department for?
>
> *Official*: $885,314,000.
>
> *Congressman*: What did you get from the Bureau of the Budget?
>
> *Official*: $780,000,000.
>
> *Congressman*: Between the two, they only cut you $100 million. Did you ask for too much?
>
> *Official*: No, sir.
>
> *Congressman*: Do you think you could use that $100 million if Congress voted it?
>
> *Official*: I think we could use the bulk of it yes, sir.[14]

If agencies are not always completely loyal to the budget as it is sent to Capitol Hill, it is because this document, when it arrives for congressional action, is a presidential document, reflecting presidential priorities and containing the most minute and comprehensive summary of what the President wants his administration to accomplish in the fiscal year ahead.

Just before the President sends the budget to Congress, he may take special pains to acquaint key congressmen with its major provisions and with the economic and political premises on which these provisions are based. While the budget is being put in final shape, the Economic Report of the President and his State of the Union Message are receiving their finishing

---

[13] The severe disruptions that followed the attempt of one President, Mr. Eisenhower, to ignore his part of this bargain are discussed by Neustadt, *op. cit.*, pp. 64–80.

[14] These and all other hearings quotations in this chapter were drawn from appropriations subcommittee hearings by Aaron B. Wildavsky and summarized in an unpublished essay. This essay, enlarged and refined, became Wildavsky's *The Politics of the Budgetary Process* (Boston: Little, Brown, 1964).

touches. Each of these three documents is written and designed to be read in the light of the other two. All three are delivered to Congress by the President in the opening days of each session, in early January.

CONGRESSIONAL ACTION: JANUARY–JULY (OR LATER)

The Constitution provides that "All bills for raising Revenue shall originate in the House of Representatives."[15] This has, over the years, been given a most liberal interpretation. By extension, all "money" bills—both for taxing and for spending—now begin in the House, and so it is to the House that the budget goes. It is referred to the Committee on Appropriations—with fifty members, the largest committee in the House. There it is split into thirteen bills, along agency lines, and parcelled out to subcommittees of various sizes. The membership, size, and jurisdiction of these subcommittees are partly the handiwork of custom, which helps in determining what sorts of subcommittees there will be. Partly, they are shaped by the committee-assignment process, through which energetic Majority and Minority Leaders can, over the years, pack the committee with men of their choosing. But most of all, the membership and size of the subcommittees and what they do are determined by the committee chairman, who can rearrange these sometimes recalcitrant elements to suit himself.

Clarence Cannon, Chairman of the Appropriations Committee in the Eighty-eighth Congress (and for more than twenty years preceding) was a superb example of the geologic processes of legislative time. He came to the House as a young man in 1911, as a temporary staff member in the office of the Speaker, Champ Clark of Missouri. In 1917, he was appointed Parliamentarian of the House, a signal honor and a position of great importance. When Clark died, Cannon went back to Missouri and soon thereafter, in 1923, ran for his mentor's old seat. He thus began his second career, which was crowned in 1941 by his accession to the chairmanship of the Committee on Appropriations. This post he held, except for four years in which Republicans controlled Congress, until he died in May, 1964, aged eighty-five. Cannon, in spite of the fact that he was continually at odds with Speaker Rayburn ("Sam has packed the Committee against me," he once said) and Speaker McCormack, had little difficulty in running the Appropriations Committee his way. In 1956, he reorganized the subcommittees, in the course of which he deprived Representative Vaughn Gary, who was perhaps not sufficiently staunch in opposition to the foreign-aid program, of the chairmanship of the relevant subcommittee. Cannon did it by proclaiming a rule—no committee member could serve as chairman of more than one subcommittee, and so Gary gave up the chair in the subcommittee on foreign operations.[16] Can-

---

[15] Art. I, Sec. 7. The authoritative work on the contemporary budget process from the congressional side is Richard F. Fenno, Jr., *The Power of the Purse* (Boston: Little, Brown, 1966).

[16] Gary's successor as chairman of the subcommittee was Otto Passman. In the summer of 1964, George Mahon of Texas, Cannon's successor, led a successful fight to prevent

non would have gone further, had he not been restrained by the protests of his senior colleagues on the committee. Subsequently, Representative Albert Thomas served as chairman of two subcommittees, until February 19, 1964, when Cannon, without consulting anyone, abolished one of Thomas's subcommittees. The abolished subcommittee was on deficiency appropriations, which had the power to expedite the appropriation of funds during the year supplementing those requested in the regular budget. In 1962 Cannon reached into the budget for the Defense Department and plucked out the civil defense program—which had been placed in the Pentagon expressly to avoid this fate—and assigned it to a subcommittee whose chairman opposed the program. In 1963 five liberal new members were placed on the committee by the House leadership, replacing, on the average, more conservative men. Cannon gave all but one of the new members low-level jobs in the committee's equivalent of Siberia—subcommittees on the District of Columbia, on the legislative budget, and, for a man from New York City, on agriculture. Meanwhile, senior members whose views were more congenial sat on three or four important subcommittees simultaneously. This does not necessarily reflect a conservative bias; newcomers to this committee almost always get Siberia. Nevertheless, it is worth noting that while the House leadership was liberalizing the committee, Cannon managed to hold the line on virtually every important subcommittee. In 1963, the five subcommittees whose majority members were substantially more conservative than the Democratic members of the full committee and Democratic members of the House handled 76.6 percent of the Federal budget.[17]

The committee is regarded as something of a law unto itself, even within the House. It guards all its prerogatives jealously. It resists attempts by the Senate to originate appropriations bills. It opposes a joint committee on the budget, a system that has worked out efficiently in the realm of taxation, especially from the standpoint of fiscal conservatives, as appropriations members usually are. It attacks all legislation that provides for the financing of government programs through Treasury loans or revolving funds, thus escaping the toils of the budgetary process.

The committee is universally regarded as hard-working, even by the most craftsmanlike House standards. Subcommittee hearings are famous for their detailed, lengthy, sometimes harsh, scrutiny of budget items.

> Hearings on a routine major bill may run for six weeks of nearly daily sessions. Swelled on the one hand by matter prepared in advance (like the justifications) and by information worked up later at the request of

---

Passman from slashing the foreign-aid bill of that year. His chief ally was Vaughn Gary. Then, in early 1964, Mahon packed Passman's subcommittee with friends of foreign aid— or enemies of Passman. Over the years since then foreign aid has become less popular despite the crimp this put in Passman's style. See Elizabeth Brenner Drew, "Mr. Passman Meets His Match," *The Reporter* (November 19, 1964), pp. 40–43.

[17] A neat demonstration of this point is contained in Paul D. O'Brien, "Party Leadership and the Committee Selection Process in the House of Representatives," unpublished B.A. thesis, Honors College, Wesleyan University, Middletown, Connecticut (June, 1964), pp. 61–66.

committee members during the hearings (usually inserted at the point where the question appears), the printed hearings have become monumental.[18]

With the possible exceptions of the traditionally generous subcommittees in charge of defense and health-research budgets, each of the subcommittees is united in a common task—

> . . . to guard the Federal Treasury. Committee members state their goals in the essentially negative terms of guardianship—screening requests for money, checking against ill-advised expenditures, and protecting the taxpayer's dollar. In the language of the committee's official history, the job of each member is "Constantly and courageously to protect the Federal Treasury against thousands of appeals and imperative demands for unnecessary, unwise and excessive expenditure."[19]

Agency heads from the executive departments appear at subcommittee hearings and, just as they have done "downtown," defend their budgetary requests. The arduousness of this experience can be suggested by a few excerpts from the transcripts of hearings:

> *Congressman:* I find a gentleman here, an FSO-6. He got an A in Chinese and you assigned him to London.
> *State Department Official:* Yes, sir. That officer will have opportunities in London—not as many as he would have in Hong Kong, for example—
> *Congressman:* What will he do? Spend his time in Chinatown?
> *Official:* No, sir. There will be opportunities in dealing with officers in the British Foreign Office who are concerned with Far Eastern Affairs. The British have foreign language specialists as well as we do.
> *Congressman:* So instead of speaking English to one another, they will sit in the London office and talk Chinese?
> *Official:* Yes, sir.
> *Congressman:* Is that not fantastic?
> *Official:* No, sir. They are anxious to keep up their practice.
> *Congressman:* Are they playing games or is this serious business?
> *Official:* This is serious business.
> *Congressman:* Can you describe how this would happen? This officer, who is an FSO-6, probably would not be on too important a mission to the British Foreign Office, would he?
> *Official:* That is correct.
> *Congressman:* But he has a counterpart in the British Foreign Office

[18] Arthur W. Macmahon, "Congressional Oversight of Administration: The Power of the Purse," *Political Science Quarterly*, vol. 58 (July, September, 1943), reprinted in R. L. Peabody and N. W. Polsby (eds.), *New Perspectives on the House of Representatives* (Chicago: Rand McNally, 1963), p. 351.

[19] Richard F. Fenno, Jr., "The House Appropriations Committee as a Political System," *American Political Science Review*, vol. 50 (June, 1962), pp. 310—324, reprinted in *ibid.*, p. 82.

who also is studying Chinese and they sit down and they talk Chinese together; is that right?
Official: Yes.
Congressman: They go out to Chinese restaurants and have chop suey together?
Official: Yes, sir.
Congressman: And that is all at the expense of the American taxpayer?

Congressman: I wrote you gentlemen . . . a polite letter about it thinking that maybe you would [circulate Savannah, Ga. weather reports to Northern cities] . . . and no action was taken on it. Now Savannah may be unimportant to the Weather Bureau but it is important to me. . . .
Weather Bureau Official: I can almost commit ourselves to seeing to it that the Savannah weather report gets distribution in the northeastern United States.

Congressman: Can you give us a few recent results of your research?
Bureau of Mines Official: [Reads a prepared statement]
Congressman: . . . that is something that you are going to undertake, is it not?
Official: It is something that is underway.
Congressman: But there are no results. . . .
Official: That is correct. There have been no immediate results by industry at the present time but as the program proceeds, new findings are made continually which will lead to further research on the subject.
Congressman: . . . Were there any results . . .?

Congressman: I note you have 60 people handling 268 loans; that represents about 4½ loans per person. Are they not a little overworked . . .?
Housing and Home Finance Official: . . . This . . . is . . . the most difficult program . . . with which I ever had any experience. . . .

The appropriations subcommittees exercise to the full their prerogative of examining the justifications for Federal programs. This may mean making requests for specific services to constituents and looking into work loads—both of which are checks into the ongoing performance of executive bureaucrats. But there are severe limits on the time of subcommittee members and staff. They cannot hope to inquire into every aspect of executive performance. They cut corners by asking about items they may know something about or by trying to find things that look "fishy" or by concentrating on deviations in requests or performance from prior years.

The powers of the subcommittees extend further. As the "saucers that cool the legislative tea," in the colorful phrase of a subcommittee chairman,[20] these subcommittees may effectively nullify the expressed will of Congress by refusing to appropriate money authorized by law. On the other hand, they

---

[20] This colorful phrase has been around quite a while. George Washington used it to refer to the Senate as contrasted with the House.

may not appropriate where there is no authorization; to do so would be legislating in an appropriations measure an act that can be blocked on the House floor by a simple point of order. On such occasions the offending section is removed on the floor. But when the committee wants blanket protection against points of order, they go to the Rules Committee for a special order waiving points of order against it.

Hearings are followed by mark-up sessions, as in the case of authorization bills. Here, however, the thirteen subcommittees do the real work. Each of these subcommittees, once it is put together with the blessing of the chairman, is quite independent. "One sub-committeeman chairman exclaimed: 'Why, you'd be branded an imposter if you went into one of those other subcommittee meetings. . . . Each one does its work apart from all others.' "[21] The subcommittees do their work free of partisan discord. "Since they deal immediately with dollars and cents, it is easy for the members to hold to the idea that they are not dealing with programmatic questions, that theirs is a 'business' rather than a 'policy' committee."[22]

When all the bargains are finally struck in the subcommittee, the bill is presented to the full committee for ratification, not for change. "It's a matter of 'you respect my work and I'll respect yours.' 'It's frowned upon if you offer an amendment in the full Committee if you aren't on the subcommittee.' 'It's considered presumptuous to pose as an expert if you aren't on the subcommittee. . . .' Members agree that sub-committee recommendations are 'very rarely changed.' "[23] Two observers of the Eighty-eighth Congress have given an excellent picture of how full committee compliance is assured:

> Most sessions of the 50-member Committee are as ritualistic and meaningless as a gathering of the Supreme Soviet in Moscow. A subcommittee's report on a bill isn't even seen by the full Committee until members file into the meeting room. Before they have a chance to glance at the report Cannon gavels the bill through. The entire process takes about five minutes.
>
> This system makes it impossible for a Committee member to influence the contents of a spending bill unless he happens to be a member of the sub-committee involved—with one little exception. The exception is Clarence Cannon himself, who wanders in and out of all subcommittee meetings, making a suggestion here and influencing a decision there. He and only he is familiar with the full scope of the Committee's work.[24]

A junior member of the committee said, "When the main committee meets, the sub-committee report is on your desk. You've never seen it before. You know how thick it is? This thick! [about two inches.] Well, you thumb through

---

[21] Fenno, in Peabody and Polsby (eds.), *op. cit.*, p. 90.
[22] *Ibid.*, p. 84.
[23] *Ibid.*, p. 94.
[24] Rowland Evans and Robert Novak, "Inside Report: King Clarence," *Washington Post* (June 5, 1963).

it, and meanwhile Cannon asks if there are any questions. You can't even ask an intelligent question."[25]

Just as the subcommittees are rarely challenged in full committee, the full Appropriations Committee is seldom reversed on the floor. When an appropriations bill is ready to be reported, the chairman arranges for time on the floor directly with the Speaker and Majority Leader. His committee has privileged access to the floor without recourse to the Rules Committee.[26] The Appropriations Committee rarely releases its reports before the day on which debate is to be held. As a result, few congressmen are inclined to challenge the committee's united front on the floor. Almost always the committee gets its way. A tabulation of the appropriations histories of thirty-six bureaus dealing with domestic policies for sixteen years (1947–1962) showed that the House deviated from committee recommendations only 10.1 percent of the time. The rest of the time, Appropriations Committee recommendations prevailed to the last dollar.[27]

When appropriations bills reach the Senate, they have been thoroughly worked over. Senatorial scrutiny is much less detailed and generally much more sympathetic to the agencies. In appropriations, the Senate regards itself as an appeals body. Agencies are expected to complain in hearings about those aspects of the House bill that seem likely to do them the most damage. The Senate often restores these cuts.[28]

In part, the Senate Appropriations Committee is more liberal than its counterpart in the House because of its position as legislatively second in line and because of the way the House Appropriations Committee defines *its* role. But there are other reasons as well. In the House, appropriations is an exclusive committee, occupying all of a legislator's time, absorbing all his committee loyalties. Not so in the Senate. Appropriations Committee members all serve elsewhere. Subcommittees are manned predominantly by senators who are members of the substantive Senate committees that passed the bills enacting the programs whose appropriations are before them. Where this is not the case, senators from the appropriate legislative committees are invited to sit in. Thus, in the House, money bills are seen primarily in the context of assaults on the treasury; in the Senate, they are seen as financial extensions of programs, as expressions of legitimate social and political demands.[29]

[25] Author's interview, July 16, 1963. The congressman exaggerated somewhat. Subcommittee reports average perhaps one-half inch in thickness.

[26] The Ways and Means Committee also has privileged access on tax bills, but they always go through the Rules Committee anyway in order to obtain a special order barring amendments on the floor.

[27] Fenno, *The Power of the Purse, op. cit.*, p. 450.

[28] Ralph K. Huitt, "Congressional Organization and Operations in the Field of Money and Credit," *Fiscal and Debt Management Policies* (Englewood Cliffs, N.J.: Prentice-Hall, 1963), pp. 433–434, summarizes evidence on this point. See also Robert Ash Wallace, *Congressional Control of Federal Spending* (Detroit, Mich.: Wayne State University Press, 1960), pp. 27–28, and Fenno, *The Power of the Purse, op. cit.*

[29] In addition, subcommittee vacancies in the Senate are filled according to seniority—a process that tends to allocate senators according to their programmatic interests. In the House committee, subcommittee rosters are made up by the chairman (for the majority) and, usually, the ranking minority member (for the minority). This tends to allocate House members according to the programmatic interests of the chairman and his minority-party counterpart.

The mechanics of the conference process are the same for appropriations bills as for other bills. When House and Senate bills are not identical, representatives of both sides meet and hammer out a compromise. The result then goes directly to each house for a final vote, without amendment.[30] Because appropriations are necessary for the very running of the government, the likelihood that such bills will be rejected by the House or Senate at the last stage or vetoed by the President is remote. This places an extra measure of responsibility and power on members of appropriations conferences.

Occasionally—and increasingly of late—this process is not complete by the beginning of the fiscal year in July. When a bill is not ready, the Appropriations Committees report continuing resolutions, which provide for financing of government activities month-by-month on the same basis as the preceding year. There is also a procedure by which agencies can request appro-

---

[30] The only live option other than passing an appropriations bill is to send it back to the conference committee. If it is defeated, it means that the Federal agencies affected have to go out of business, and this is likely to inconvenience a substantial number of constituents.

Table 10   The Extent to Which Federal Budgets Predict Actual Federal Expenditures, 1953–1963 (in Billions of Dollars)

| | | | | | Source of Error | |
Year	Federal Budget	Predicted Surplus (Deficit)	Actually Spent	Actual Surplus (Deficit)	Over (Under) Spending	Over (Under) Estimate of Receipts
1953	84.6	(14.4)	74.1	(9.4)	(10.5)	5.4
1954	77.6	(9.9)	67.5	(3.1)	(10.1)	3.4
1955	65.4	(2.9)	64.4	(4.2)	(1.0)	2.2
1956	62.1	(2.4)	66.2	1.6	4.1	(8.1)
1957	64.6	0.4	69.0	1.6	4.4	(5.6)
1958	71.2	1.8	71.4	(2.8)	0.2	(4.4)
1959	73.6	0.5	80.3	(12.4)	6.7	(6.2)
1960	76.3	0.1	76.5	1.2	—	1.3
1961	79.1	4.2	81.5	(3.9)	2.4	(5.7)
1962	80.9	1.5	87.8	(6.4)	6.9	(1.0)
1963	92.5	0.5	92.6	(6.2)	0.1	(6.6)
1964	98.8	(11.9)	97.7	(8.3)	(1.1)	(2.5)
1965	97.9	(4.9)	96.5	(3.4)	(1.4)	(0.1)
1966	99.7	(5.3)	130.9[a]	(3.8)[a]	34.9[a]	(36.3)[a]
1967	153.6	(3.8)	158.4	(8.8)	4.8	(0.2)
1968	169.2	(2.1)	178.9	(25.2)	9.7	(13.4)

Sources: *Congressional Quarterly Weekly Report*, vol. 22 (January 17, 1964), p. 109, and *Congressional Quarterly Almanac* (annually since 1964). The figures for "sources of error" are arrived at in the following way. Over (under) spending is the difference between the Federal budget and the actually spent columns. Over (under) estimate of receipts is the budget plus the predicted surplus (or minus the predicted deficit) minus the sum of the actually spent and actual surplus (deficit) columns.
    [a] In 1967, the BOB abandoned the "administrative budget," which portrays a smaller portion of Federal spending, and began calculating on the basis of "national income accounts," which include transactions in the large Federal trust funds.

priations to supplement their annual allotment. This process is essentially the same as I have already outlined, only it proceeds at a somewhat faster pace and as the result of a special request not included in the budget. Presidents can submit balanced budgets to Congress and then unbalance them by making heavy use of supplemental requests. Having what looks like a balanced budget at the start of the budgeting cycle is a useful propaganda device. The government frequently spends more than the budget asks for, however. There are, as well, some reallocations among programs as the result of the budgetary process. And often, receipts are less than predicted. Table 10 gives the figures for a recent sixteen-year period.

SUMMARY: THE POLITICS OF BUDGET-MAKING

The budgetary process comes close to being the ideal illustration of the maxim that power in the American political system is dispersed and shared among a large number of participants with widely varying obligations, constituencies, and policy preferences. It also shows how political leaders sample selectively among numerous opportunities to make decisions.

Budget-making is often admired on the presidential side because of what is regarded as excellent presidential coordination of budget policy; at the same time, the alleged fragmentation of the congressional appropriations process is often roundly criticized. In fact, the contrasts between the ways in which Congress and the President handle budgetary policy are not as compelling as the similarities between the two branches. Neither Congress nor the President considers all programs in relation to all other programs. Both, in practice, take account of expected revenues in deciding how much to spend. Disagreements between congressional appropriations and presidential requests do not reflect "more adequate" presidential information, but rather differing responses to the demands of various groups in society for Federal programs, differing evaluations of the same sorts of information, and differing preferences about what sorts of public policy are desirable.

If there are real differences in the policies preferred by congressmen and Presidents, there are also real similarities in the processes by which they arrive at their decisions. Both executive and legislative policy-makers accept the major outlines of the budget from year to year. In making their contributions to the marginal adjustments of budget allocations, both Congress and the President take account of (1) What agencies received last year. Deviations from former allocations draw attention. It is, practically speaking, rarely possible to ask an agency to justify *all* its activities in detail. But they can be asked to explain why they want more or less than what they have previously succeeded in justifying and receiving. (2) World developments. When Sputnik went up, so did the budget for the National Aeronautics and Space Administration. When war broke out in Korea, this fact was rapidly reflected in the Defense Department's budget. (3) Agency reputations for accurate estimating, hard work, "integrity." Just as some agencies are "glamorous" and reap the rewards of headline attention and others are dull and prosaic in the image they project, so also on a more professional level some agencies make better reputations than others and gain and suffer accordingly. Agencies may develop different relationships with their OMB examiners and their appropriations subcommittee, but in both cases, the criterion comes into play in decision-making. (4) Prior programmatic commitments. It is rare that a well-established program will be crippled in the appropriations process. (5) Interest-group demands. Some interest groups have better access to Republicans, some to Democrats, some to Congress, some to the President, some direct to agencies; and so their demands are likely to be met selectively in the different arenas.

CONFLICT
AND
COOPERATION

Conflict and cooperation between Congress and the President are not merely the result of whim or wilfulness at one end or the other of Pennsylvania Avenue. There are institutional reasons that make it difficult for Congress and the President to see eye to eye, and there are characteristic practices and tactics that help on some occasions to overcome these differences. It is difficult to deal with the question of conflict between these two institutions dispassionately, for an enormous volume of rhetoric favoring one side or the other has accumulated in both the popular press and the writings of political scientists. Much of this rhetoric revolves around the legitimacy of disagreement between Congress and the President; there is not much question over the fact of disagreement. But it may be useful nonetheless for us to begin with that fact. From there I propose to discuss possible sources of disagreement, or reasons for disagreement, between Congress and the President. Then, briefly, I will take up the methods and instruments by which disagreement is expressed and move to a discussion of the legitimacy of conflict between the two branches of government. The chapter ends with a discussion of cooperation between Congress and the President.

DIMENSIONS OF CONFLICT

Disagreement between Congress and the President is generally measured in two ways. The platform of the party winning the Presidency normally contains a great number of policy proposals. If, as usually happens, the same party wins a majority in Congress, the gap between presidential platforms and legislative output is often held to reflect the extent of disagreement between the President and Congress. This gap is normally very wide. As a matter of fact, it is not unusual for the presidential platforms of *both* political parties to be in substantial agreement on a wide range of issues, yet the policies they recommend are not enacted by Congress. How can this be so?

A presidential platform is an unusual document. It is written at the national party convention, and its avowed purpose is to appeal to voters and groups of voters who will be electing a President. Platforms must be appealing—they need not be terribly practical. They need not promise only those policies that are likely to be enacted. They need not mention any of the costs of what they propose, only the benefits. They need not reflect the actual relative strength of demands made on the political system once the election is over. They need not even reflect the priorities of the man who is elected President. And they are certainly not intended to reflect the goals or priorities of all the persons who are elected to Congress. Given all these peculiarities of party platforms, it is easy to see why they do not anticipate legislation more closely. They are written by the presidential wing of the party as an appeal—not to Congress or even to the congressional wing of the President's party, but to voters.

A more sophisticated measure of disagreement between Congress and the President can be achieved by turning to those appeals that the President makes directly to Congress and seeing which proposals, or how many of them, are enacted. The newspapers and magazines keep a running box score while Congress is in session, and much of the comment that flows from Washington revolves around the state of this box score. Presidential "triumphs" occur when a bill is enacted. Congressional "obstruction" occurs when a policy that the President has asked for is held up at one point or another in the legislative process. When a bill is "watered down," as congressmen seek a formula that can command the successive majorities that must be mobilized in Congress, it is not clear who wins in the box score.

These box scores are, to be sure, somewhat arbitrary in that they reflect somebody's judgment on which measures are to be included and which excluded. On the whole, box scores appearing in the popular press are somewhat unrealistic in that they are usually weighted heavily toward presidential priorities and newly proposed legislation. Renewals of old programs, although they may occupy much congressional time and effort, rarely appear in the accounts, nor does noncontroversial legislation. Box scores are, in other words, designed less to monitor congressional output than to keep tabs on presidential success in moving a program through Congress. In general, between one-third and two-thirds of presidential proposals are enacted in some recognizable form by Congress, with the median for the last 17 years lying below the 50 percent mark, as Table 11 shows.

Many of the controversial items that fail repeatedly of enactment cast the President in a conventionally "liberal" and Congress in a "conservative" role. The President wishes to expand the role of the Federal government in protecting the civil rights of Negroes; congressional objections refer to states' rights and property rights. The President asks for medical care for the aged under Social Security; congressional objections call forth the spectre of socialized medicine. The President seeks expanded Federal aid to education;

Table 11   Disagreement between President and Congress

Year	President	Presidential Proposals Submitted	Approved by Congress	Approval Score
1954	Eisenhower (R)	232	150	64.7%
1955		207	96	46.3
1956		225	103	45.7
1957		206	76	36.9
1958		234	110	47.0
1959		228	93	40.8
1960		183	56	30.6
1961	Kennedy (D)	355	172	48.4
1962		298	132	44.3
1963	Kennedy/Johnson (D)	401	109	27.2
1964	Johnson	217	125	57.6
1965		469	323	68.9
1966		371	207	55.8
1967		431	205	47.6
1968		414	231	55.8
1969	Nixon (R)	171	55	32.2

Sources: *Congressional Quarterly Weekly Report* (January 24, 1964), p. 181 and (January 12, 1968), p. 43; *Congressional Quarterly Almanac* (1965), p. 97; *Congressional Quarterly Almanac* (1968), p. 97; *Congressional Quarterly Almanac* (1969), p. 115.

Congress worries the question of states' rights in the face of the possible imposition of Federal requirements, desegregation of school systems, and aid to parochial schools. The President attempts to mount a "war on Poverty"; congressmen claim beneficiaries of the program have police records.

These conflicts have reality not merely because principled and dedicated men stand on both sides of each issue. They also reflect differences between Congress and the Presidency as institutions. These issues, and many others like them—foreign aid, reciprocal trade, and tax reform are three other examples—customarily divide Presidents and significant segments of Congress along liberal and conservative lines. This is easiest to see when the President is Democratic and especially sensitive to the most probable winning presidential coalition, which is predominantly liberal, activist, and urban in its orientation. This coalition may be contrasted with typical winning coalitions in Congress, which depend so heavily on seniority and expertise. There are clear advantages in this system for congressmen and senators from one-party states with small electorates. The attention of these men is not so constantly diverted from legislative business; their ties back home are easier to maintain, and their chances of falling by the wayside in massive party turnovers are, of course, much less than those of their brethren from competitive two-party areas. And so they rise to positions of power in the all-important committee system of Congress.

In sparsely populated and one-party areas, the interests that dominate—for example, tobacco, textiles, and segregation in the South—are quite different from those that dominate in urban, two-party areas, which consist of such groups as laborers employed in manufacturing and racial and ethnic minorities.[1] Thus the germ of conflict over policy is contained in the very rules by which congressmen, senators, and Presidents are elected and sustained in office.

When the President is Republican and both houses of Congress are controlled by Democrats, it is much harder to generalize about their respective policy positions. The basic winning coalition in national politics is still unquestionably liberal, but a Republican President, even one elected with only a minority of the vote, may nevertheless feel tempted by a "Southern strategy." He may hedge, let us say, on the enforcement of school desegregation while, on the other hand, sponsoring a liberal program of payments to replace the unsuccessful welfare system currently in use. Likewise, congressmen, especially senators, may find themselves very pleasantly in the limelight as they mount attacks on mediocre (and conservative) Supreme Court appointments, press for the end of an unpopular war, or fight for more aid to education.

INSTITUTIONAL SOURCES OF CONFLICT

Even in those unusual times when the probability of building liberal and conservative coalitions is evenly divided between Congress and the President, *institutional* factors facilitate conflict between the two branches. These factors may drive a wedge even between a President and those men in Congress who were elected as supporters of presidential programs from constituencies like the President's own.

Perhaps the most fundamental of these institutional sources of conflict can be described as a difference in the time perspectives of members of the two branches. Consider the "efficient minority" of congressmen—both liberals and conservatives—who regard Congress as their vocation and who have risen in the hierarchies of the House or Senate sufficiently to have a noticeable impact on legislative outcomes. The unit of time to which a member of this group is most attentive in gauging the consequences of his behavior is the career. Normally, he will think of his career as open-ended and having no fixed terminal point. The questions he must continually pose to himself are: How will my behavior today affect my standing in this house tomorrow, the

---

[1] It is nevertheless true that there are a substantial number of one-party congressional districts from urban areas. One of the problems of contemporary congressional research is to determine why—as is apparently the case—big-city congressmen are by and large less effective than Southern congressmen. One possible answer might be that big-city machines tend to send people to Congress who are, on the average, older and thus much less likely to be able to build up seniority. See Leo M. Snowiss, "Congressional Recruitment and Representation," *American Political Science Review*, vol. 60 (September, 1966), pp. 627–639. Raymond E. Wolfinger and Joan Heifetz argue that the dominance of the South in Congress may be less a pervasive social pattern than a historically bounded phenomenon that is rapidly passing from the scene as more and more one-party areas are established in the North. See Wolfinger and Heifetz, "Safe Seats, Seniority, and Power in Congress," *American Political Science Review*, vol. 59 (June, 1965), pp. 337–349.

next day, and in years to come? How may I act so as to enhance my esteem in the eyes of my colleagues? How may I lay up the treasures of obligation and friendship against my day of need? Or, if he is oriented to public policy, how may I enhance the future chances of policies *I* favor?

In contrast, the President and his agents must focus on the presidential term of office as the unit of time most relevant to them. Eight years is the very most they have in which to do what they want to do. Subtract one year as a lame-duck period. Discount the period of time just before and just after elections—especially the critical period just prior to the decision whether there is to be a second term or not. And, finally, subtract whatever time has elapsed already. How much time remains? Not very much, and yet there are so many programs that they may want to advocate, so many policies they desire to put into practice.

The conflict that arises from the difference in time perspectives even between responsible, loyal, and decent members of the two branches is this: The President is intent on the problem of the moment, which is to pass high-priority items in his program. He asks his congressional allies to spend power in behalf of this goal. The congressman, who has to worry about the possibility of a future transfer to a desirable committee or a private bill that he thinks may mean political life or death at some future time, is naturally inclined to hoard power or to invest it so as to increase his future stock of resources. Meanwhile, the President's opponents in Congress are not so constrained. If they are of the opposition party, they may content themselves with simple party regularity. If they are of the President's party, they need only refrain from bestirring themselves. Or if they fight, they can fight in behalf of their own preferences or those of their district—but not necessarily those of the President.

A second institutional dilemma that strains presidential-congressional relations is the age-old strategic question—"Help thy friends or woo thine enemies?" No matter which horn of the dilemma the President chooses to confront, the other is bound to cause him grief. Dean Acheson gave a famous example.

> Dealing with the two senior foreign relations Senators took a good deal of time. . . . The simple thing would have been to talk with them together; but simplicity would have been, if not disastrous, at least hazardous. Connally loved to heckle Vandenberg. Vandenberg when aroused could respond in a way calculated to move Connally another notch toward disagreement for its own sake. So the procedure was first to see them separately, to get each so far committed that only the sheerest wilfulness could undo it. But which to see first? Here was a tricky decision. Both were fairly good about not leaking the content of our talk to the press. But each found it hard to resist leaking the fact of a private talk. Once this was done, the second to be seen knew that he was the second. With Connally, this was instant cause for offense. We were members of the same party; he was loyal and proved; yet I turned to his rival first—if, indeed, I had done so. It was to him a poor ex-

planation that Vandenberg was the Chairman of the committee, in the years in which he was.[2]

Here is an instance from the Kennedy administration.

> Some of the Executive's relations with Congress have not helped the aid program. For example, its chief ball carrier in Passman's House Appropriations sub-committee, the major fortress of aid opponents, is Representative Silvio O. Conte, a three-term liberal Republican from Massachusetts. Yet Conte is rarely consulted on strategy and on occasion has been snubbed by thoughtless underlings in AID. When the University of Massachusetts, located in Conte's district, received a $178,-000 AID contract for a farm training project in Nyasaland last February, Conte read about it in his home-town newspaper in the form of a joint "announcement" by the state's Senior Senator, Republican Leverett Saltonstall, and the newly-arrived Senator Edward M. Kennedy. Five days later Conte's office received a routine press release containing the same information.[3]

Immediately upon taking office, President Nixon was faced with similar problems. The standard-bearer of the minority party in this country, elected with only 43.4 percent of the popular vote, it was clearly desirable for Nixon to broaden the base of his support as he put together his administration. The complaints were not long in coming.

> To hear some Republicans tell it, Democrats were the only guys getting jobs in this Republican administration. Senator Robert Dole of Kansas, only half jokingly, has been urging fellow GOP lawmakers to include this line in their letters of recommendation: "Even though Zilch is a Republican, he's highly qualified for the job."
> According to Mr. Flemming [of the White House] the complaint isn't grounded in fact, since Democrats have received only about 8% of the jobs. Yet the Democrats still control Congress, so Mr. Nixon must give them some patronage in hope of winning support for his legislative program. "You can't just go around with a meat ax when you have to work with them," Senator Bellmon remarks. . . .
> Not everyone is happy. Senator Dole laments his inability to place a single Kansan in the Administration so far. "There must be a spot for one between now and 1976," he says. "A janitor maybe?"[4]

---

[2] Dean Acheson, *Sketches from Life of Men I Have Known* (New York: Harper & Row, 1961), pp. 144–145.

[3] Paul Duke, "The Foreign Aid Fiasco," *The Reporter* (January 16, 1964), p. 22.

[4] John Pierson, "Nixon Talent Hunt: Off to a Good Finish," *The Wall Street Journal* (May 9, 1969). Other newspaper accounts of the early tribulations of the Nixon administration in the same vein include Marjorie Hunter, "Dirksen Holds Up Rights Appointment," *The New York Times* (May 2, 1969), and Warren Unna, "Postal Rate Increase Is Jeopardized by Congressional Anger at Blount," *The Washington Post* (May 17, 1969).

Presumably the ideal way to handle the problem is for the President to keep both his friends and his enemies happy. But then the question is bound to arise whether the President's friends are being sufficiently differentiated from his enemies. What profit accrues to a congressman who regularly sticks his neck out for the administration if congressmen who do not are amply rewarded, just as he is? In practice, limits on the time and other resources available to the President and his aides set boundaries on the extent to which *either* activity is pursued. Mistakes are bound to occur.

A third institutional factor encumbering presidential-congressional relations concerns the gains and costs of uncertainty to both. Congressmen and senators often find it useful to refrain from committing themselves on legislation in order to bargain with interest groups and within the House or Senate or perhaps simply in order to avoid potentially dangerous controversy. The President, on the other hand, has a stake in knowing the lay of the land as early as possible so he can see what he needs to do to win. And so the conflict between secrecy and disclosure can be added to the ones already mentioned.

Relations between the President's men and the men of Congress have seldom been easy. One recalls widespread congressional resentment, in former administrations, of Harry Hopkins, Dean Acheson, and Sherman Adams. One way for people in the White House to avoid problems with congressmen is to ask far less of them in the way of performance, and clearly some Presidents have taken this tack. But this course of action—or rather inaction— hazards the displeasure of the President's natural allies among interest groups. If carried to an extreme, it may even jeopardize the President's control of his own administration and his own or his party's chances of retaining the Presidency itself.

INSTRUMENTS OF CONFLICT

The means that Congress and the President have available with which they can express disagreements and induce cooperation—in short, their weapons in the intramural political struggles of Washington politics—are probably well enough known to demand only a brief recapitulation.

The President can veto legislation desired by congressmen. He can prevent the spending of funds appropriated by Congress for purposes he does not approve. And he has an enormous range of discretion over the activities of the executive branch. This includes his power of appointment, a power which reaches into every state and locality, embracing postmasterships, United States attorneys, Federal judges, and collectors of ports. Other appointments made mostly at presidential discretion include those to the Supreme Court, to independent regulatory commissions, to top managerial posts in the various departments and agencies of the government, and to honorific boards and commissions—some of them *ad hoc*, such as the Presidential Commission on Intergovernmental Relations, and some more permanent, such as the Fine Arts Commission, which advises on the design of public buildings in Washington, D.C.

A President can create good will and forge alliances by prudent use of his appointment powers. He has the obligation, in order to protect his own political position, to find appointees who are competent and also politically acceptable. Normally, these matters proceed on a state-by-state basis; some attempt is made to strengthen the hand of the party and distribute rewards in states where the party leaders are allies of the President.

Sometimes "clearance" with state party leaders is quite formal and elaborate, sometimes not. Minor appointments have been delegated to the congressman from the district involved, if he is of the President's party. This congressional patronage helps to build a bridge between the President and his party's members in Congress. In like manner, senators of the President's party clear the Federal judgeships and most of the other important Federal appointments made to citizens of their respective states.

When senatorial confirmation is required by law, as it is in the case of the more important appointments, senators employ a cooperative device to ensure clearance. This is senatorial "courtesy," so called. When a senator from the President's own party announces that a nominee to high office from his state is personally obnoxious or embarrassing to him, the Senate customarily refuses to confirm. This is a powerful weapon but is used sparingly; senators prefer to encourage consultation by less visible means, by arranging for delays in the confirmation process while appropriate apologies or even more concrete tokens of contrition are proffered them by minions of the executive branch.

Presidential discretion does not end with the appointment process. All the manifold programs of the government have differential impacts on the various geographic areas of the nation, and so it is possible to reward and punish congressional friends and foes quite vigorously. Small Business Administration and Area Redevelopment Administration loans to certain areas may get more and more diffcult to obtain, as applications fail to "qualify." Pilot programs and demonstration projects may be funneled here rather than there. Defense contracts and public works may be accelerated in some areas, retarded in others. Administrative decisions to open offices or consolidate operations of various Federal agencies may be made. All these activities are indispensable to the running of any large administrative apparatus, and it may be a matter of indifference administratively whether an installation is opened in Dallas or Houston, whether a regional headquarters is in Portland or Seattle. But these administrative decisions have great political impact, because they affect the prosperity of the areas where they are put into effect and they are often of acute concern to local political leaders. And so they can become weapons in the hands of a politically astute President.

The sheer high status of the Presidency is of course a formidable weapon. Only the crustiest and most independent congressmen and senators fail to warm to considerate personal treatment by a President of the United States. A private breakfast, a walk in the White House rose garden, an intimate conference—all duly and widely reported in the press—give a man a sense of importance that not only may flatter his ego but also may remind him of his responsibilities as a national legislator, as a trustee of the common weal. He may then moderate his opposition or stiffen his resolve to support the President. Of course this does not always work. President Eisenhower once tried the personal touch with the indefatigable and colorful Representative Otto Passman, chief opponent of foreign aid.

> In 1957, as the foreign aid bill was getting its final touches, President Eisenhower and his advisors decided to try an advance truce talk with Otto. They gave him the full treatment, and he recalls it with a nice touch of sadness, even today.
>
> "It was kind of embarrassing, you understand," he told me in his musical southern voice. "I refer to it as the Passman trial. They sent for me in a long black Cadillac, I guess the first time I had ever been in one. I felt real important, which is not my usual way of feeling. When I got to the President's study at the White House, all the big shots were there. Admiral Radford and Secretary Dulles and the leaders of Congress. We had tea and little cakes, and they sat me right across from the President. They went around the room, asking for comments, one minute each. When they got to me, I said I would need more than one minute, maybe six or seven minutes, to tell what was wrong with their program. . . ."
>
> Passman's lecture was complete with footnotes and fine print, figures down to the last thin dime, unobligated balances in the various foreign aid accounts, carry-over funds, re-obligated, de-obligated obligations, supplies in the pipe-line, uncommitted balances, and so on—in that mysterious verbal shorthand that only a man who lives and breathes foreign aid could comprehend. . . . After . . . everyone left, the President turned to his staff and said,
>
> "Remind me never to invite that fellow down here again."[5]

This example is not typical. Congressmen and senators generally find it hard to say no directly to the President of the United States, especially when he asks them nicely. But they may simply fail to do what he wants.

Another way of exploiting the prestige of the Presidency is the gambit of "going to the people." This process is usually described in a misleading way. What a President does when he goes to the people is try to focus the attention of the mass media and relevant interest groups on an issue. It is not really possible in the course of one or a few fireside chats to provoke a ground swell of opinion change that promises to rearrange the composition of Congress unless congressmen knuckle under. The ties that congressmen and senators have back home are typically multiple, strong, and of long standing. It is hard for a President to change all this while explaining the intricacies of a particular issue over television. He can, however, communicate his concern about the issue. He can increase its general visibility, stir up interest-group activity, and, to a certain extent, set the terms in which it will be debated.

Congressional weapons have already been covered to a substantial de-

[5] Rowland Evans, Jr., "Louisiana's Passman: The Scourge of Foreign Aid," *Harper's* (January, 1962), pp. 78–83.

gree. They include the power to delay and to fail to act, the power to cut appropriations and thus to curtail programs, the power to require the executive agencies to comply with stringent requirements, either by writing technical and specific laws or by legally requiring frequent reports and repeated authorizations.

Senatorial courtesy is a significant constraint on the presidential appointment power. Throughout the legislative labyrinth, different congressmen and senators are strategically placed to delay, modify, or defeat legislation and appropriations. There is also the power of impeachment, which has only been used once against a President (in 1868), but that once almost succeeded in deposing President Andrew Johnson. The power is now moribund, however. It is an extreme constitutional safeguard; its employment, or even its serious consideration, would signal a severe breakdown of the political system and its constraints on behavior, as we know it today.

One other weapon in the congressional arsenal deserves brief consideration—the power to investigate. This is a significant congressional activity, although one that has perhaps suffered from a surfeit of publicity. Investigations may move in many directions. Perhaps the most famous of these in recent years have been the Kefauver and McClellan investigations of crime and racketeering, various House Committee on Un-American Activities investigations of communism in the United States, and the Army-McCarthy hearings of 1954. Of these, only the last involved any sort of congressional scrutiny of the executive branch, and this was also an inquiry into the practices of a senator and a subcommittee of the Senate that was under his leadership.

The President and his Executive Office are immune from congressional investigation; the precedents for this stretch back to George Washington. But Congress may inquire minutely into the workings of the rest of the executive branch, may probe for conflict of interest, may seek to reconstruct the premises on which decisions were made, may ferret out interoffice disagreements and expose all to the glare of publicity. Sometimes the public ventilation of policy disagreement is the purpose of congressional investigations—as was true of hearings after the dismissal of General MacArthur during the Korean War and of hearings by the Senate Foreign Relations Committee during the Vietnam War in which the Secretary of State and other members of the executive branch were subjected to sharp interrogation. Insofar as the President needs the various departments and agencies of the executive branch to execute his policies, this power of Congress to investigate constrains him.[6]

So, finally, does the congressional power of post-audit. The General Accounting Office, an agency of Congress, continuously audits the expenditure of Federal funds after they are made to ascertain that they have been spent in accordance with law. This office may disallow expenditures and require restitution.[7]

[6] On investigations in general, see Telford Taylor, *Grand Inquest* (New York: Simon and Schuster, 1955).

[7] See Gerald G. Schulsinger, *The General Accounting Office: Two Glimpses* (University, Alabama: University of Alabama Press, 1956), ICP case 35.

THE LEGITIMACY OF CONFLICT

Let us now examine the legitimacy of conflict between Congress and the President. Curiously, the fact of conflict itself has a bad name with writers on political questions. In behalf of the President and his policies, Congress is charged with wilful parochialism, with neglect of national needs, with a variety of immoral, illegal, and undignified activities—all of which are indicative, it is often held, of an overriding need for general reform of the legislative branch. In the words of a few book titles, Congress is "on trial,"[8] a sink of "corruption and compromise,"[9] responsible for the "deadlock of democracy,"[10] a "sapless branch"[11] of government. It is "in crisis"[12] and has a "house out of order."[13] "Congress," says a title, "needs help."[14]

In behalf of Congress, it is urged that the country is, as is Congress, "essentially moderate." The President is trying to impose a tyranny of the majority. He wishes to go "too far, too fast." He cares not for the Constitution, for public order, for the American way. His actions verge on usurpation. Nobody, however, suggests in this connection that the Presidency be weakened as an institution; rather, it is urged that incumbents pull up their socks and act less like Presidents.[15]

In the light of our constitutional history, however, conflict between the two branches should come as no surprise. Indeed, the system was designed so that different branches would be captured by different interests and so that they would have to come to terms with one another peaceably in order to operate the system at all. This theory is explicitly stated in *The Federalist* (1788), which is the authoritative commentary on the Constitution by Founding Fathers:

> To what expedient, then, shall we finally resort, for maintaining in practice the necessary partition of power among the several departments, as laid down in the Constitution . . . ? [B]y so contriving the interior structure of the government as that its several constituent parts may, by their mutual relations, be the means of keeping each other in

[8] James M. Burns, *Congress on Trial* (New York: Harper & Row, 1949).

[9] H. H. Wilson, *Congress: Corruption and Compromise* (New York: Holt, 1951).

[10] James M. Burns, *The Deadlock of Democracy* (Englewood Cliffs, N.J.: Prentice-Hall, 1963).

[11] Joseph S. Clark, *Congress: The Sapless Branch* (New York: Harper & Row, 1964).

[12] Roger H. Davidson, David M. Kovenock, and Michael K. O'Leary, *Congress in Crisis* (Belmont, Calif.: Wadsworth, 1966).

[13] Richard Bolling, *House Out of Order* (New York: Dutton, 1965).

[14] Philip Donham and Robert J. Fahey, *Congress Needs Help* (New York: Random House, 1966). See also Harold Laski, *The American Presidency* (New York: Harper & Row, 1949); Drew Pearson and Jack Anderson, *The Case against Congress* (New York: Simon and Schuster, 1968).

[15] With varying degrees of emphasis, this point of view can be found in occasional newspaper columns of (among others) William S. White, David Lawrence, and Roscoe Drummond. See also Ernest S. Griffith, *Congress: Its Contemporary Role* (New York: New York University Press, 1961); James Burnham, *Congress and the American Tradition* (Chicago: Regnery, 1949).

their proper places. . . . In order to lay a due foundation for that separate and distinct exercise of the different powers of government, which
to a certain extent is admitted on all hands to be essential to the preser-
vation of liberty, it is evident that each department should have a will
of its own. . . . [T]he great security against a gradual concentration of
the several powers in the same department, consists in giving to those
who administer each department the necessary constitutional means and
personal motives to resist encroachments of the others. . . . Ambition
must be made to counteract ambition.[16]

Indeed, if the Constitution can be said to grant legitimacy to anything, surely
it legitimizes conflict between Congress and the President.

It is often argued, however, that majoritarian principles are violated by
one or another of the two great branches. A presidential veto may render
ineffectual congressional majorities in both houses. Or an administration bill
may be stalled somewhere in the toils of the legislative process by a small
minority. Aside from any general skepticism one may harbor that majority
rule is always a good thing, there is often in any particular case a problem in
identifying a relevant majority whose decisions are to be regarded as legitimate.

Different doctrines suggest different solutions. There is, for example, the
doctrine of *party responsibility.* According to this doctrine, the will of the
majority of the majority party within Congress, if it is the same as the President's party, should prevail. On the other hand, a doctrine of *congressional
responsibility* would hold that the will of the majority within Congress as a
whole should prevail.

As it happens, in present-day American politics, these two majorities
are generally at loggerheads.[17] The majority within Congress as a whole is
frequently composed of a coalition of Republicans and Southern Democrats.
Northern and Western Democrats, who make up a clear majority of the majority party, often cannot get a majority on the floor. As Clem Miller says:

What the correspondents need to do is to sit down with a stubby
pencil and do some simple addition and subtraction. What we will find
is that the combination of southern Democrats and northern Republicans can always squeak out a majority when they want to, and they want
to on a great number of significant issues. . . . Actually, the Democratic
party as nonsoutherners define it is a minority in the House.[18]

---

[16] *The Federalist,* 51. The authorship of this number has been disputed between Alexander Hamilton and James Madison. Madison is now regarded as the most likely author.
See Jacob Cooke's "Introduction" to *The Federalist* (Middletown, Conn.: Wesleyan University Press, 1961) and a recent ingenious attempt to resolve the issue by Frederick Mos-
teller and David L. Wallace, "Inference in an Authorship Problem," *Journal of The American Statistical Association,* vol. 58 (June, 1963), pp. 275–309.

[17] An exploration of this problem—along with several other issues—is contained in Will-
moore Kendall, "The Two Majorities," *Midwest Journal of Political Science,* vol. 4 (November, 1960), pp. 317–345.

[18] Clem Miller, *Member of the House,* in John W. Baker, ed. (New York: Scribner, 1962),
p. 123.

One way to resolve this dilemma would be to regard the relevant majority as existing in the electorate. Those for whom the majority of people vote, nationwide, should prevail. Now it is true that the President is elected on a nationwide basis and congressmen and senators individually are not, but congressmen and senators act in concert; collectively, they are elected on a national basis. At this point, the argument must become intricate. The legitimacy of the presidential majority may be impugned because the electoral college in effect nullifies the votes accruing to presidential candidates that lose states by narrow margins. Even when this does not actually deprive the winner of the popular vote of public office—as it did last in 1888—it can lead to the election of a President who receives less than a majority of all the popular votes. This in fact has happened at least thirteen times, most recently in 1968, when Richard Nixon received 43.4 percent of the votes, and Hubert Humphrey received 42.7 percent, the rest going to other candidates.

The legitimacy of the congressional majority can be questioned on at least two grounds. Malapportionment in the states, it can be argued, forbids the expression of true majority sentiment in electing congressmen and senators.[19] And after they are elected, various characteristics of decision-making processes in the respective houses make the expression of the will of the majority of even these truncated representatives difficult and on some occasions impossible.

All these charges, it should be said, are perfectly true. It appears that nobody enters into the arena of national policy-making with an absolutely clean and unsullied right to have his will prevail because he was elected by majority sentiment. Furthermore, who knows why men are elected to public office? Most people vote the way they do out of party habit, not because they endorse any particular set of campaign promises or projected policies. Typically, small minorities care about selected policies. But it is perfectly possible for a candidate to be elected by a majority that disagrees with *all* his policy preferences. It is also perfectly possible for a particular electorate to elect a President, a senator, and a congressman, none of whom agrees with either of the others to a significant extent about any public policies.[20] And so an attempt to justify particular policies advocated by congressmen or Presidents based solely on their supposed link to the electorate seems dubious.

What about reforms? Would it be possible to change a few features of the political system so that Congress and the President could at least claim

---

[19] Even so, 31,850,140 popular votes in 1968 were cast for Republican candidates for seats in the House of Representatives; only 31,004,304 popular votes were cast for Mr. Nixon. For the Democrats, the 1968 figures were 30,691,699 for Vice President Humphrey, 33,045,-283 for Democratic congressional candidates. The source of these figures is "Complete Returns of the 1968 Elections by Congressional District," *Congressional Quarterly Weekly Report*, 27 (June 6, 1969).

[20] The literature on these points is immense. See, in particular, Angus Campbell, Philip Converse, Warren Miller, and Donald Stokes, *The American Voter* (New York: Wiley, 1960); and V. O. Key, Jr., *Public Opinion and American Democracy* (New York: Knopf, 1961). In a later book, Key attempts to introduce a modification into this picture of the electorate, mainly by analyzing the small minority of voters who switch from one election to the next. See V. O. Key, Jr., *The Responsible Electorate* (Cambridge, Mass.: Belknap Press, Harvard University Press, 1966).

legitimacy for their actions, if not on the grounds that they expressed accurately the will of a majority, then on the grounds that they represented more closely the majority choice of their respective electorates? On the presidential side, this would entail at least scrapping the electoral college and substituting direct popular election. In some quarters the move would be popular. It would probably have the effect of loosening the hold that the current presidential coalition has on the office. Of course, the incentives to interest groups in the large, two-party states to give up their present access to the Presidency were not very great so long as they were at a severe disadvantage in the other parts of the system.[21]

But the reapportionment decisions were aimed at equalizing the influence of voters in the elections of all legislatures, state and Federal, save only the United States Senate. Meanwhile, owing to the third-party candidacy of George Wallace in fifty states in the 1968 election, Americans began to confront the possibility that in some future election no candidate would receive a majority in the electoral college, thus throwing the election into the House of Representatives; there, according to the constitutional requirement, each state, no matter how populous, is entitled to only one vote.[22] On election night in 1968, commentators horrified themselves with this specter and may well have produced a ground swell of interest in direct elections. Direct elections, however, may not solve all the difficulties complained of in the present system. The unit rule of the electoral college, by providing a winner-take-all procedure within each state, actually discourages splinter parties. Only those parties that are securely anchored in at least one section of the country have even the smallest hope of scoring in the electoral college. Under the present system, splinter parties may draw marginal support away from one party or another in closely contested states, but, in general, that is all they can do. Under direct-election rules, however, any number can run, so this system seems unlikely to do away with minority Presidents, if that is the contemplated end in view.

A second set of reforms looks toward changing Congress's internal decision-making procedures. In general, reform proposals seeking to bring congressional policy-making more closely into line with presidential preferences suggest procedures to bring measures to the floor easily and to weaken the grip of the committees on them. These proposals identify Congress as a great forum for debate.[23] It would be instructive to list all such proposals to see how many of them would cancel out in their effects. It is not certain, for example, that a joint committee on the budget would lead either to a com-

---

[21] This and other proposed reforms of the presidential party and electoral system are examined in Nelson W. Polsby and Aaron B. Wildavsky, *Presidential Elections* (New York: Scribner, 1968), Chap. 5. See also Alexander M. Bickel, *The New Age of Political Reform* (New York: Harper & Row, 1968).

[22] See Neil Peirce, *The Peoples' President* (New York: Simon and Schuster, 1968) for the parade of horrors.

[23] Examples of this style of argument may be found in Woodrow Wilson, *Congressional Government* (New York: Meridian, 1956; originally published 1885); in Holbert N. Carroll, *The House of Representatives and Foreign Affairs* (Pittsburgh, Pa.: University of Pittsburgh Press, 1958); and in many of the writings of George Galloway. See, for example, his *The Legislative Process in Congress* (New York: Crowell, 1953).

prehensive congressional overview or to a congressional appropriations process more sympathetic to presidential programs.[24]

The difficulties with suggestions of this kind are substantial. Insofar as congressmen weaken their committees, they weaken the one device they have to scrutinize the merits of legislative proposals. Committees encourage specialization and technical sophistication, even expertise. They are convenient agencies through which bridges can be built to the executive branch, making possible a flow of information so that Congress can act intelligently.

Typically, suggestions for congressional reform have their beginnings in modest dissatisfactions over the President's inability to persuade Congress to enact parts of his program. But like the comedian who begins by tugging at a stray thread and ends up unraveling his entire wardrobe, congressional reformers soon find themselves dismantling the entire political system in their mind's eye and suggesting instead a system modeled on the British government, where the legislature takes orders from the Cabinet, and the Cabinet from the Prime Minister. This vision of tidiness is, however, not well suited to a nation in which conflict is a legitimate feature of the day-to-day processes of governing, in which sectional traditions are strong, and in which a substantial variety and number of interest groups have learned to expect that one or another part of the government will always be accessible to them.

Actually, most specific proposals for reform would, if enacted, fall far short of provoking a constitutional crisis. They are not adopted primarily because they require the assent of leaders whose powers they would curb. Thus it seems highly improbable that a proposal in the Senate to make it a bit easier to close off filibusters would not itself be subjected to the filibuster. A resolution changing the rules of the House so as to clip the wings of the Rules Committee must be reported in the first instance by the Rules Committee. Proposals to curtail the powers of committee chairmen seem likely to be opposed by committee chairmen, with all the skills, rewards, and penalties they command. It may be that better government in some meaningful sense would emerge if many of the specific reforms that have been offered were adopted —but few of them are likely to be.

SOURCES OF COOPERATION

The extent of conflict between Congress and the Presidents is, in any event, easily overestimated. There are an impressive number of forces in the political system that encourage cooperation between the branches and that keep the conflict that does exist at a tolerable level. Certainly high on any list of such forces would be the effects of party membership.

Because American political parties are not highly organized, have no clear standards for membership, and are not highly ideological, it is easy to underestimate their claims on the loyalties of the faithful. But these claims are

[24] "Coordination" of revenue policies of the two houses through a Joint Committee on Internal Revenue Taxation has certainly not had this effect. See Ralph K. Huitt, "Congressional Organization and Operations in the Field of Money and Credit," in Commission on Money and Credit, *Fiscal and Debt Management Policies* (Englewood Cliffs, N.J.: Prentice-Hall, 1963), pp. 451–455.

important and especially so to men who hold office bearing the party label. Students of roll-call voting have repeatedly found that the best single predictor of the vote of a member of Congress is his party membership.[25] And because major portions of the congressional agenda are set by the President, it is clear that the party designation he shares with members of Congress is of enormous aid in promoting cooperation between the branches.

Party loyalty is, indeed, a very conscious part of congressional behavior. When congressmen speak—as they often do—of making a record to run on, they are referring as much to the winning of the Presidency or of Congress as a whole for their party as to the winning of their own seat. The party label and the party record are meaningful entities to them, and much of the sharpest kind of partisan conflict on Capitol Hill revolves not around the specific merits of legislation so much as around the question of credit. Members of the minority party must ask themselves whether they can afford to support programs that may help to perpetuate the administration in office. Thus party lines cut across the gulf between Congress and the Presidency.

To be sure, party loyalty is not so pervasive as to preclude opposition within segments of the President's own party in Congress to parts of the President's program. Sectional, local, and factional preferences, strongly held within the constituencies of congressmen, including those of the President's own party, place a constraint on the cooperation congressmen can give to a President. Sometimes the very political survival of the congressman, who is, after all, subject to renomination and reelection on the local level, demands that he break on one or more issues with a President of his own party. On the other hand, winning coalitions in Congress can often be forged from bipartisan components. This tends to mute the effects of partisanship; it forces bipartisan participation in the formulation of legislation, which enables members of both parties to claim credit for programs that are popular with the presidential coalition but controversial within Congress. Cross-party alliances thus damp down conflict in general within the political system. Political leaders never know when they will need a few extra votes from the other side of the aisle—and they can rarely be sure precisely who among the opposition will defect on a large number of unspecified future issues. And so it pays to fight fairly, to play only as roughly as they absolutely have to. This general rule applies to Presidents when dealing with opposition congressmen as well as to congressmen when dealing with opposition Presidents.

One congressman who understood this rule of the game particularly well was Joseph Martin, long-time Republican leader of the House. In his memoirs he spoke of his relations with Franklin Roosevelt.

> When he became President, I liked Roosevelt personally and admired —ruefully at times—his dynamic political skill. . . . Like myself, he was a practical politician. That is what politicians should be. During his years in office, we met often. . . . As members of the same trade, we under-

[25] See Julius Turner, *Party and Constituency: Pressures on Congress* (Baltimore: Johns Hopkins, 1951); David B. Truman, *The Congressional Party* (New York: Wiley, 1959); Lewis A. Froman, Jr., *Congressmen and Their Constituencies* (Chicago: Rand McNally, 1963), pp. 88–89; Avery Leiserson, *Parties and Politics* (New York: Knopf, 1958), p. 379.

stood one another well. . . . One day I told him I needed a new road in the southern part of my district. He called in Louis McHenry Howe. "Louis," he said, "call MacDonald"—Thomas H. MacDonald, head of the Bureau of Public Roads—"and tell him I am sending down a black Republican, and I want to give him a road." And I got it. . . .[26]

Another rule of the game tending to confine conflict between Congress and the President is a kind of unwritten moratorium on partisanship that takes place at the start of a President's term of office. During this "honeymoon" period, while the President is organizing his administration, it is customary for most presidential nominees for the various top-level jobs in his administration to be confirmed with only the most perfunctory scrutiny. Even in cases when some senators have sincere reservations or when their political interests in their home states could be better served by other nominees, the custom is to withhold objection and to allow the President to surround himself with men of his own choosing.

There is also a rather sizable number of occasions requiring joint presidential-congressional action in which neither partisanship nor sectional differences play a part. These occur most often in the realm of foreign affairs. When the President acts in international crises—as in Mr. Truman's decision to send troops to Korea, or Mr. Eisenhower's decision not to send troops to Indo-China, or Mr. Kennedy's decision to blockade Cuba, or Mr. Johnson's decision to retaliate after the Bay of Tonkin incident—he customarily consults with congressional leaders of both parties; and he can usually count on their strong support, at least for the duration of the crisis. Lack of consultation can be correspondingly costly, as Mr. Nixon may have discovered in the spring of 1970 when he sent American troops into Cambodia. There are also instances —seldom crises—when the President is hemmed in by Congress in foreign affairs, for example, in our policies toward Communist China, in our relations with Germany and Britain before World War II, or in our capacity to fight limited wars after a few inconclusive years of heavy investment, as in the case of Vietnam.

Finally, there are occasional periods of severe domestic difficulty in which presidential proposals find ready acceptance in Congress. One such period was the famous first 100 days of Franklin Roosevelt's first term of office, when the presidential honeymoon coincided with the depths of a depression. An impressive volume of legislation was enacted during this period, some of it remarkably innovative. But it would be wrong to suggest, as it sometimes is, that the 100 days were merely a demonstration of presidential mastery over Congress. Rather, both Congress and the President responded in much the same way to the urgency of external events. Once the crisis had abated, a more familiar pattern of congressional response to presidential initiatives was gradually reestablished.[27]

---

[26] Joe Martin (as told to Robert J. Donovan), *My First Fifty Years in Politics* (New York: McGraw-Hill, 1960), pp. 68–71.

[27] See Pendleton Herring, *Presidential Leadership* (New York: Farrar and Rinehart, 1940), pp. 31–32, 42–45, 52–59, and *passim*.

Congress and the Presidency are like two gears, each whirling at its own rate of speed.[28] It is not surprising that, on coming together, they often clash. Remarkably, however, this is not always the case. Devices that harmonize their differences are present within the system; the effects of party loyalty and party leadership within Congress, presidential practices of consultation, the careful restriction of partisan opposition by both congressional parties, and the readily evoked overriding patriotism of all participants within the system in periods—which nowadays, regrettably, come with some frequency—universally defined as crises.

With all the snags and thickets that complicate relations between Congress and the Presidency, it is worth noting that cooperation between the two branches does take place. This remarkable fact can be explained only in part by referring to incentives built into the machinery of the system. In addition, the underlying political culture discourages ideological extremism and fanatical intransigence and places a premium on the political skills of negotiation, maneuver, and accommodation. These permit Congress and the President to get along in spite of their differences, to unite in times of national emergency, and yet to return another day to disagree.

[28] Herring, who uses a similar image, remarks that "In looking at the operations of Congress and the executive, we may see with Ezekiel, De little wheel run by faith/ And de big wheel run by de grace ob God/ 'Tis a wheel in a wheel/ Way in de middle of de air." *Ibid.*, p. x.

To explore further

Good general analyses of the basic principles of American national government are scarce. Let me recommend Lewis A. Froman, Jr.'s, *People and Politics* (Englewood Cliffs, N.J.: Prentice-Hall, 1962); E. Pendleton Herring's *The Politics of Democracy* (New York: Holt, 1940); Robert A. Dahl's *A Preface to Democratic Theory* (Chicago: University of Chicago Press, 1956); and Dahl's less schematic, more historical, *Pluralist Democracy in the United States* (Chicago: Rand McNally, 1967).

For treatment of some of the cultural and social factors underlying American governmental institutions, see Alexis de Tocqueville, *Democracy in America*, 2 vols. (New York: Vintage Books, Random House, 1956); Seymour Martin Lipset, *The First New Nation* (New York: Basic Books, 1963); and David Potter, *People of Plenty* (Chicago: Phoenix Books, University of Chicago Press, 1958). David B. Truman in *The Governmental Process* (New York: Knopf, 1953), written with a theory of interest groups firmly in mind, tells a great deal about "rules of the game." David Braybrooke and Charles E. Lindblom in *A Strategy of Decision* (New York: Free Press, 1963) spell out the theory that undergirds my discussion of national decision-making, and Lindblom's book in this series, *The Policy-Making Process* (Englewood Cliffs, N.J.: Prentice-Hall, 1968), applies his own theory to American government.

The most ambitious analytical work on the contemporary Presidency is Richard Neustadt's *Presidential Power* (New York: Wiley, 1960). It draws on a rich backlog of case material and on Neustadt's own experience as an aide to President Truman, but, curiously, it has not stimulated a critical dialogue. Other treatments of the same subject are Francis Heller's *The Presidency* (New York: Random House, 1960); Clinton Rossiter's *The American Presidency* (New York: Harvest Books, Harcourt, Brace & World, 1960); and Sidney Hyman's *The American President* (New York: Harper & Row, 1954).

Neustadt, in addition, has contributed several impressive articles to the study of the Presidency: "Presidency and Legislation: The Growth of Central Clearance," *American Political Science Review,* vol. 48 (September, 1954); "Presidency and Legislation: Planning the President's Program," *American Political Science Review,* vol. 49 (December, 1955); and "The Presidency at Mid-Century," *Law and Contemporary Problems,* vol. 21 (Autumn, 1956). Four articles by Elmer E. Cornwell are also useful and relevant: "Wilson, Creel and the Presidency," *Public Opinion Quarterly,* vol. 23 (Summer, 1959); "Coolidge and Presidential Leadership," *Public Opinion Quarterly,* vol. 21 (Summer, 1957); "Presidential News: The Expanding Public Image," *Journalism Quarterly,* vol. 36 (Summer, 1959); and "The Presidential Press Conference: A Study in Institutionalization," *Midwest Journal of Political Science,* vol. 4 (November, 1960). See also Elmer E. Cornwell, *Presidential Leadership of Public Opinion* (Bloomington, Ind.: Indiana University Press, 1965).

On institutionalization, see Lester G. Seligman, "Developments in the Presidency and the Conception of Political Leadership," *American Sociological Review,* vol. 20 (December, 1955); and Henry Fairlie, "Thoughts on the Presidency," *The Public Interest,* no. 9 (Fall, 1967), pp. 28–48.

Revealing information about presidential decision-making often turns up in case studies. For example, see Herman Somers's *Presidential Agency* (Cambridge, Mass.: Harvard University Press, 1950), which discusses the operations of the Office of War Mobilization and Reconversion; Bernard C. Cohen's *The Political Process and Foreign Policy* (Princeton, N.J.: Princeton, 1957), on the domestic politics of the Japanese peace treaty; Joseph Jones's *The Fifteen Weeks* (New York: Viking, 1955) on the establishment of the Marshall Plan; Aaron Wildavsky's *Dixon Yates: A Study in Power Politics* (New Haven, Conn.: Yale, 1962); and Samuel P. Huntington's *The Common Defense* (New York: Columbia, 1961). Dean Acheson, *Present at the Creation* (New York: Norton, 1969), is a valuable account of policy-making in the Truman presidency and contains a superb capsule description of Mr. Truman as President.

Basic sources on the Kennedy Presidency are Theodore Sorensen's *Kennedy* (New York: Harper & Row, 1965), and Arthur Schlesinger, Jr.'s, *A Thousand Days* (Boston: Houghton Mifflin, 1965). Both are unremittingly adoring accounts. Less cloying is Hugh Sidey's *John F. Kennedy: President* (New York: Atheneum, 1963). On foreign policy aspects of the Kennedy Presidency, see Roger Hilsman, *To Move a Nation* (Garden City, N.Y.: Doubleday, 1967) and for a good overview of economic aspects, see Seymour E. Harris, *Economics of the Kennedy Years* (New York: Harper & Row, 1964).

The best book on the Johnson Presidency is undoubtedly Rowland Evans's and Robert Novak's *Lyndon B. Johnson: The Exercise of Power* (New York: New American Library, 1966). Eric Goldman's *The Tragedy of Lyndon Johnson* (New York: Knopf, 1968) has some useful passages; and Philip Geyelin's *Lyndon B. Johnson and the World* (New York: Praeger, 1966) is excellent on foreign affairs. An important case study is Townsend Hoopes, *The Limits of Intervention* (New York: McKay, 1969). See also the following: "The American Presidency in the Last Half-Century," *Current History,* vol. 39 (October, 1960); "The Office of the American Presidency," *Annals,* vol. 30 (September, 1956); "The Presidential Office," *Law and Contemporary Problems,* vol. 21 (Autumn, 1956); and "The Presidency in Transition," *Journal of Politics,* vol. 21 (February, 1949). Edward Corwin's classic, *The President: Office and Powers* (New York: New York University Press, 1957), is the foremost source on the legal and constitutional aspects of the presidential office. There are now a number of good readers on the Presidency that reprint many of the articles mentioned here: Don Johnson and Jack Walker (eds.), *The Dynamics of the American Presidency* (New York: Wiley, 1964); Elmer E. Cornwell (ed.), *The American Presidency: Vital Center* (Chicago: Scott, Foresman, 1966); and Aaron Wildavsky, *The Presidency* (Boston: Little, Brown, 1969).

Two sources that provide much raw material for speculation on problems of presidential power are Robert Donovan's *Eisenhower: The Inside Story* (New York: Harper & Row, 1956), an account of Cabinet-level decision-making drawn from stenographic records of meetings of the Eisenhower Cabinet; and John Hersey's "Mr. President," *The New Yorker,* 5 parts (April 7–May 5, 1951), a diary of a few days spent with President Truman. On staffing the Executive Office, see Edward Hobbes, *Behind the President* (Washington, D.C.: Public Affairs Press, 1954), and Lauren Henry, *Presidential Transitions* (Washington, D.C.: Brookings, 1960). Richard F. Fenno, Jr., *The President's Cabinet* (New York: Vintage Books, Random House, 1959), is a useful synthesis. For analytical articles on the Executive Office, see Don K. Price, "Staffing the Presidency," *American Political Science Review,* vol. 40 (December, 1946); Price, "The Office of the Chief Executive," *Public Administration Review,* vol. 14 (Autumn, 1954); Warren Cikens, "The Council of Economic Advisors: Political Economy at the Crossroads," *Public Policy,* vol 4 (1953); Corrine Silverman's ICP case, *The President's Economic Advisors* (University, Ala.: University of Alabama Press, 1959); Bertram Gross and John Lewis, "The President's Executive Staff during the Truman Administration," *American Political Science Review,* vol. 48 (March, 1954); and George A. Graham, "The Presidency and the Executive Office of the President," *Journal of Politics,* vol. 22 (November, 1950). More recent material includes books cited in the text by Walter Heller, Charles Schultze, and Paul Y. Hammond.

Material on presidential nominating politics and on the presidential coalition are summarized in Nelson W. Polsby and Aaron Wildavsky, *Presidential Elections* (New York: Scribner, 1964). Paul David, Ralph Goldman, and Richard Bain have written a voluminous treatment of nominations in *The Politics of National Party Conventions* (Washington, D.C.: Brookings, 1960).

The best scholarly work on the United States Senate has been done by Ralph K. Huitt, primarily in a series of articles, which at long last have been collected and reprinted in Huitt and Robert L. Peabody, *Congress: Two Decades of Analysis* (New York: Harper & Row, 1969). See also Donald R. Matthews's *U.S. Senators and Their World* (Chapel Hill, N.C.: University of North Carolina Press, 1960). It and William S. White's more informally written *Citadel* (New York: Harper & Row, 1957) are of major importance in guiding contemporary thinking on the Senate, although each has deficiencies. Bertram Gross's *The Legislative Struggle* (New York: McGraw-Hill, 1953) is oriented toward legislative strategy and toward reform. H. Bradford Westerfield's *For-*

eign Policy and Party Politics (New Haven, Conn.: Yale, 1955) is an acute study of senatorial behavior in a particular issue area. Two of the better senatorial biographies happen to be about mavericks: Richard Rovere, *Senator Joe McCarthy* (New York: Harcourt, Brace & World, 1959); and Robert A. Smith, *The Tiger in the Senate* (Garden City, N.Y.: Doubleday, 1962), about Wayne Morse. On McCarthy, Michael Straight's remarkable *Trial by Television* (Boston: Beacon Press, 1954) is perhaps the most revealing study yet published.

On the house, see *Member of the House* by the late Clem Miller (New York: Scribner, 1962), the newsletters of a gifted young congressman; this book does not merely explain the House as an institution, it evokes it. Robert L. Peabody and Nelson W. Polsby (eds.) have, in *New Perspectives on the House of Representatives*, 2d. ed. (Chicago: Rand McNally, 1969), gathered together a dozen essays and a short bibliography on aspects of contemporary House politics. Neil MacNeil in *Forge of Democracy* (New York: McKay, 1963) does for the House what William White did for the Senate, with less flair for generalization but greater attention to historical anecdotage. George Galloway's *History of the House of Representatives* (New York: Crowell, 1961) is predominantly procedural in its concerns, as are his *Congress at the Crossroads* (New York: Crowell, 1946), an authoritative commentary on the Legislative Reorganization Act of that year, and *The Legislative Process in Congress* (New York: Crowell, 1962). Another valuable set of congressional memoirs is Jerry Voorhis's *Confessions of a Congressman* (Garden City, N.Y.: Doubleday, 1948). Holbert N. Carroll's *The House of Representatives and Foreign Affairs* (Pittsburgh, Pa.: University of Pittsburgh Press, 1958) is more inclusive than its title indicates. Edith Carper's ICP case, *The Defense Appropriations Rider* (University, Ala.: University of Alabama Press, 1960) is written with wit and verve. John Bibby and Roger Davidson's *On Capitol Hill* (New York: Holt, 1967) contains a good set of original case studies. Lewis A. Froman, Jr.'s, useful *The Congressional Process* (Boston: Little, Brown, 1967) lays out strategic implications of congressional rules and procedures. Two standard works are Ernest Griffith's *Congress: Its Contemporary Role,* 3d. ed. (New York: New York University Press, 1961), and Roland Young's *The American Congress* (New York: Harper & Row, 1958). A collection of general materials on Congress, including six previously unpublished letters by Clem Miller, is Nelson W. Polsby (ed.), *Congressional Behavior* (New York: Random House, 1971). Roll-call analysis is an important element in David Truman's *The Congressional Party* (New York: Wiley, 1959); Duncan MacRae's *Dimensions of Congressional Voting* (Berkeley, Calif.: University of California Press, 1958); Julius Turner's *Party and Constituency: Pressures on Congress* (Baltimore: Johns Hopkins Studies in Historical and Political Science: Series LXIX, No. 1, 1951); and David Mayhew's *Party Loyalty among Congressmen* (Cambridge, Mass.: Harvard, 1966). Lewis A. Froman, Jr., uses a variety of aggregate data to test hypotheses about congressional voting in *Congressmen and Their Constituencies* (Chicago: Rand McNally, 1963).

Perhaps the most original and noteworthy contemporary generalizations about congressional politics are contained in the work of Lewis A. Dexter.

Some of this is reprinted in Peabody and Polsby (eds.), *op. cit.*, but more still can be found in the latter parts of Raymond Bauer, Ithiel de Sola Pool, and Lewis A. Dexter, *American Business and Public Policy* (New York: Atherton, 1963). This book, a study of interest-group communication in reciprocal-trade legislation, is of great general interest. See also, Dexter's *The Sociology and Politics of Congress* (Chicago: Rand McNally, 1969).

Most treatments of the process by which a bill becomes a law are case studies; an example is Stephen K. Bailey's well-written *Congress Makes a Law* (New York: Columbia, 1950). Less detailed, and also less partisan, is H. Douglas Price's colorful "Race, Religion and the Rules Committee: The Kennedy Aid-to-Education Bills," in A. Westin (ed.), *The Uses of Power* (New York: Harcourt, Brace & World, 1962), pp. 1–71. General discussions can be found in Gross, *op cit.*, Froman, *The Congressional Process*, and Charles Zinn's lucid exposition of the technical points, *How Our Laws Are Made* (Washington, D.C.: Government Printing Office, 1956).

Two major works on the budgetary process are Richard F. Fenno, Jr.'s, detailed and thoughtful *The Power of the Purse* (Boston: Little, Brown, 1966), on the congressional side of the appropriations process; and Aaron B. Wildavsky's *The Politics of the Budgetary Process* (Boston: Little, Brown, 1964), which deals more extensively with the executive side. Wildavsky's "Political Implications of Budgetary Reform," *Public Administration Review*, vol. 21 (Autumn, 1961), gives a summary of his theoretical position and a critique of the reform orientation in, among other works, Arthur Smithies's *The Budgetary Process in the United States* (New York: McGraw-Hill, 1955), also a major contribution. The reader should also consult *Organizing for National Security, Hearings before the Subcommittee on National Policy Machinery of the Senate Committee on Government Operations,* "The Budget and the Policy Process," part 8 (Washington, D.C.: Government Printing Office, 1961); and the task force reports and reports to Congress of the Commission on the Organization of the Executive Branch of the Government (second Hoover Commission, 1955). The relevant reports are titled "Budget and Accounting" (Washington, D.C.: Government Printing Office, 1955). Ralph K. Huitt's research study, "Congressional Organization and Operations on the Field of Money and Credit," in the Commission on Money and Credit, *Fiscal and Debt Management Policies* (Englewood Cliffs, N.J.: Prentice-Hall, 1963), pp. 399–495, gives an excellent overview of the organization of Congress on financial matters. More recent material on budgetary reform is contained in David Novick (ed.), *Program Budgeting*; Charles Schultze, *The Politics and Economics of Public Spending;* and in *The Public Administration Review* symposia, cited in the text.

Much of the discussion by academic political scientists of conflict and cooperation follows Woodrow Wilson's *Congressional Government* (New York: Meridian, 1956). Works already cited by Gross, Carroll, Bailey, Smithies, and Galloway express ideas congenial to Wilson's perspective. So also, with modifications that attempt to take explicit account of the American historical experience, does James M. Burns in *Deadlock of Democracy* (Englewood

Cliffs, N.J.: Prentice-Hall, 1963). Defense of Congress is offered by Ernest Griffith, William White, and Neil MacNeil in works already cited.

The Congressional Record contains moderately reliable verbatim records of debates in Congress and much extraneous material—some of it quite entertaining. But it cannot be read with profit by the serious beginner without concurrent use of the daily newspapers as a guide. The Congressional Directory and The U.S. Government Organizational Manual provide basic facts. All three are available by mail from the Government Printing Office in Washington, D.C. One private source, The Congressional Quarterly Weekly Reports and annual Almanac, is outstanding in the accuracy, sophistication, and breadth of its coverage. The National Journal, also a weekly, provides thorough and well-documented articles on all aspects of Washington politics.

INDEX